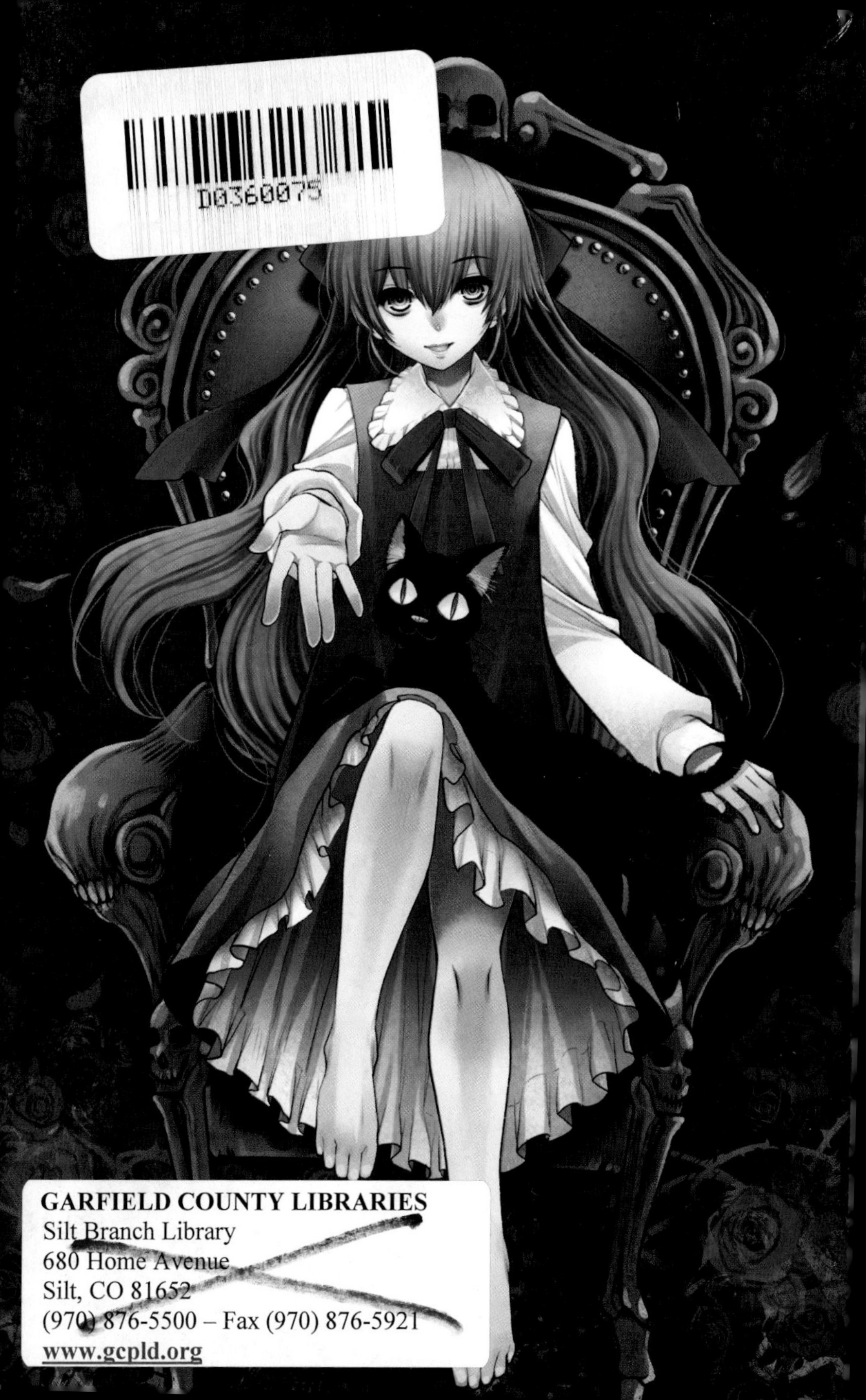

THE WITCH'S HOUSE

The Diary of Ellen

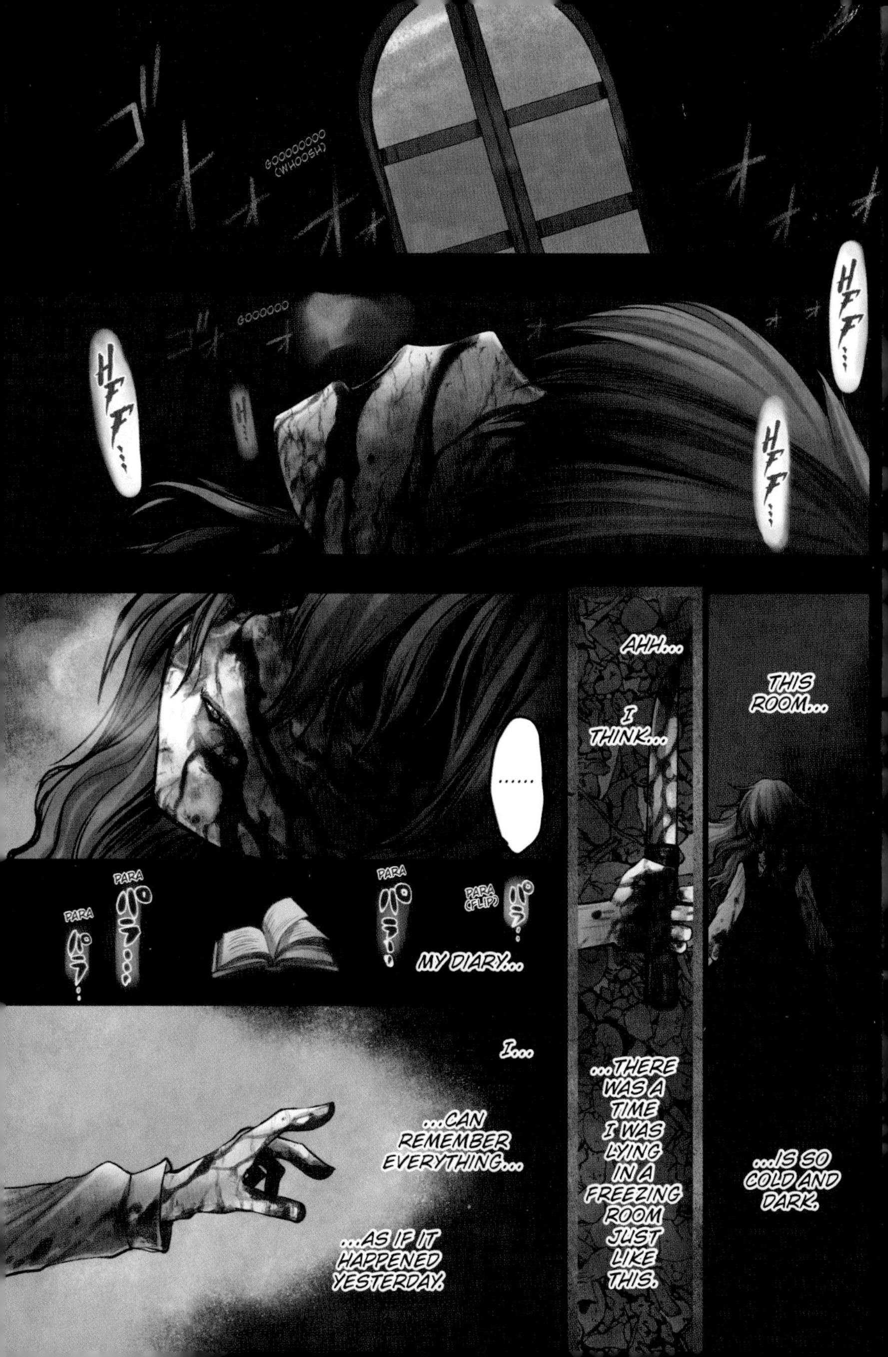
GOOOOOOOO (WHOOSH)
HFF...
HFF...
GOOOOOO
H...
HFF...
THIS ROOM...
...IS SO COLD AND DARK.
AHH...
I THINK...
...THERE WAS A TIME I WAS LYING IN A FREEZING ROOM JUST LIKE THIS.
......
PARA (FLIP)
PARA
PARA
PARA
MY DIARY...
I...
...CAN REMEMBER EVERYTHING...
...AS IF IT HAPPENED YESTERDAY.

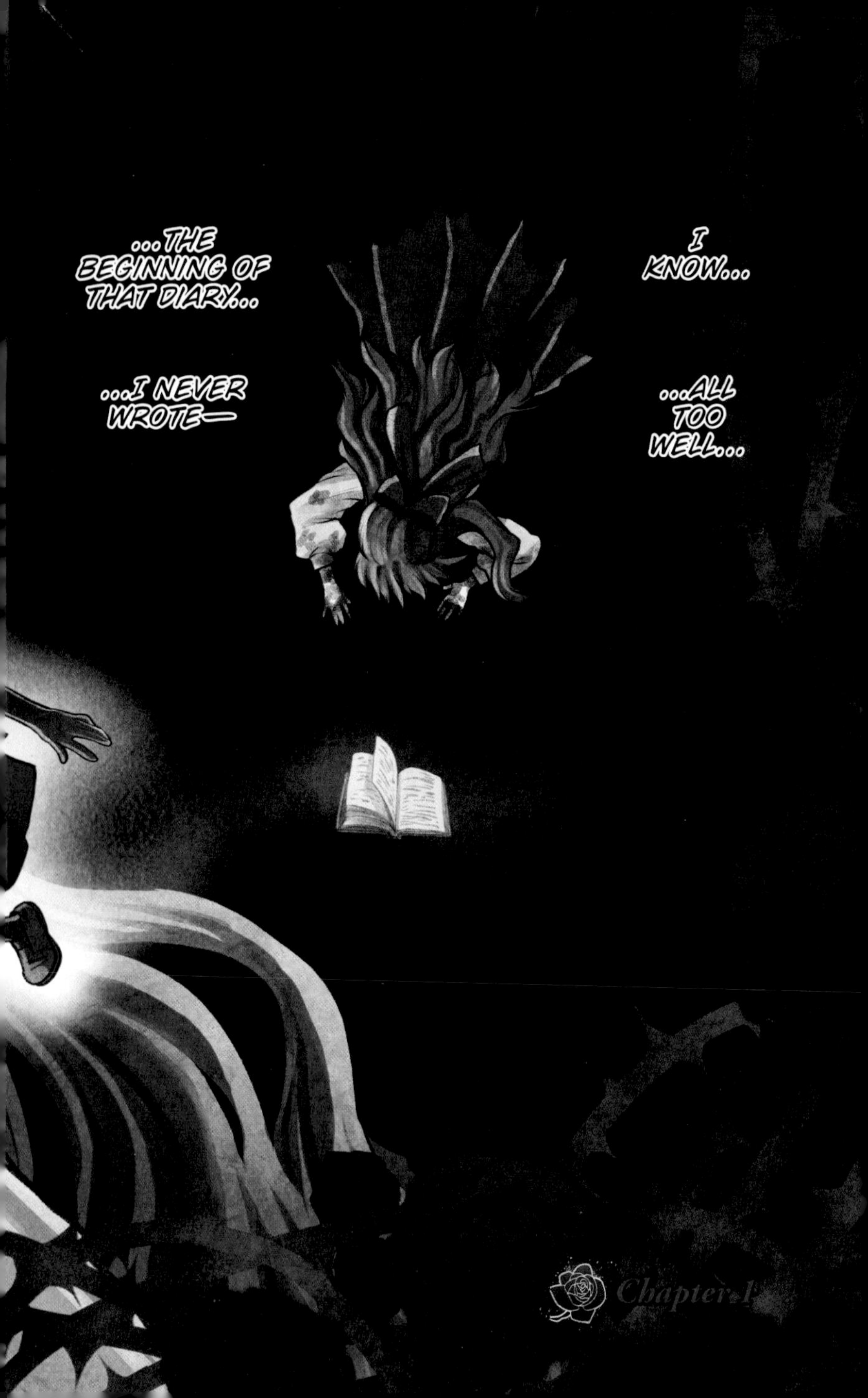
I KNOW...
...ALL TOO WELL...
...THE BEGINNING OF THAT DIARY...
...I NEVER WROTE—
Chapter 1

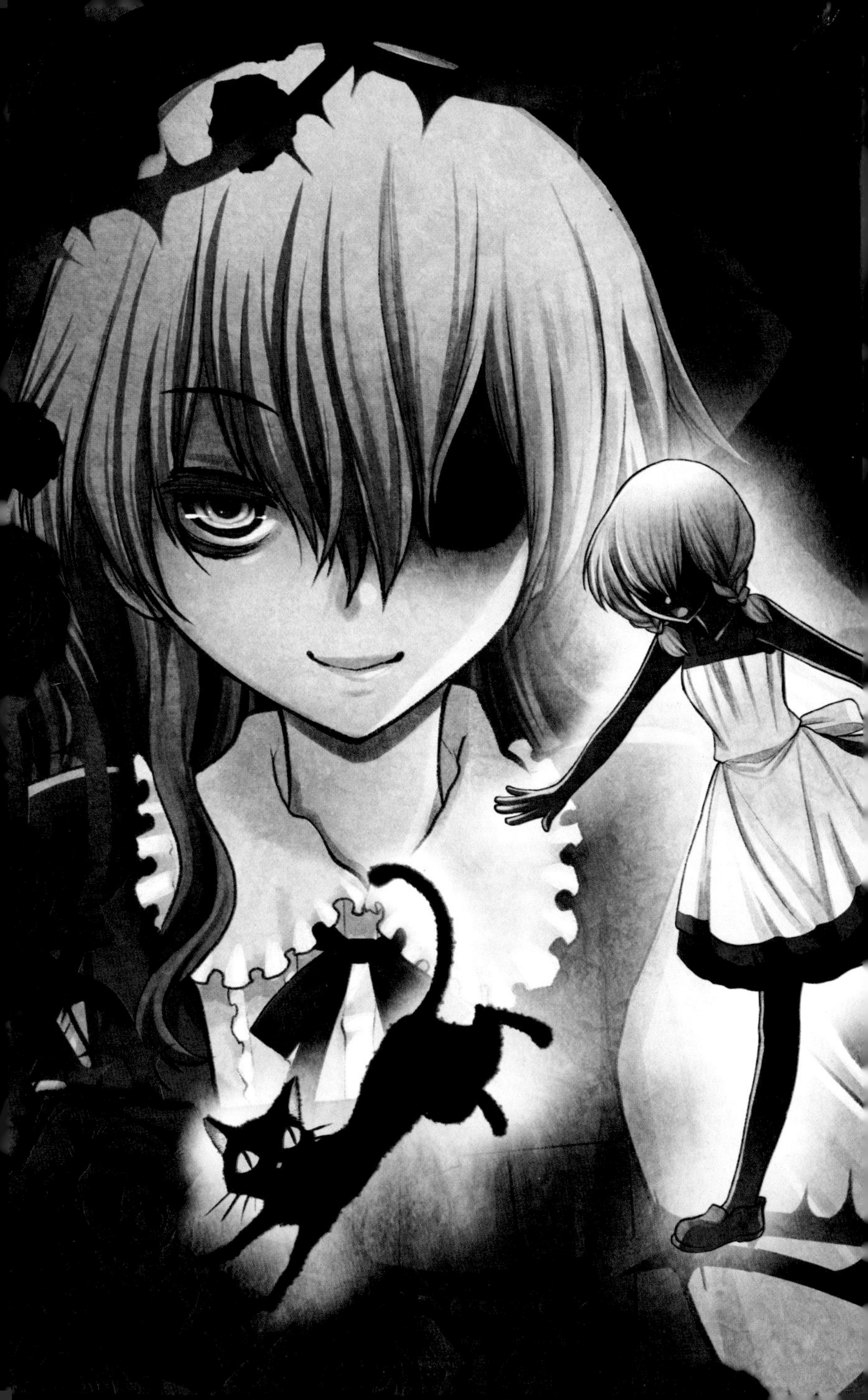

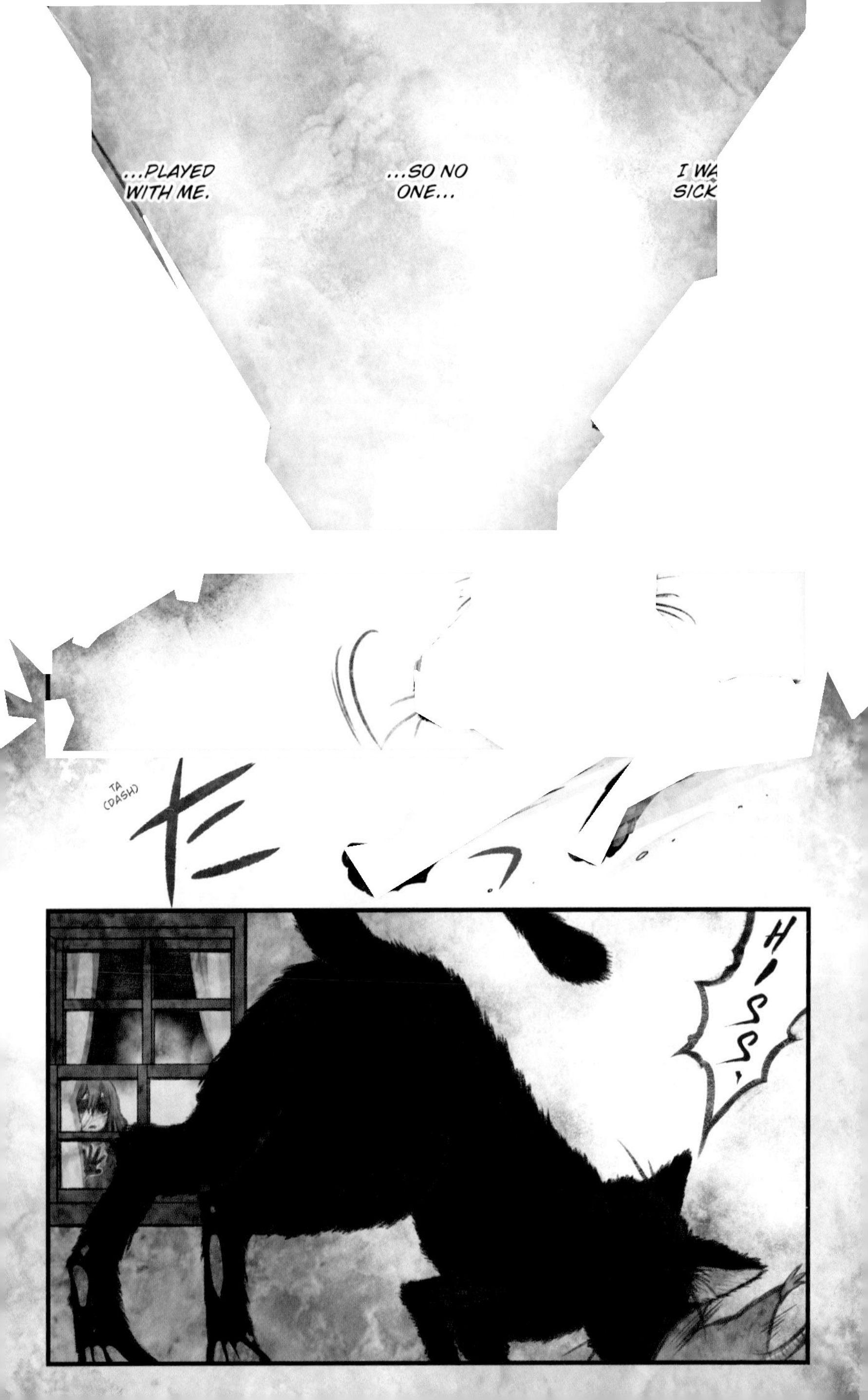
I WA
SICK
...SO NO ONE...
...PLAYED WITH ME.
TA (DASH)
HISS.

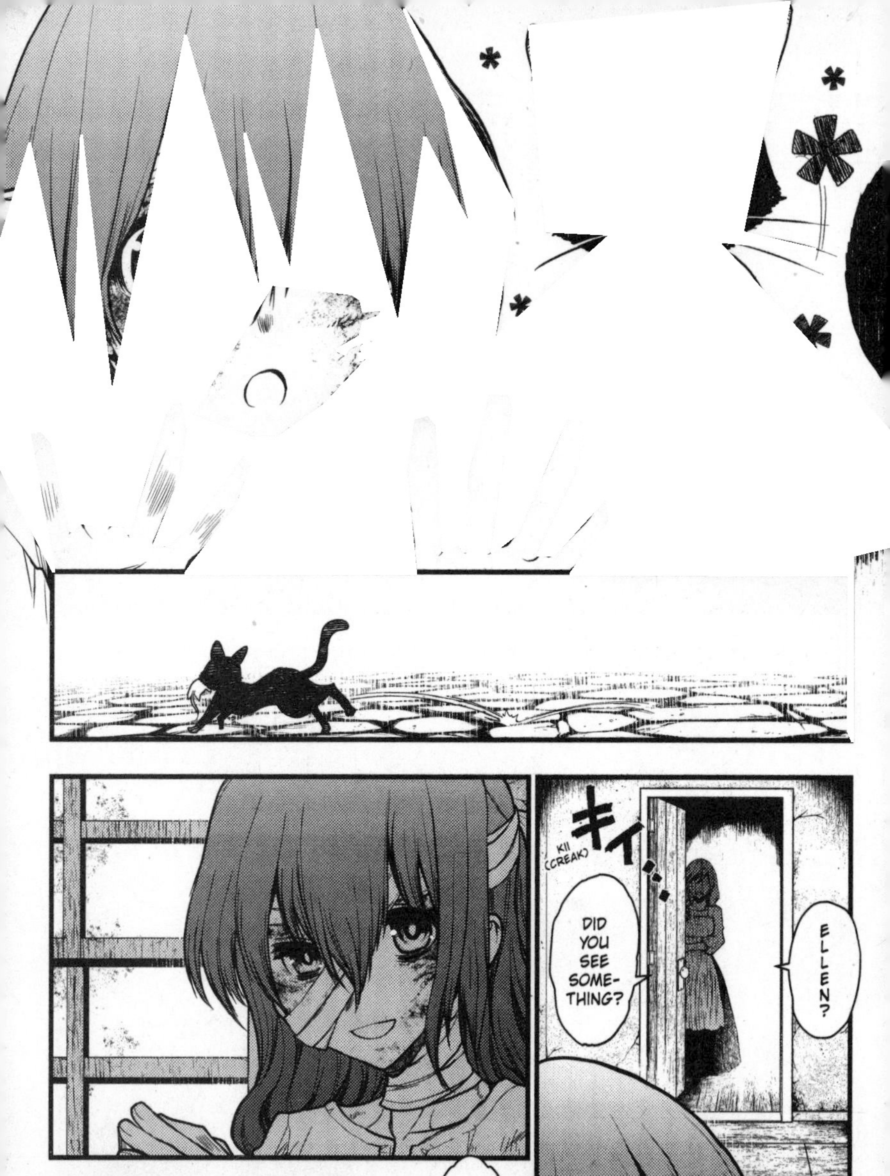

キイ
KII (CREAK)
ELLEN?
DID YOU SEE SOMETHING?
A CAT...

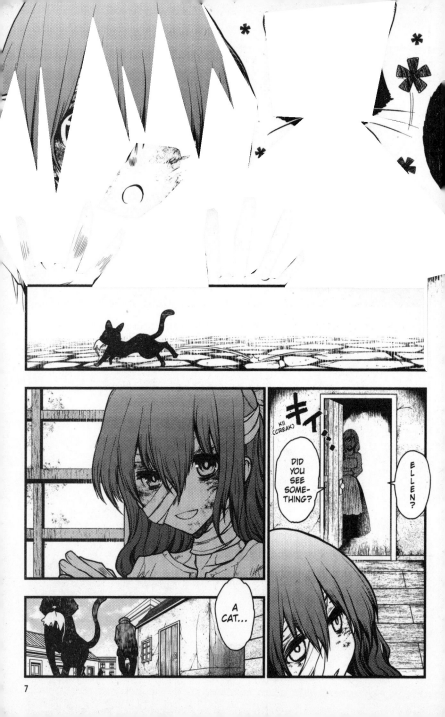

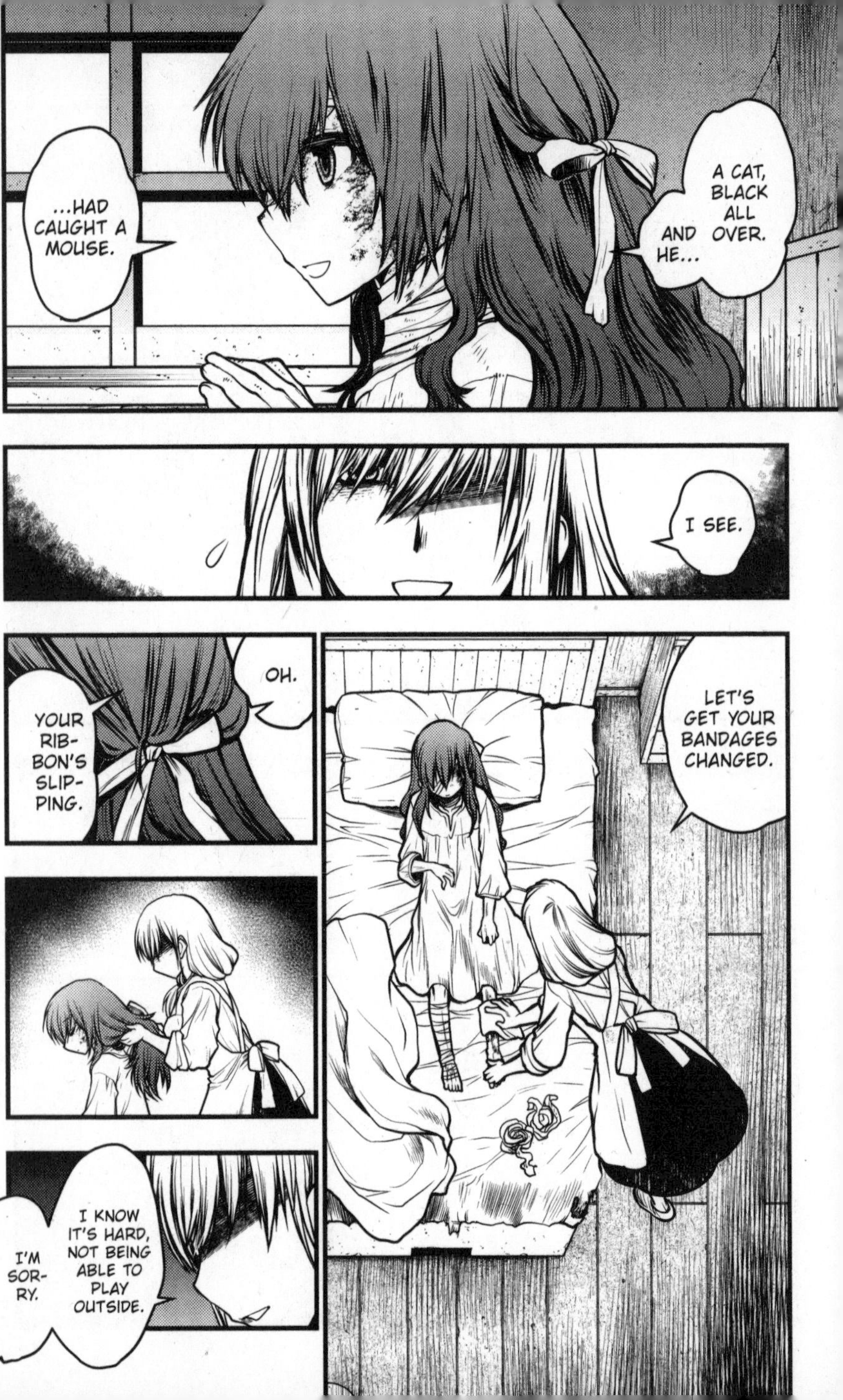
A CAT, BLACK ALL OVER. AND HE...
...HAD CAUGHT A MOUSE.
I SEE.
LET'S GET YOUR BANDAGES CHANGED.
OH.
YOUR RIB-BON'S SLIP-PING.
I KNOW IT'S HARD, NOT BEING ABLE TO PLAY OUTSIDE.
I'M SOR-RY.

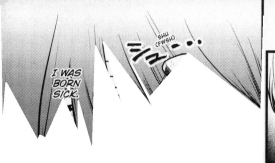

THAT'S OKAY. I ALSO LIKE...
...PLAYING INSIDE.
SHU (FWSH)
I WAS BORN SICK.
BUT IT'S NOT LIKE I WAS ALWAYS STUCK IN THIS DARK, OLD ROOM.
I CAN'T SEE THE SKY FROM THIS WINDOW, BUT...
...I KNOW HOW BLUE THE SKY IS...
...AND WHAT THE GRASS SMELLS LIKE.
BUT...
...SINCE I WAS BORN, I'D HAD RASHES ALL OVER MY FACE AND LEGS.
WALKING ALSO HURTS. SOMETHING'S WRONG WITH MY JOINTS.
NOBODY KNEW WHY.
AND THERE WAS NO CURE.
OF COURSE THERE WASN'T.
THERE WAS NO PROPER DOCTOR AROUND, AND WE WOULDN'T HAVE HAD MONEY TO PAY ANYWAY.

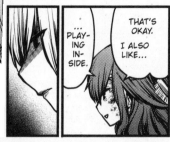

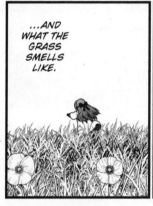

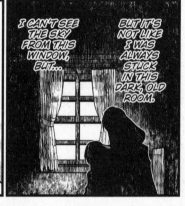

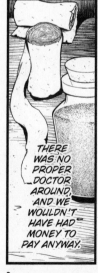

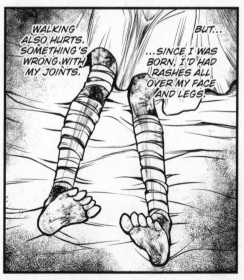

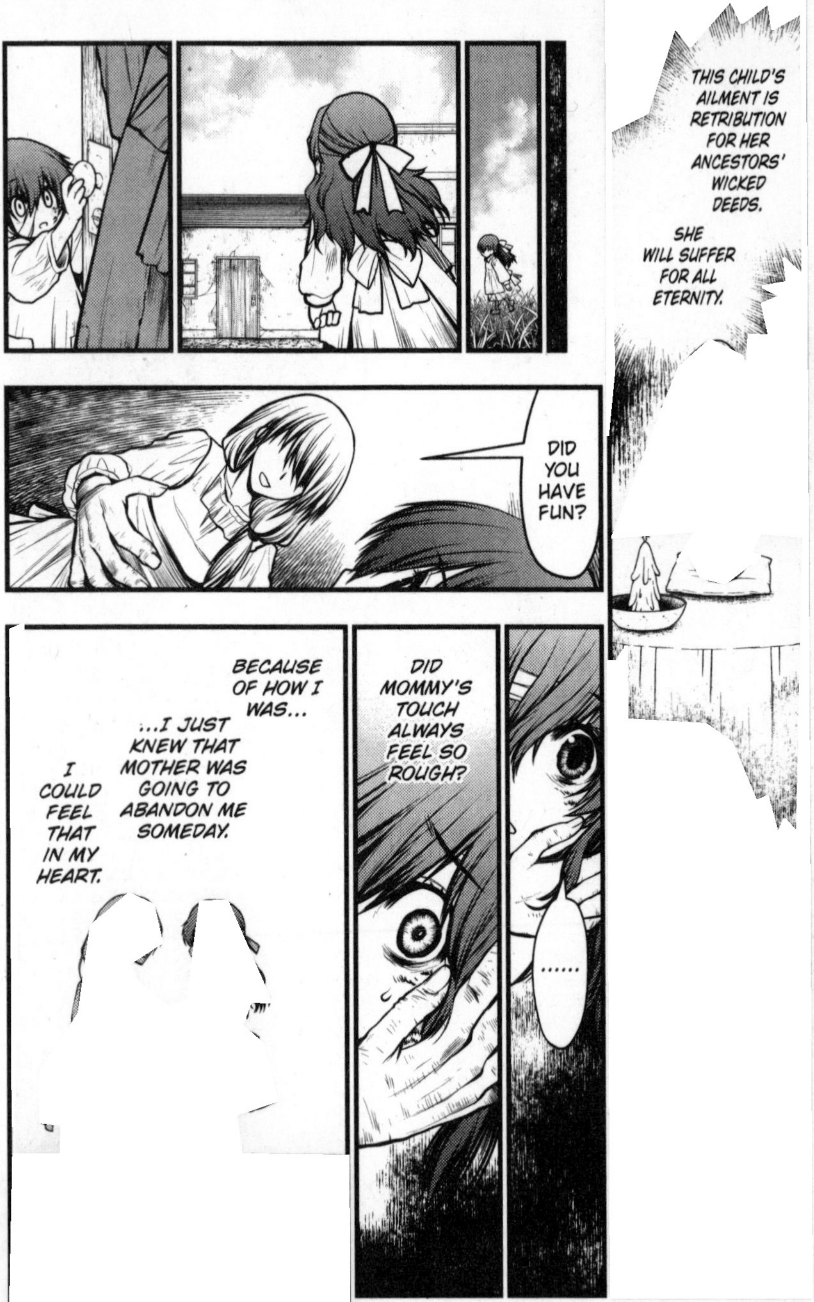
THIS CHILD'S AILMENT IS RETRIBUTION FOR HER ANCESTORS' WICKED DEEDS.
SHE WILL SUFFER FOR ALL ETERNITY.
DID YOU HAVE FUN?
......
DID MOMMY'S TOUCH ALWAYS FEEL SO ROUGH?
BECAUSE OF HOW I WAS...
...I JUST KNEW THAT MOTHER WAS GOING TO ABANDON ME SOMEDAY.
I COULD FEEL THAT IN MY HEART.

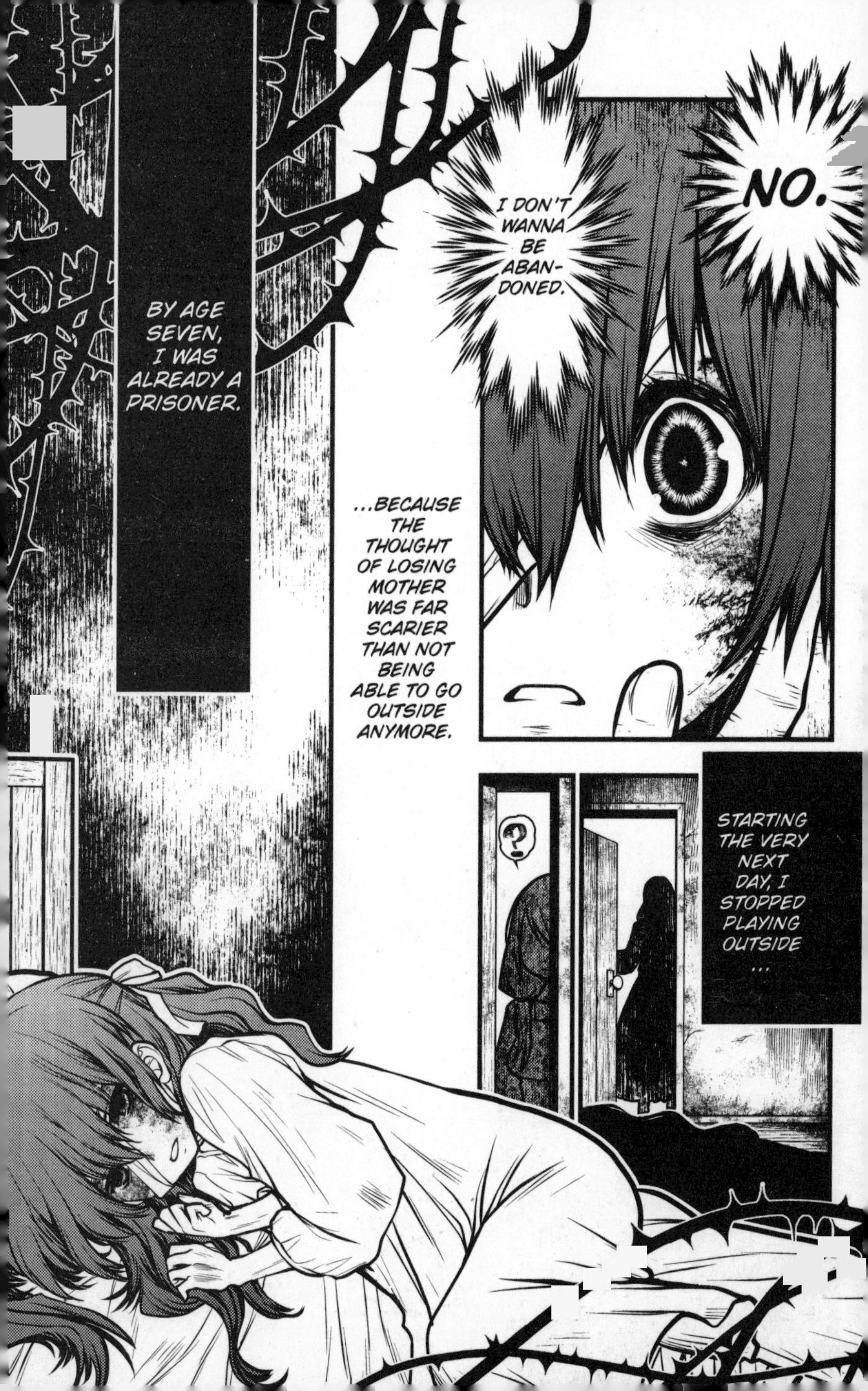
NO.
I DON'T WANNA BE ABAN-DONED.
?
STARTING THE VERY NEXT DAY, I STOPPED PLAYING OUTSIDE...
...BECAUSE THE THOUGHT OF LOSING MOTHER WAS FAR SCARIER THAN NOT BEING ABLE TO GO OUTSIDE ANYMORE.
BY AGE SEVEN, I WAS ALREADY A PRISONER.

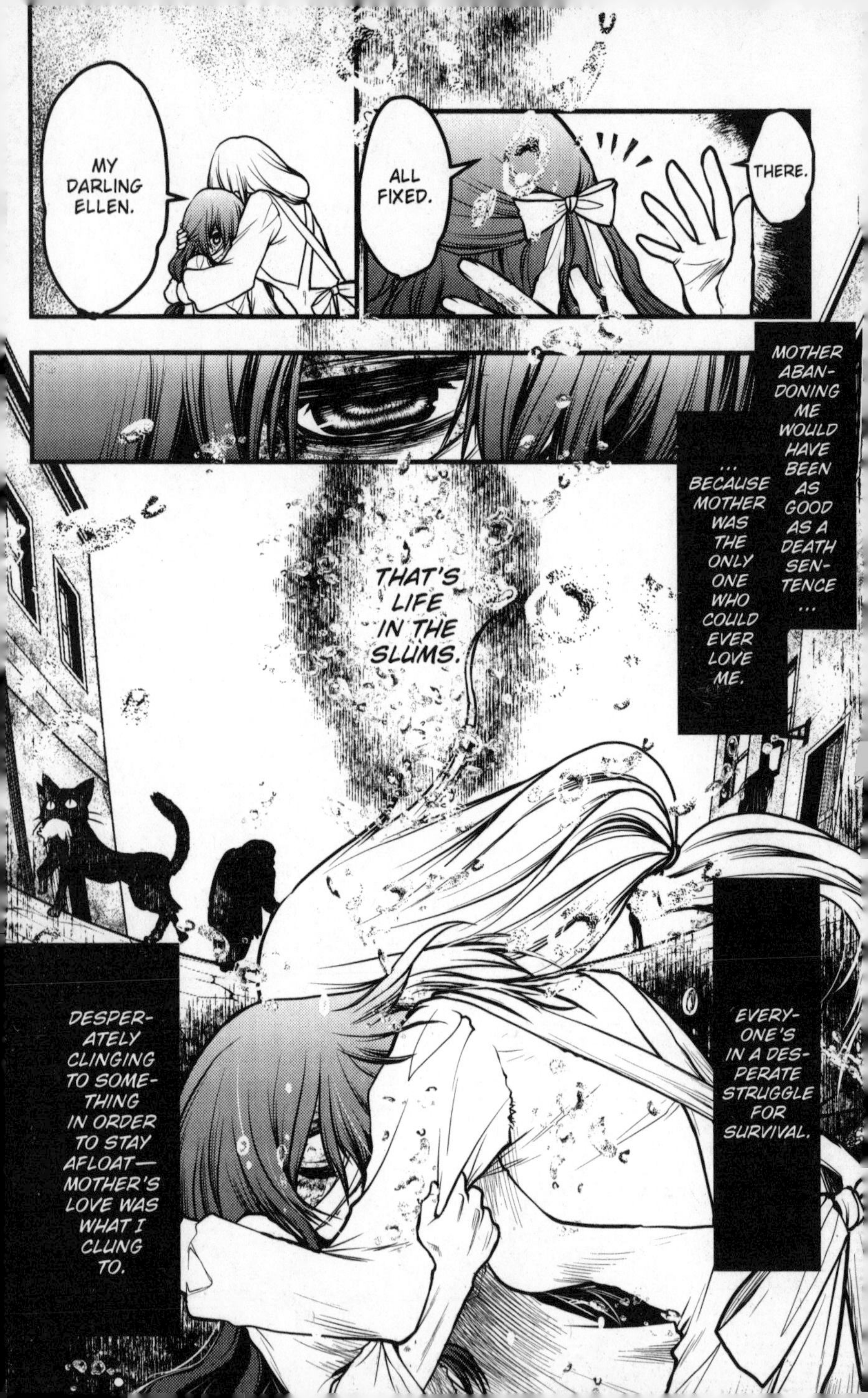
THERE.
ALL FIXED.
MY DARLING ELLEN.
MOTHER ABANDONING ME WOULD HAVE BEEN AS GOOD AS A DEATH SENTENCE...
...BECAUSE MOTHER WAS THE ONLY ONE WHO COULD EVER LOVE ME.
THAT'S LIFE IN THE SLUMS.
EVERYONE'S IN A DESPERATE STRUGGLE FOR SURVIVAL.
DESPERATELY CLINGING TO SOMETHING IN ORDER TO STAY AFLOAT—MOTHER'S LOVE WAS WHAT I CLUNG TO.

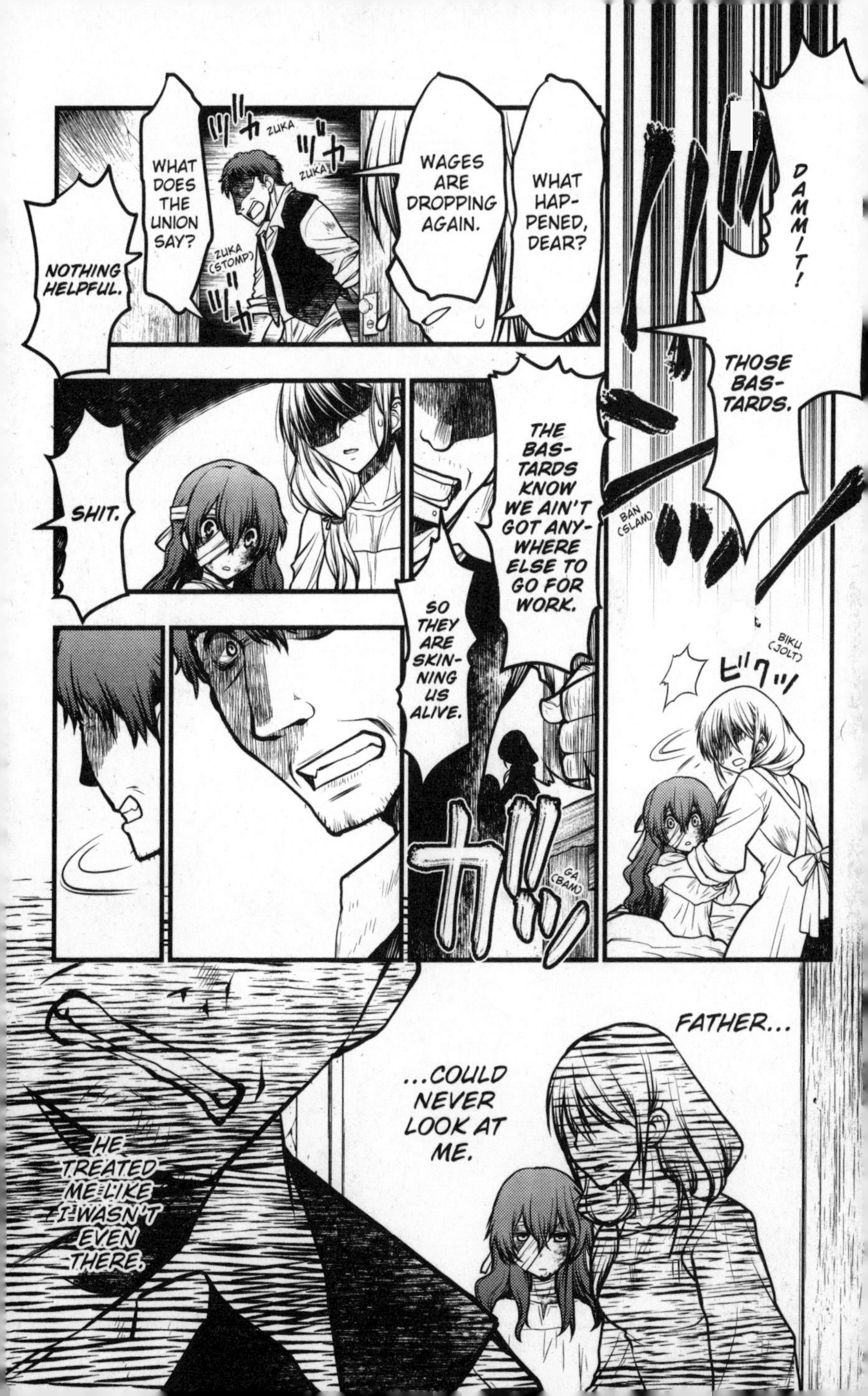
DAMMIT!
THOSE BASTARDS.
BAN (SLAM)
BIKU (JOLT)
WHAT HAPPENED, DEAR?
WAGES ARE DROPPING AGAIN.
ZUKA
ZUKA
WHAT DOES THE UNION SAY?
ZUKA (STOMP)
NOTHING HELPFUL.
THE BASTARDS KNOW WE AIN'T GOT ANYWHERE ELSE TO GO FOR WORK.
SO THEY ARE SKINNING US ALIVE.
SHIT.
GA (BAM)
FATHER...
...COULD NEVER LOOK AT ME.
HE TREATED ME LIKE I WASN'T EVEN THERE.

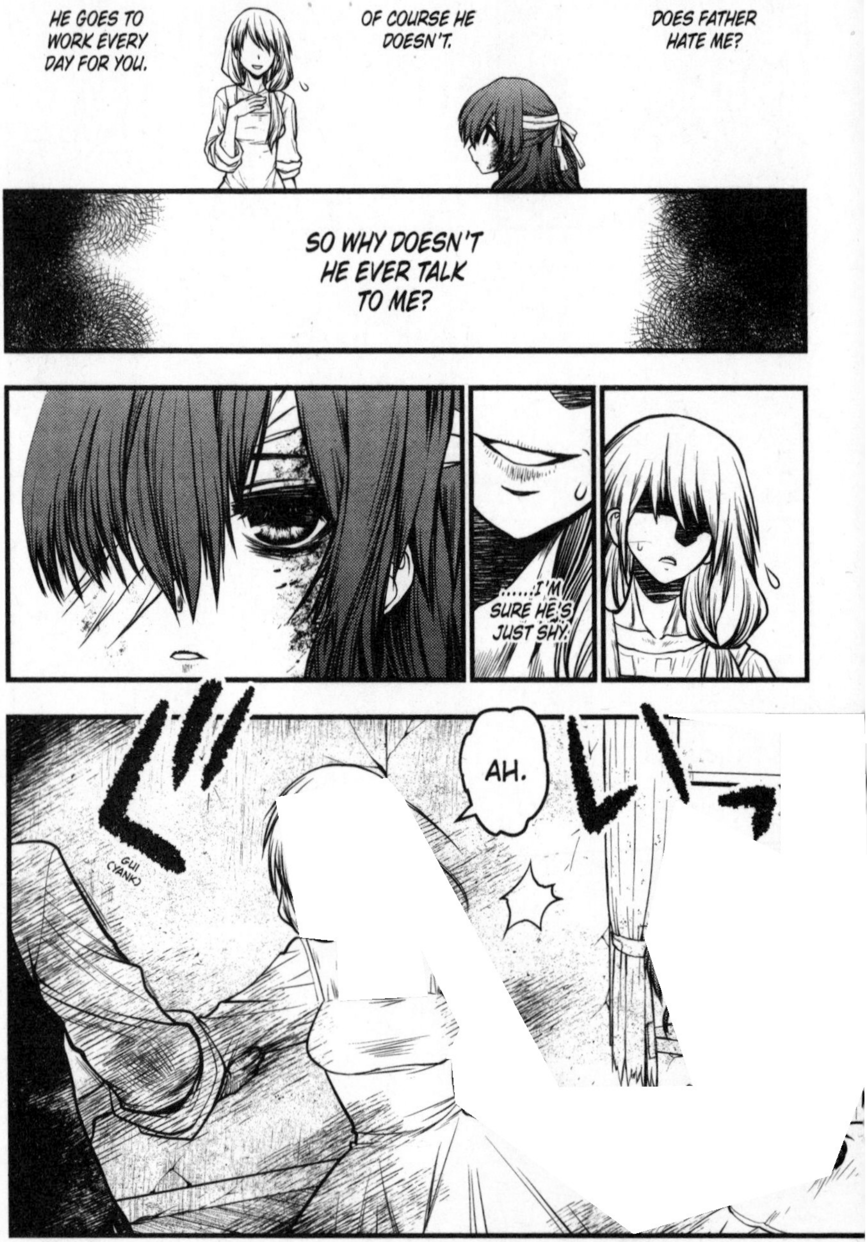
DOES FATHER HATE ME?
OF COURSE HE DOESN'T.
HE GOES TO WORK EVERY DAY FOR YOU.
SO WHY DOESN'T HE EVER TALK TO ME?
......I'M SURE HE'S JUST SHY.
AH.
GUI (YANK)

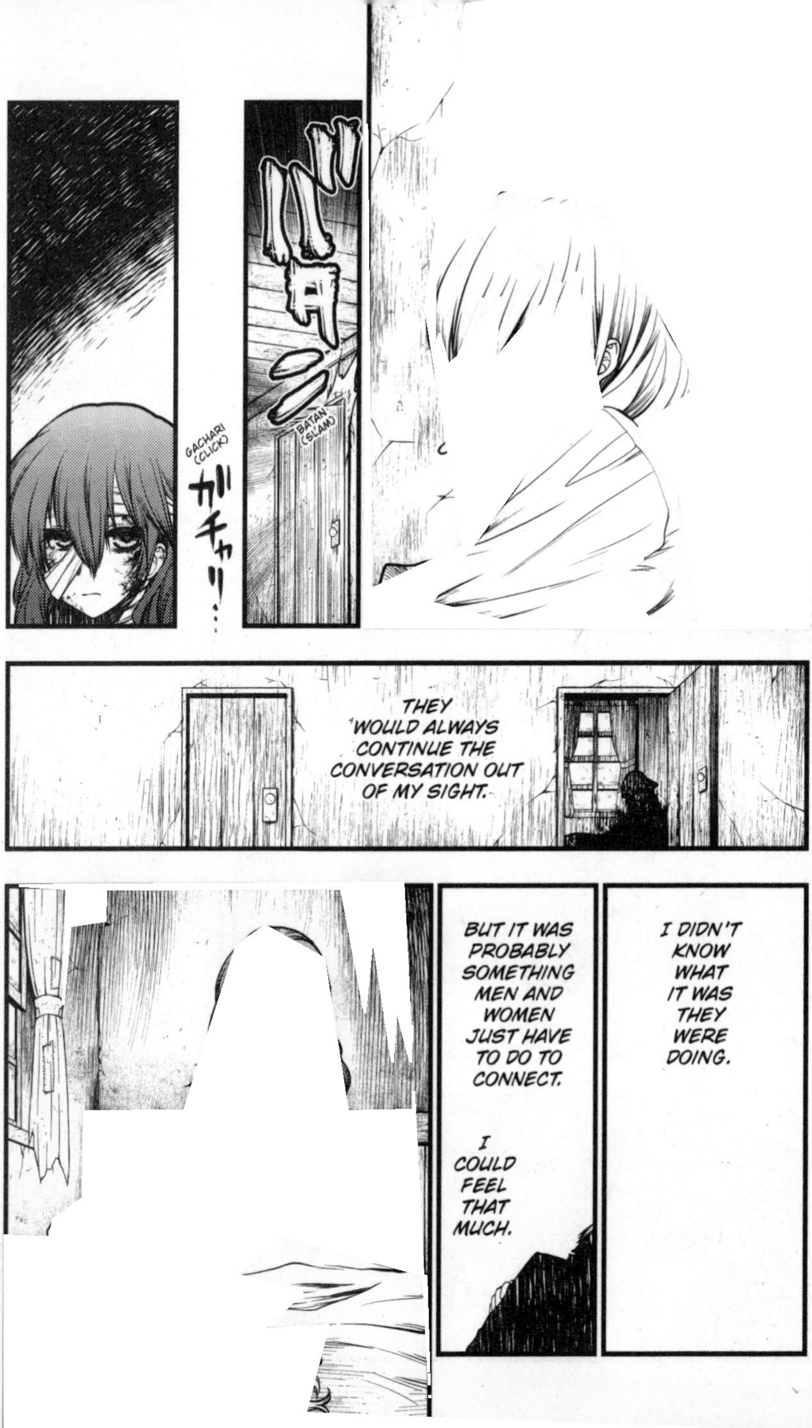

バタン
BATAN (SLAM)
ガチャリ…
GACHARI (CLICK)
THEY WOULD ALWAYS CONTINUE THE CONVERSATION OUT OF MY SIGHT.
I DIDN'T KNOW WHAT IT WAS THEY WERE DOING.
BUT IT WAS PROBABLY SOMETHING MEN AND WOMEN JUST HAVE TO DO TO CONNECT.
I COULD FEEL THAT MUCH.

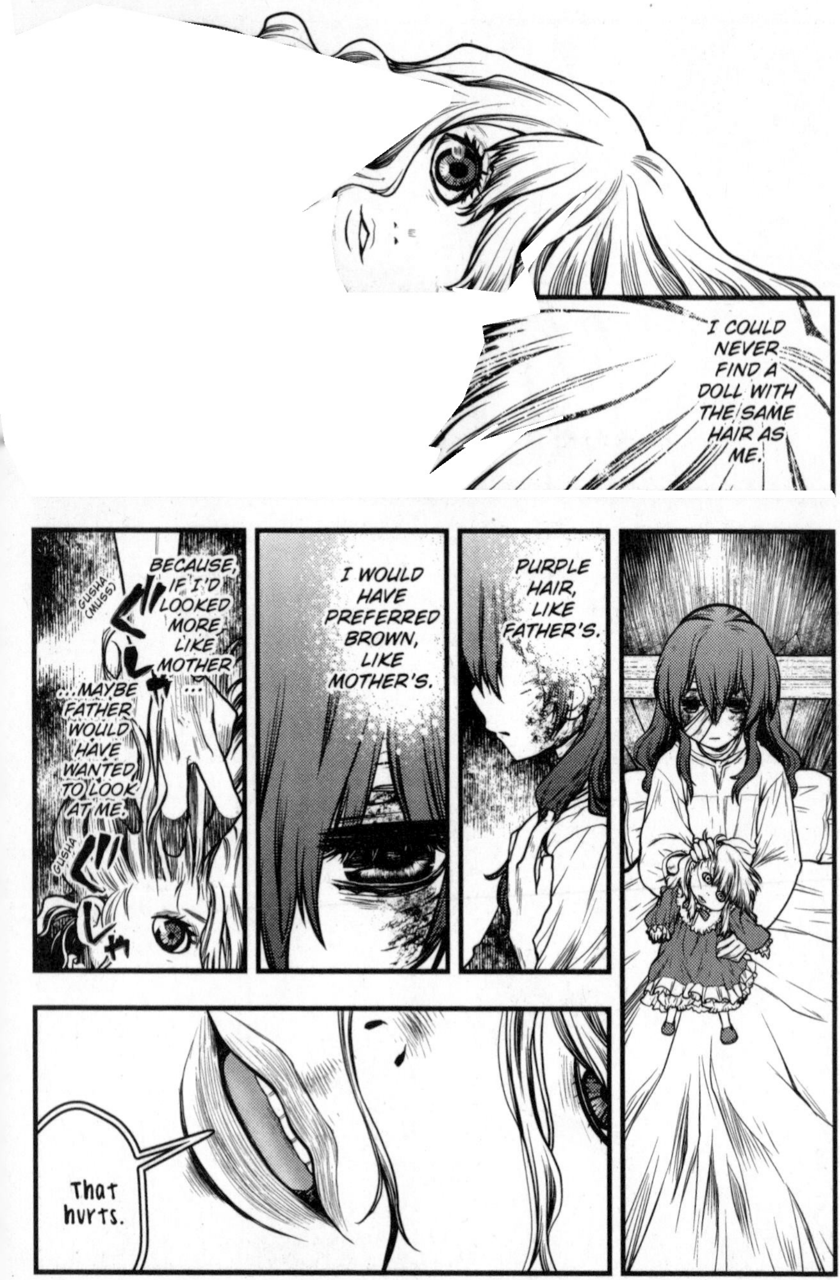
I COULD NEVER FIND A DOLL WITH THE SAME HAIR AS ME.
PURPLE HAIR, LIKE FATHER'S.
I WOULD HAVE PREFERRED BROWN, LIKE MOTHER'S.
BECAUSE, IF I'D LOOKED MORE LIKE MOTHER...
GUSHA (MUSS)
...MAYBE FATHER WOULD HAVE WANTED TO LOOK AT ME.
GUSHA
That hurts.

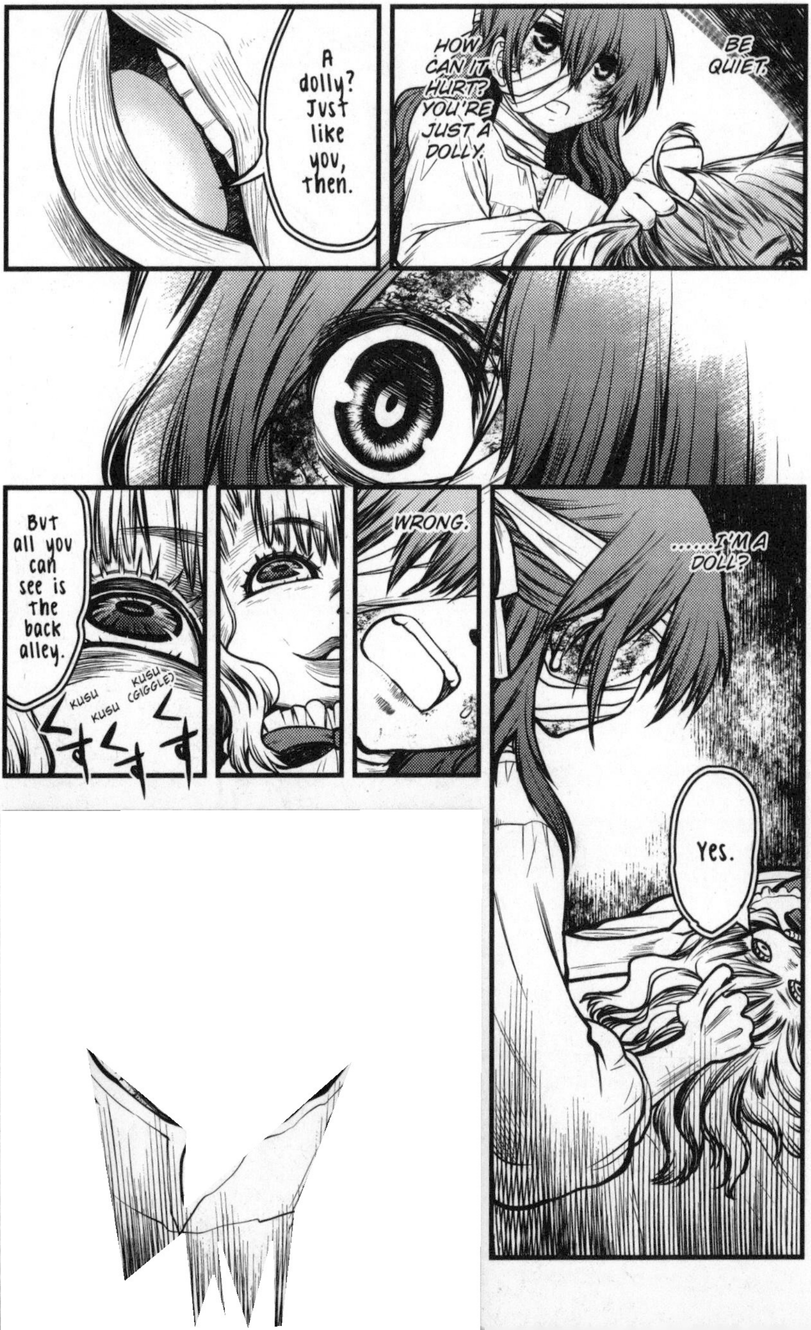
BE QUIET.
HOW CAN IT HURT? YOU'RE JUST A DOLLY.
A dolly? Just like you, then.
......I'M A DOLL?
Yes.
WRONG.
But all you can see is the back alley.
KUSU KUSU KUSU (GIGGLE)
くすくすくす

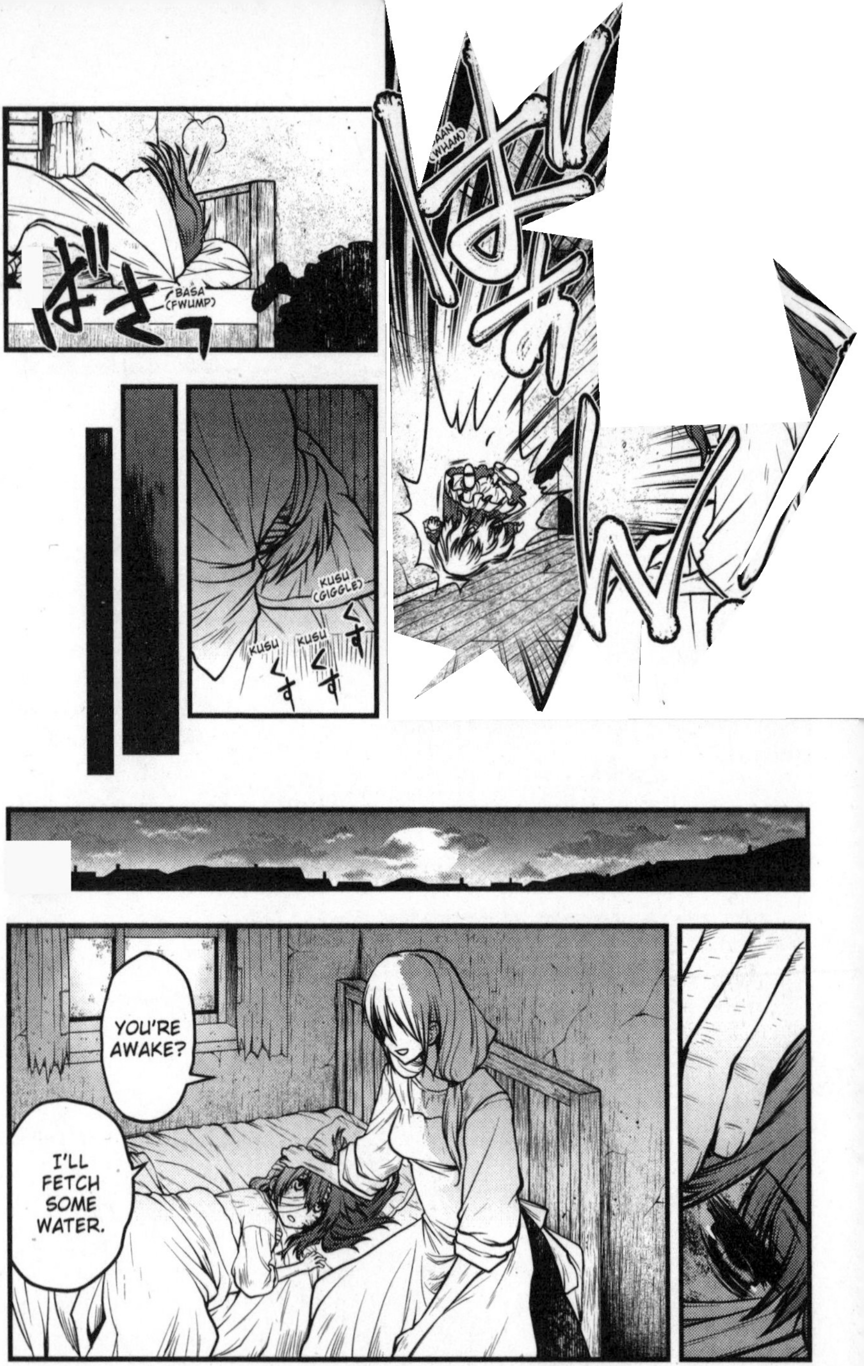
BAAN (WHAM)
ばさっ
BASA (FWUMP)
KUSU (GIGGLE)
くす
KUSU
くす
KUSU
くす
YOU'RE AWAKE?
I'LL FETCH SOME WATER.

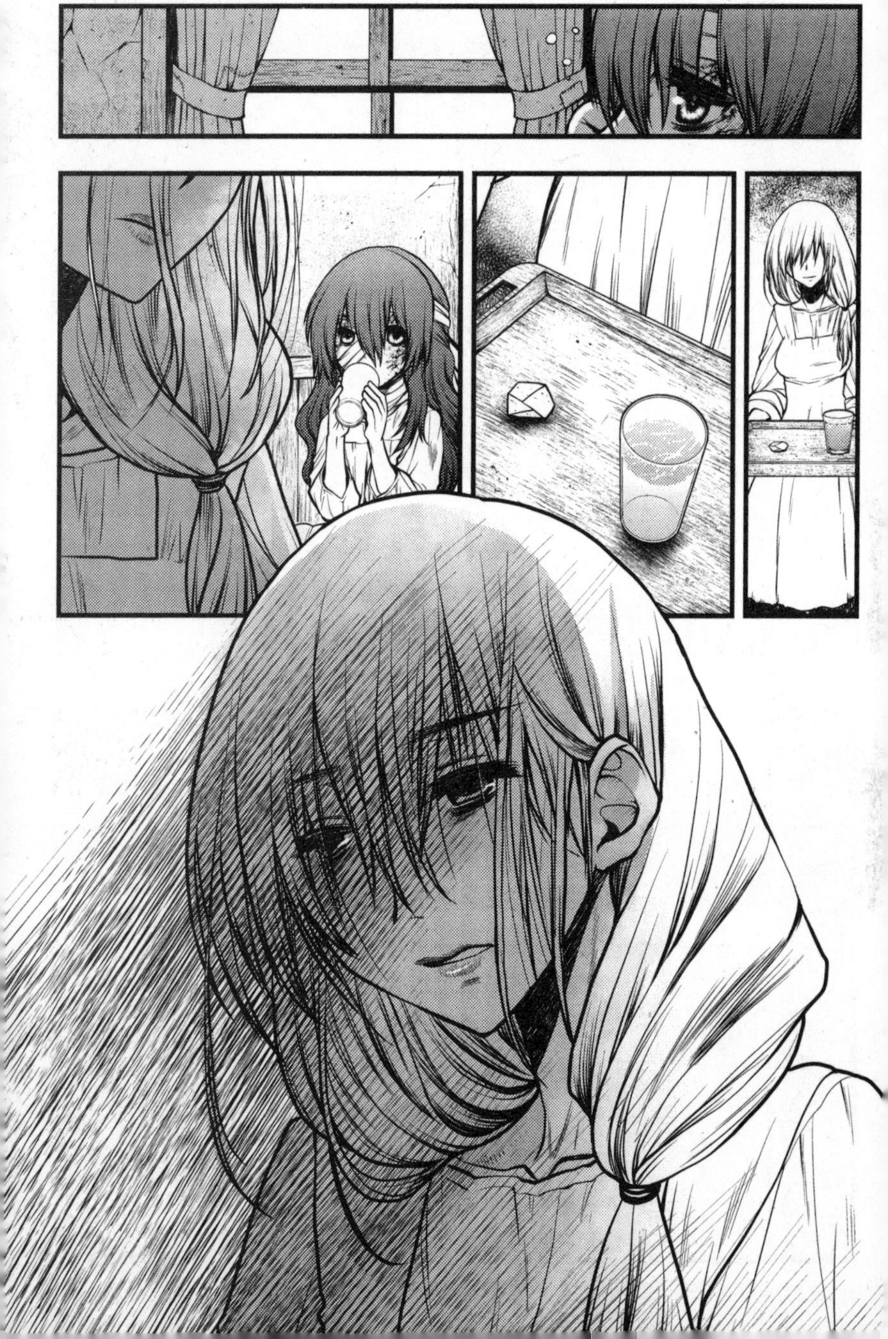

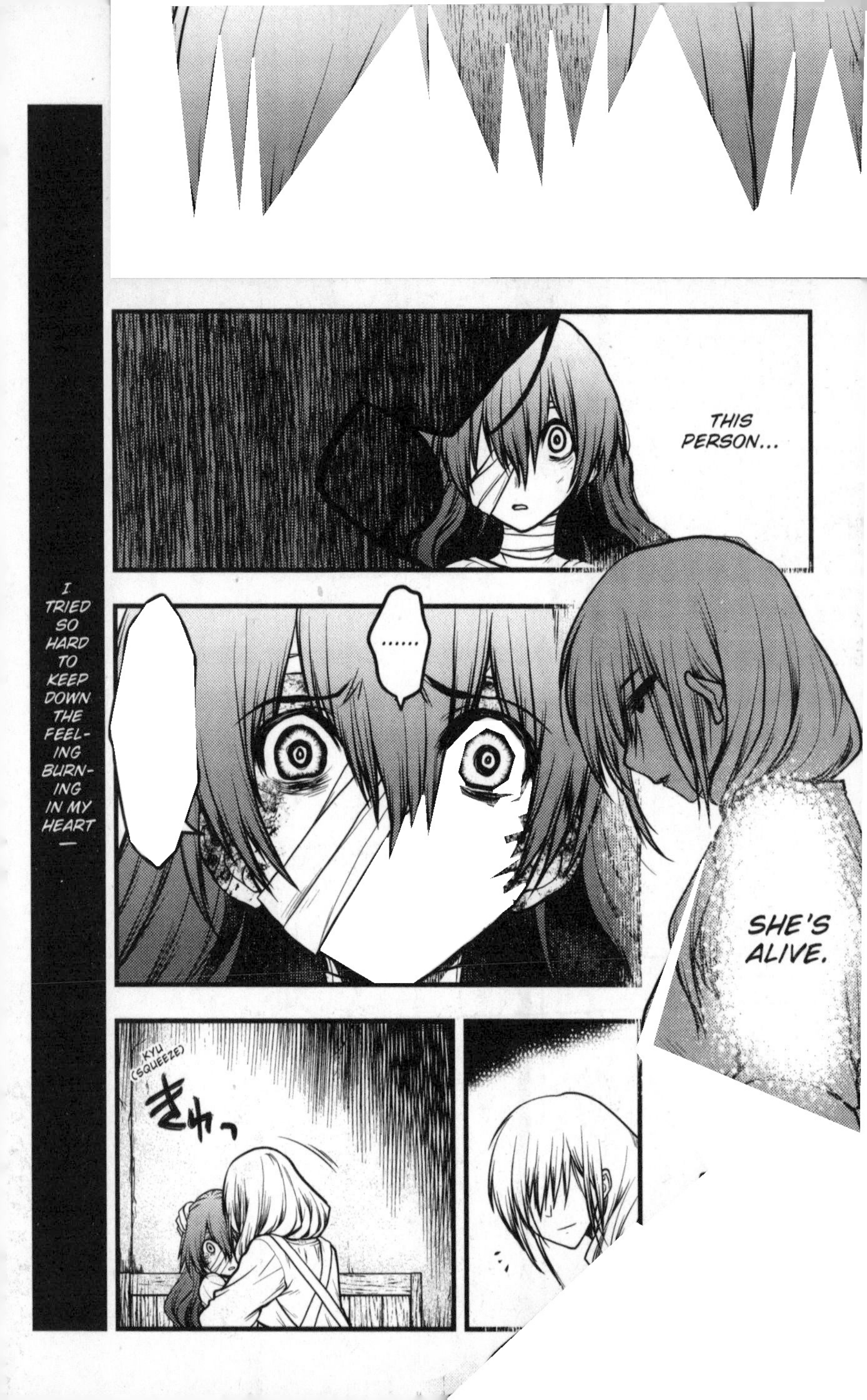
THIS PERSON...
SHE'S ALIVE.
......
I TRIED SO HARD TO KEEP DOWN THE FEELING BURNING IN MY HEART—
KYU (SQUEEZE)

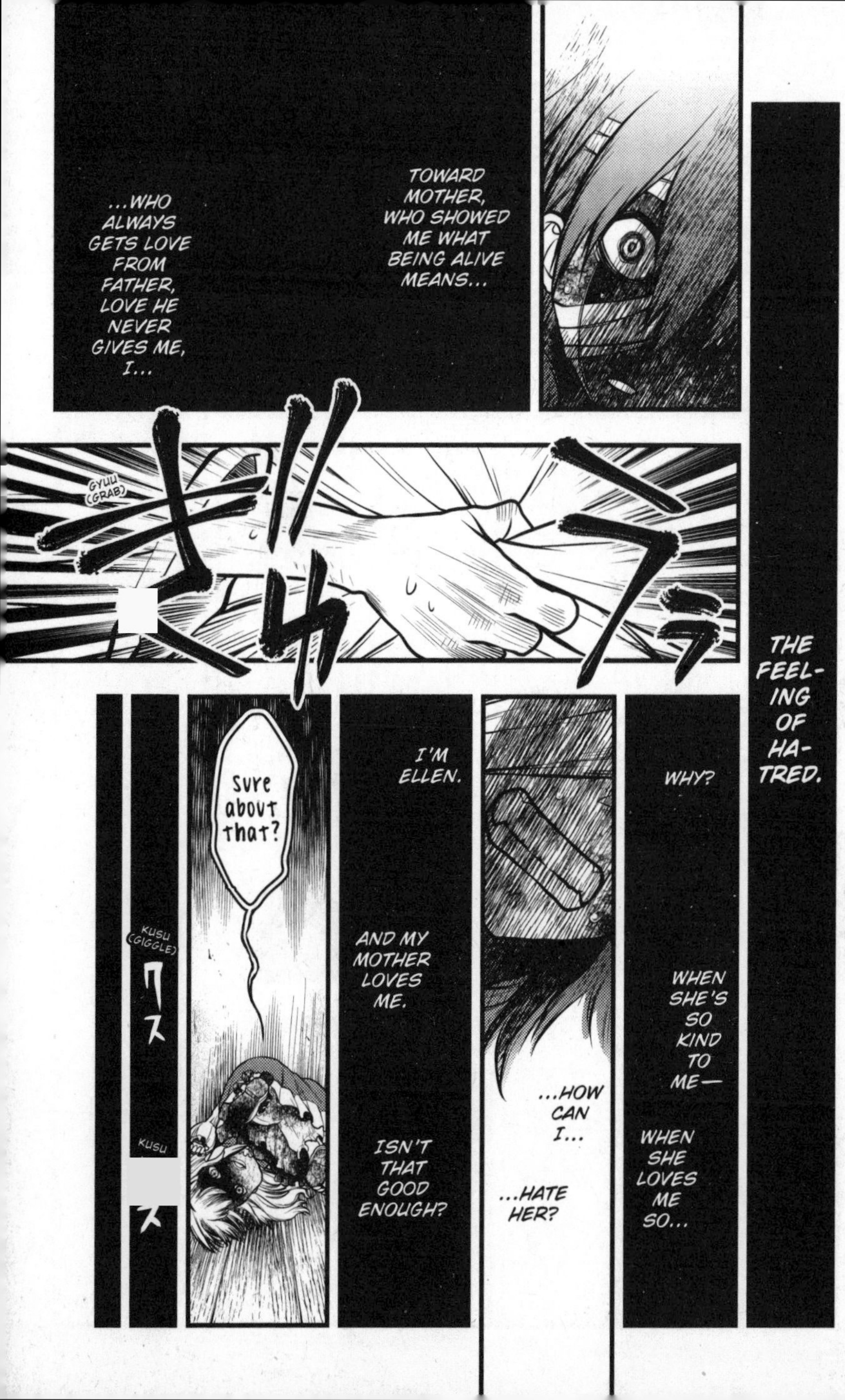
TOWARD MOTHER, WHO SHOWED ME WHAT BEING ALIVE MEANS...
...WHO ALWAYS GETS LOVE FROM FATHER, LOVE HE NEVER GIVES ME, I...
GYUU (GRAB)
THE FEEL-ING OF HA-TRED.
WHY?
WHEN SHE'S SO KIND TO ME—
WHEN SHE LOVES ME SO...
...HOW CAN I...
...HATE HER?
I'M ELLEN.
AND MY MOTHER LOVES ME.
ISN'T THAT GOOD ENOUGH?
Sure about that?
KUSU (GIGGLE)
KUSU

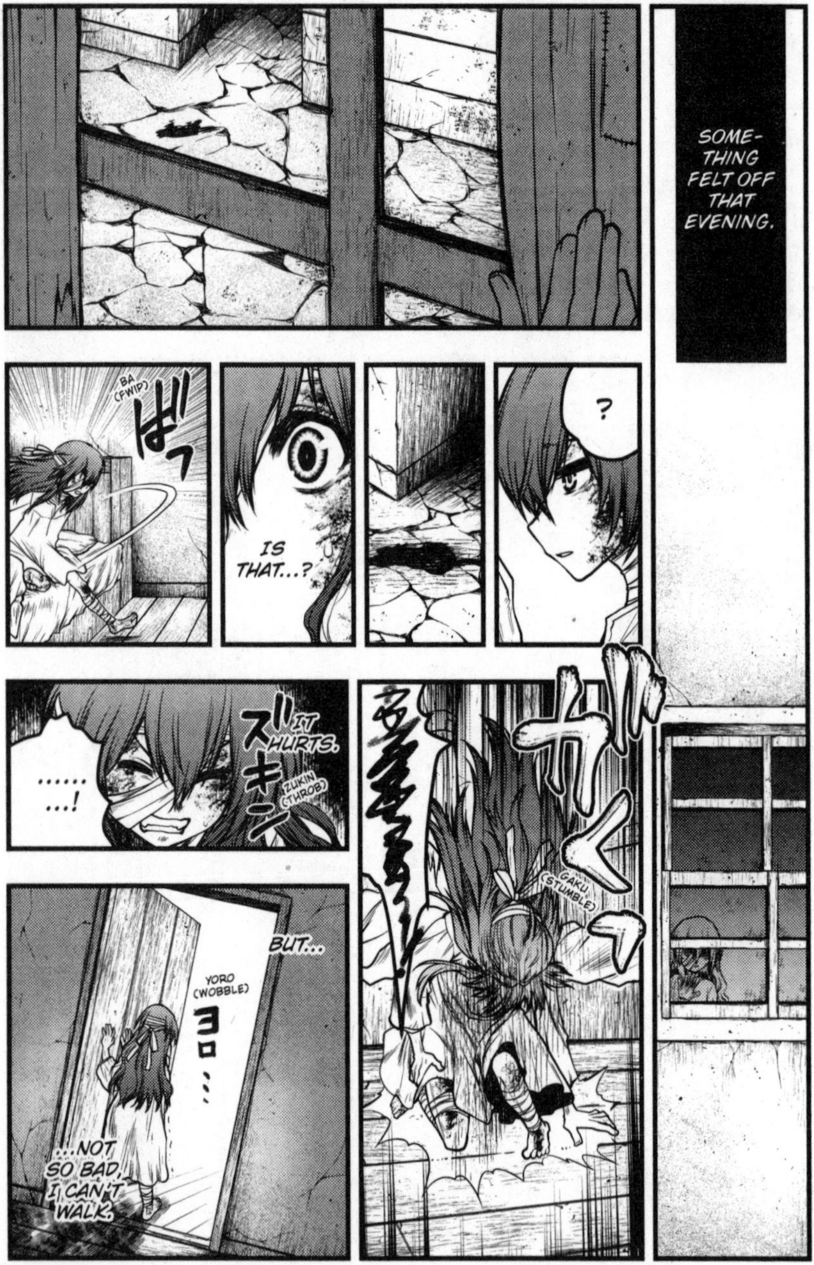
SOME-THING FELT OFF THAT EVENING.
?
IS THAT...?
BA (FWIP)
ぱっ
ガクッ
GAKU (STUMBLE)
IT HURTS.
ズキン
ZUKIN (THROB)
......
...!
BUT...
YORO (WOBBLE)
ヨロ...
...NOT SO BAD, I CAN'T WALK.

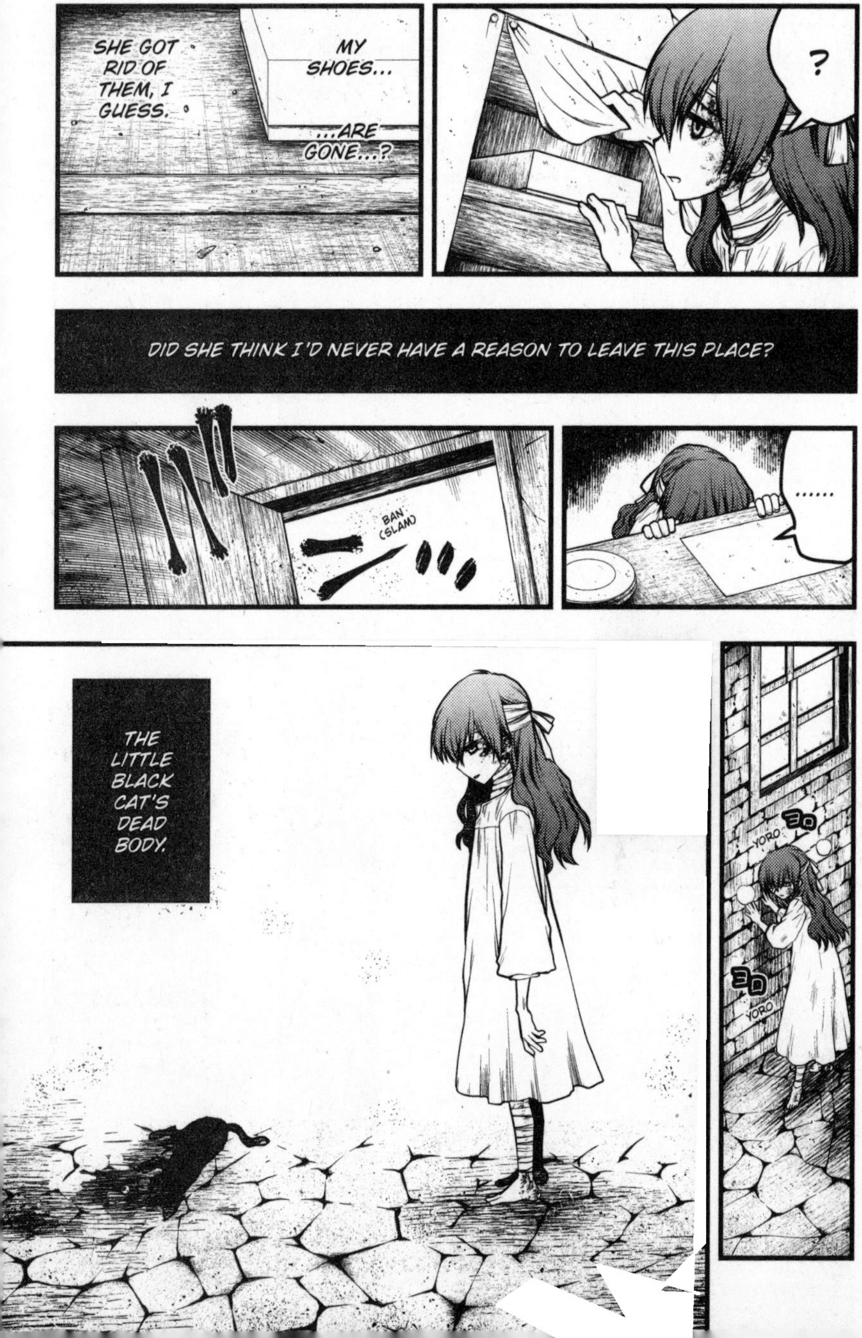
?
MY SHOES...
...ARE GONE...?
SHE GOT RID OF THEM, I GUESS.
DID SHE THINK I'D NEVER HAVE A REASON TO LEAVE THIS PLACE?
......
BAN (SLAM)
ヨロ YORO
ヨロ YORO
THE LITTLE BLACK CAT'S DEAD BODY.

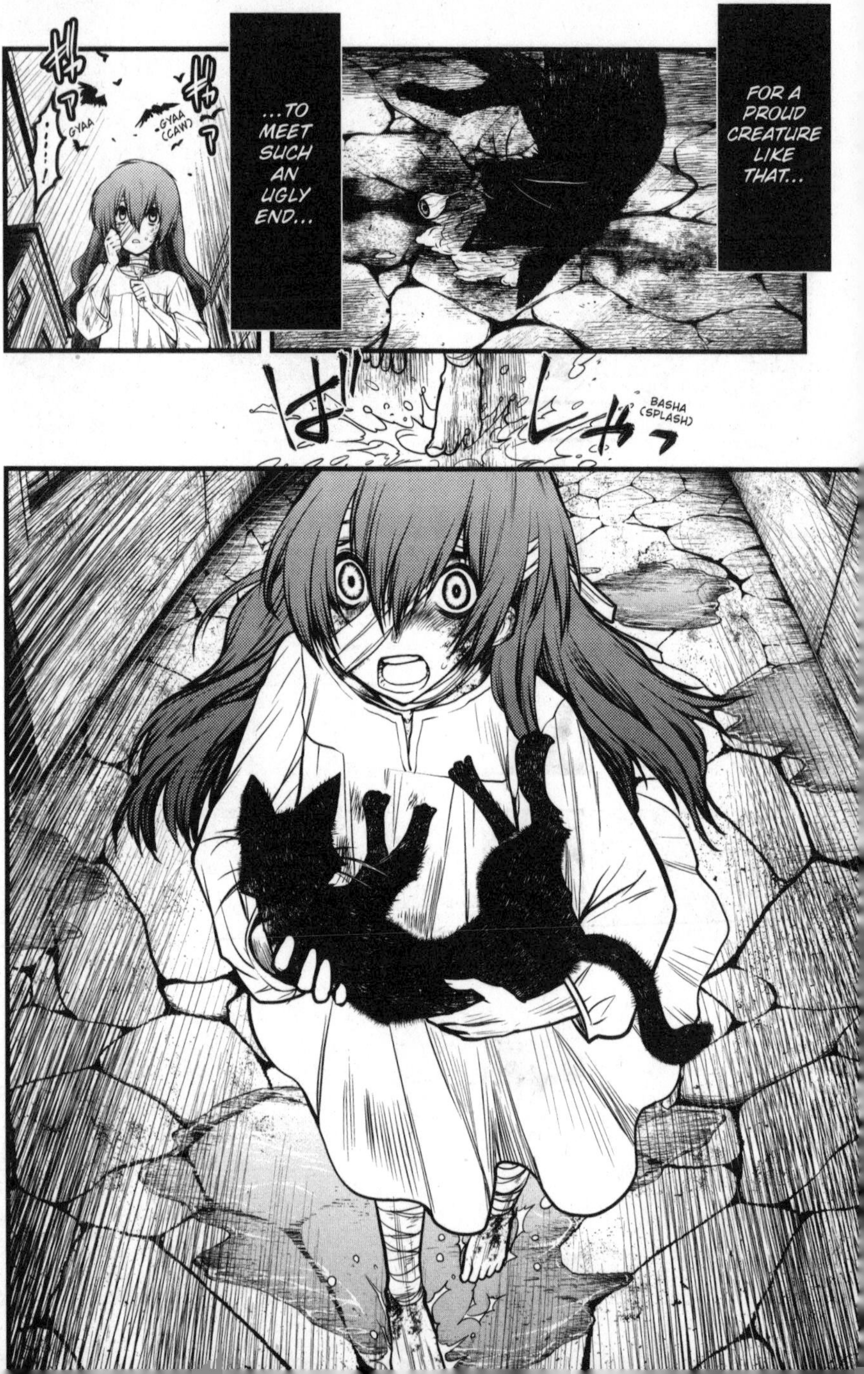
FOR A PROUD CREATURE LIKE THAT...
...TO MEET SUCH AN UGLY END...
GYAA (CAW)
GYAA
BASHA (SPLASH)

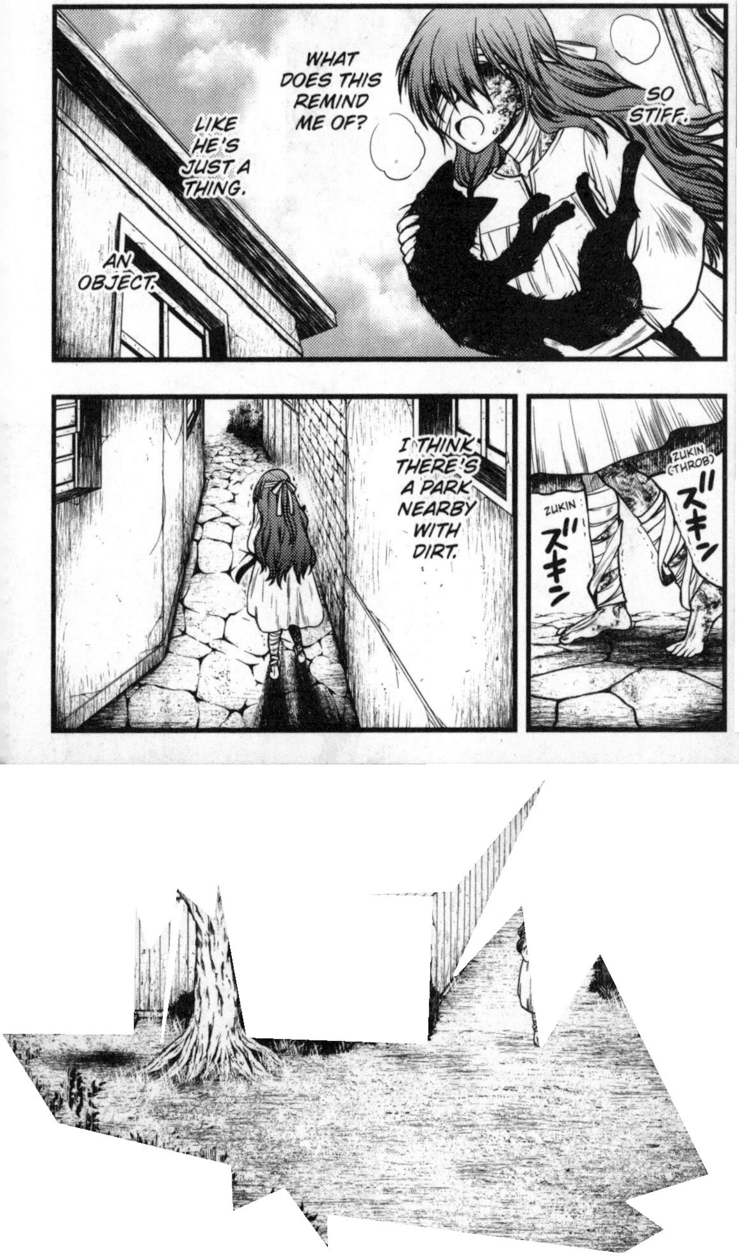
SO STIFF.
WHAT DOES THIS REMIND ME OF?
LIKE HE'S JUST A THING.
AN OBJECT.
ズキン
ZUKIN (THROB)
ズキン
ZUKIN
I THINK THERE'S A PARK NEARBY WITH DIRT.

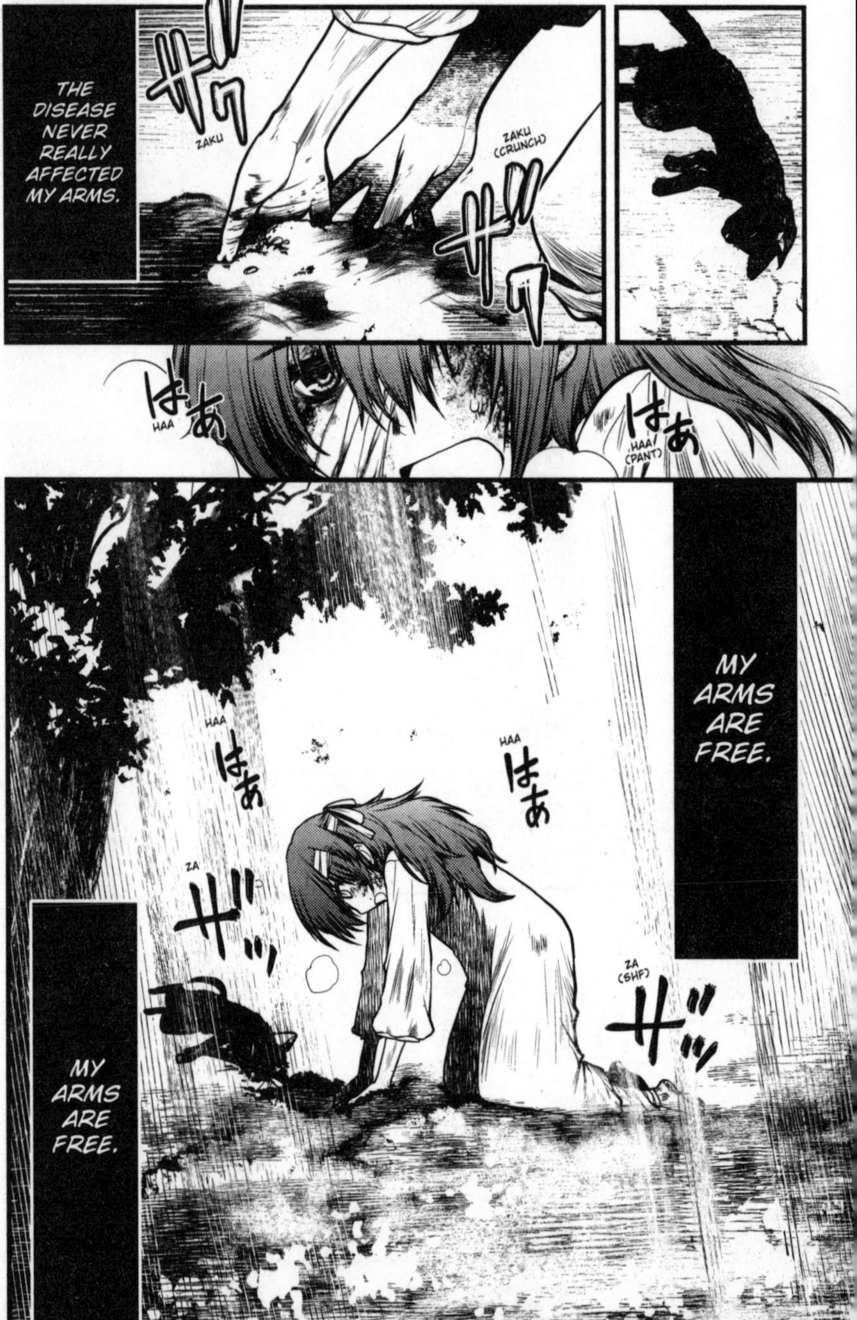
ザク
ZAKU (CRUNCH)
THE DISEASE NEVER REALLY AFFECTED MY ARMS.
ザク
ZAKU
はぁ
HAA (PANT)
はぁ
HAA
MY ARMS ARE FREE.
はぁ
HAA
はぁ
HAA
ザッ
ZA (SHF)
ザッ
ZA
MY ARMS ARE FREE.

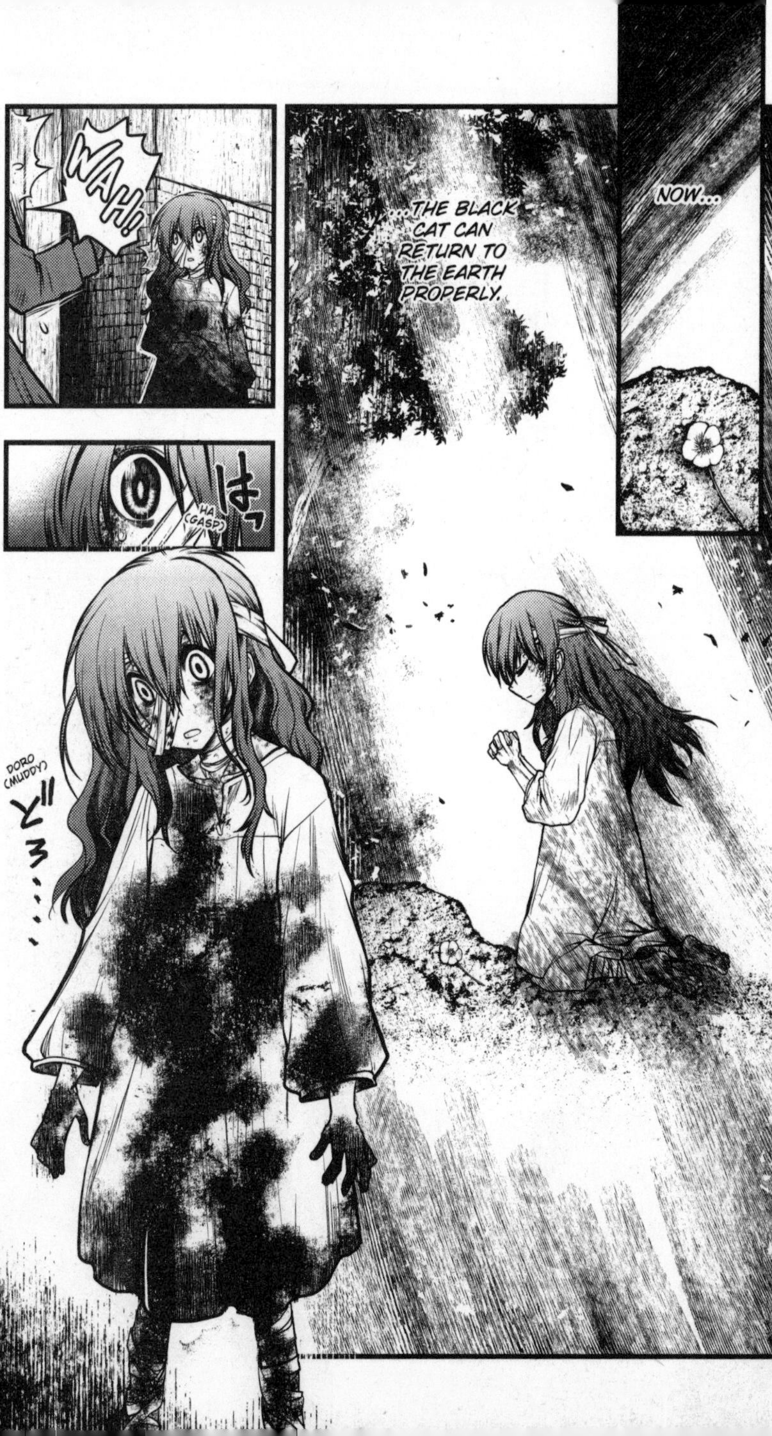
NOW...
...THE BLACK CAT CAN RETURN TO THE EARTH PROPERLY.
WAH!
はっ
HA (GASP)
どろ...
DORO (MUDDY)

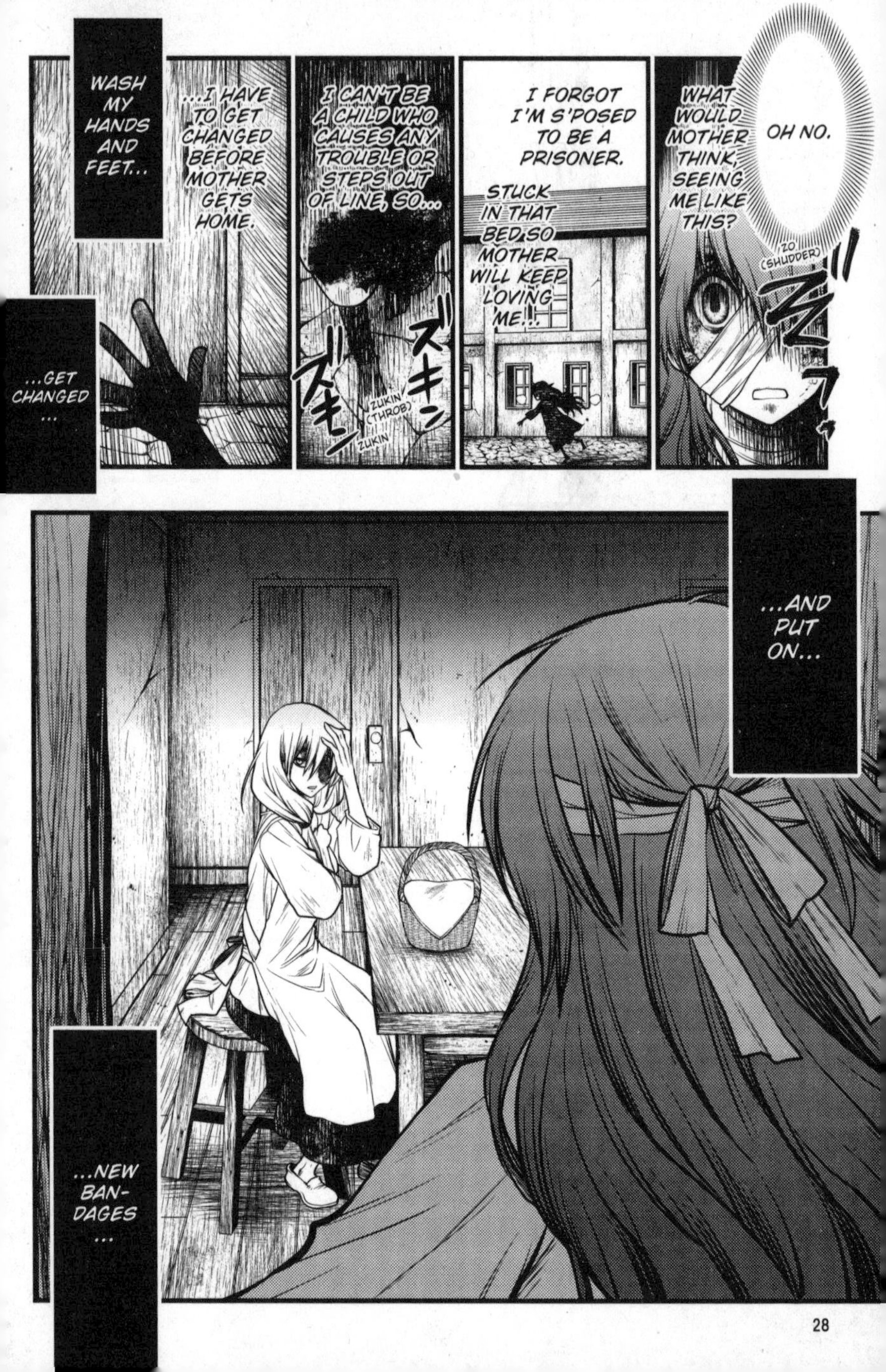
OH NO.
WHAT WOULD MOTHER THINK, SEEING ME LIKE THIS?
ZO (SHUDDER)
I FORGOT I'M S'POSED TO BE A PRISONER.
STUCK IN THAT BED SO MOTHER WILL KEEP LOVING ME...
I CAN'T BE A CHILD WHO CAUSES ANY TROUBLE OR STEPS OUT OF LINE, SO...
ZUKIN (THROB) ZUKIN
WASH MY HANDS AND FEET...
...I HAVE TO GET CHANGED BEFORE MOTHER GETS HOME.
...GET CHANGED...
...AND PUT ON...
...NEW BAN-DAGES...

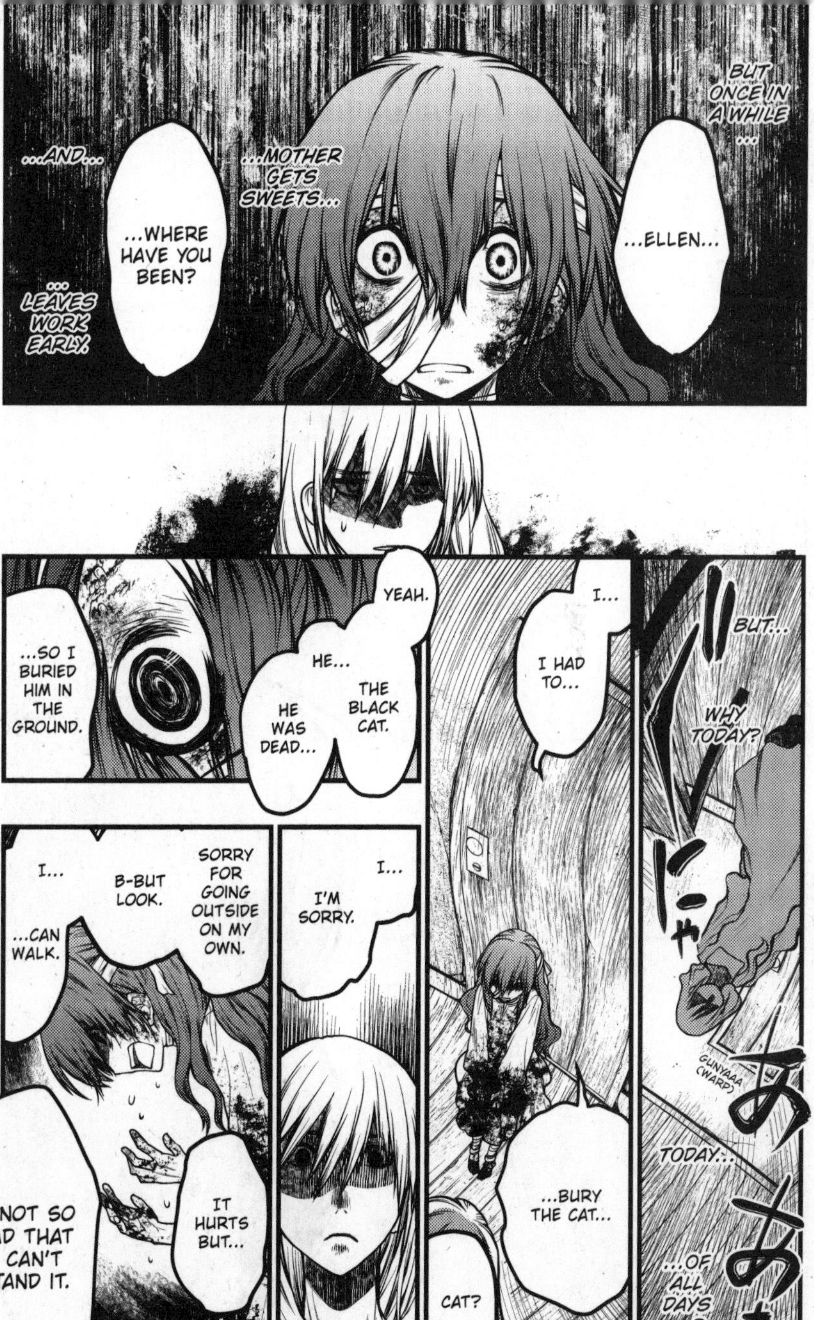
BUT ONCE IN A WHILE...
...ELLEN...
...MOTHER GETS SWEETS...
...WHERE HAVE YOU BEEN?
...AND...
...LEAVES WORK EARLY.
BUT...
WHY TODAY?
GUNYAAA (WARP)
あああ
TODAY...
...OF ALL DAYS...?
I...
I HAD TO...
...BURY THE CAT...
CAT?
YEAH.
HE...
THE BLACK CAT.
HE WAS DEAD...
...SO I BURIED HIM IN THE GROUND.
I...
I'M SORRY.
SORRY FOR GOING OUTSIDE ON MY OWN.
B-BUT LOOK.
I...
...CAN WALK.
IT HURTS BUT...
...NOT SO BAD THAT I CAN'T STAND IT.

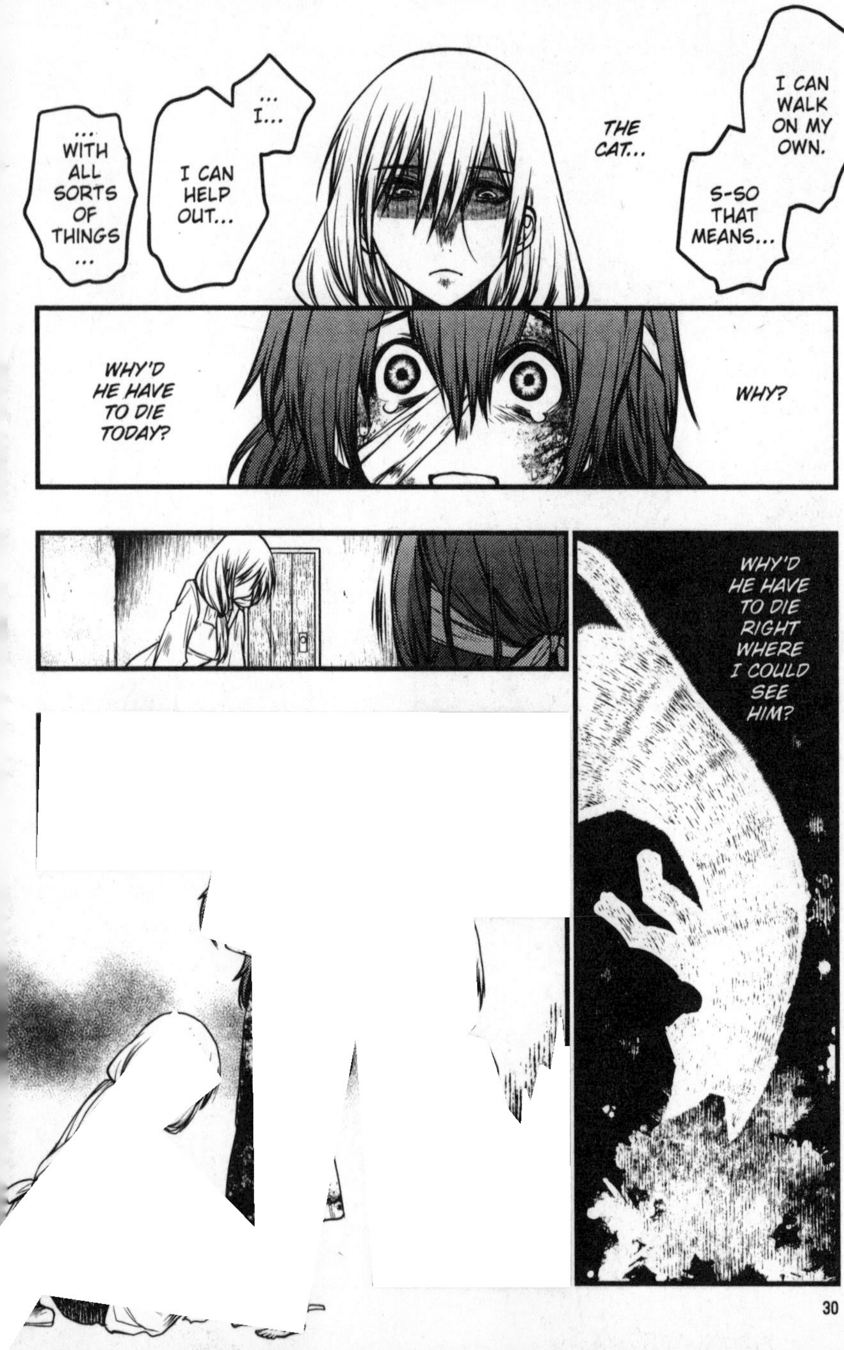
I CAN WALK ON MY OWN.
S-SO THAT MEANS...
THE CAT...
... I...
I CAN HELP OUT...
... WITH ALL SORTS OF THINGS ...
WHY?
WHY'D HE HAVE TO DIE TODAY?
WHY'D HE HAVE TO DIE RIGHT WHERE I COULD SEE HIM?

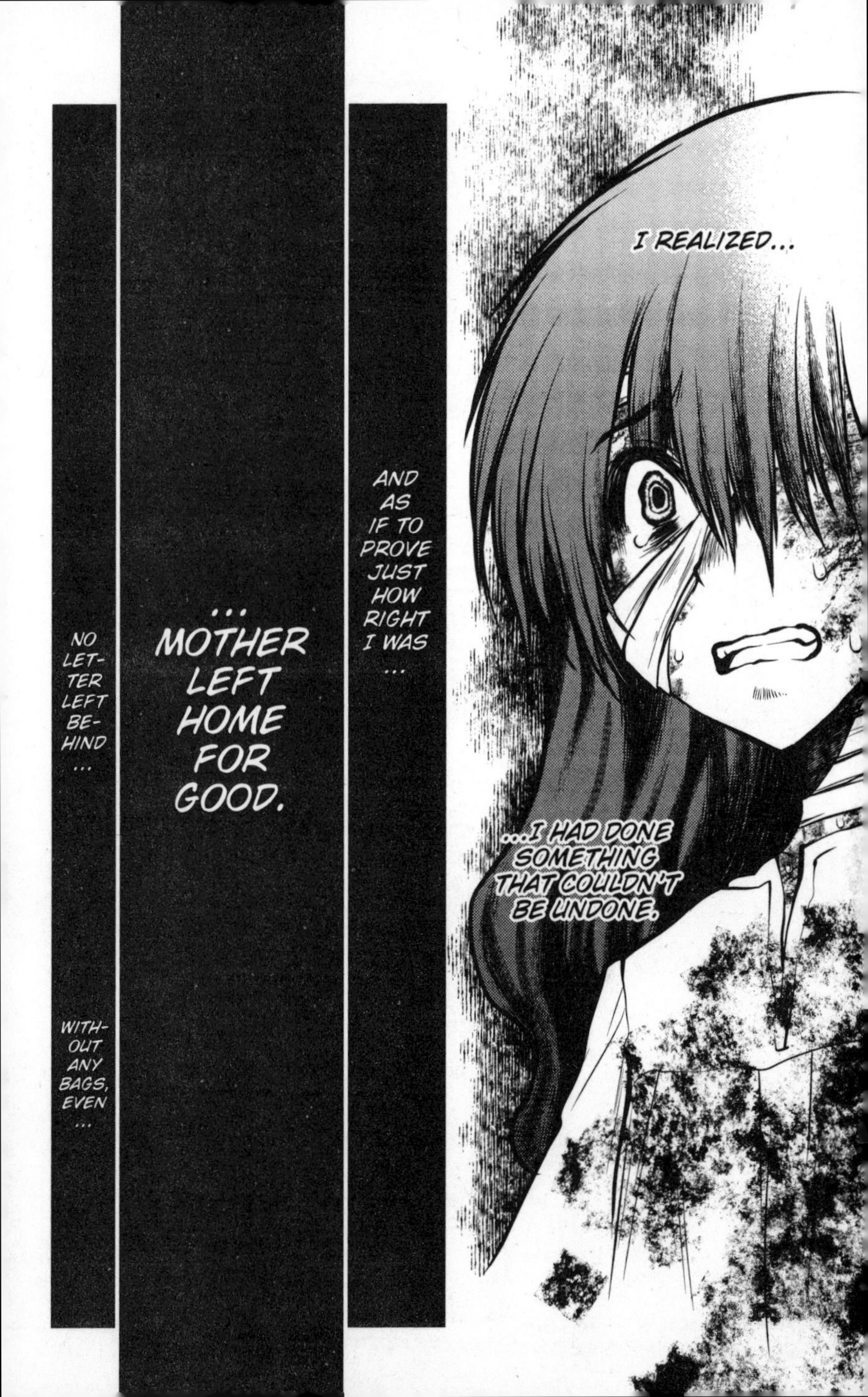
I REALIZED...
...I HAD DONE SOMETHING THAT COULDN'T BE UNDONE.
AND AS IF TO PROVE JUST HOW RIGHT I WAS ...
... MOTHER LEFT HOME FOR GOOD.
NO LETTER LEFT BEHIND ...
WITHOUT ANY BAGS, EVEN ...

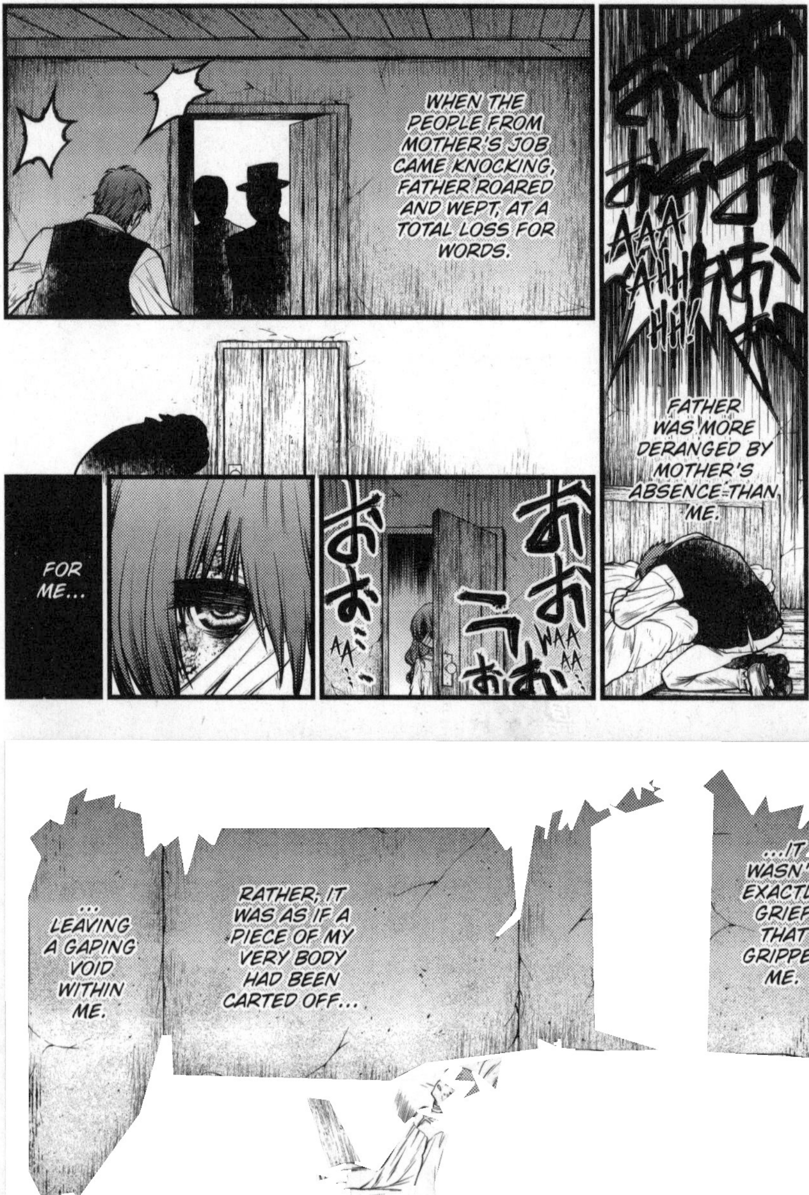

AAAAHHHH!
FATHER WAS MORE DERANGED BY MOTHER'S ABSENCE THAN ME.
WHEN THE PEOPLE FROM MOTHER'S JOB CAME KNOCKING, FATHER ROARED AND WEPT, AT A TOTAL LOSS FOR WORDS.
WAAAA...
AA...
FOR ME...
...IT WASN'T EXACTLY GRIEF THAT GRIPPED ME.
RATHER, IT WAS AS IF A PIECE OF MY VERY BODY HAD BEEN CARTED OFF...
...LEAVING A GAPING VOID WITHIN ME.

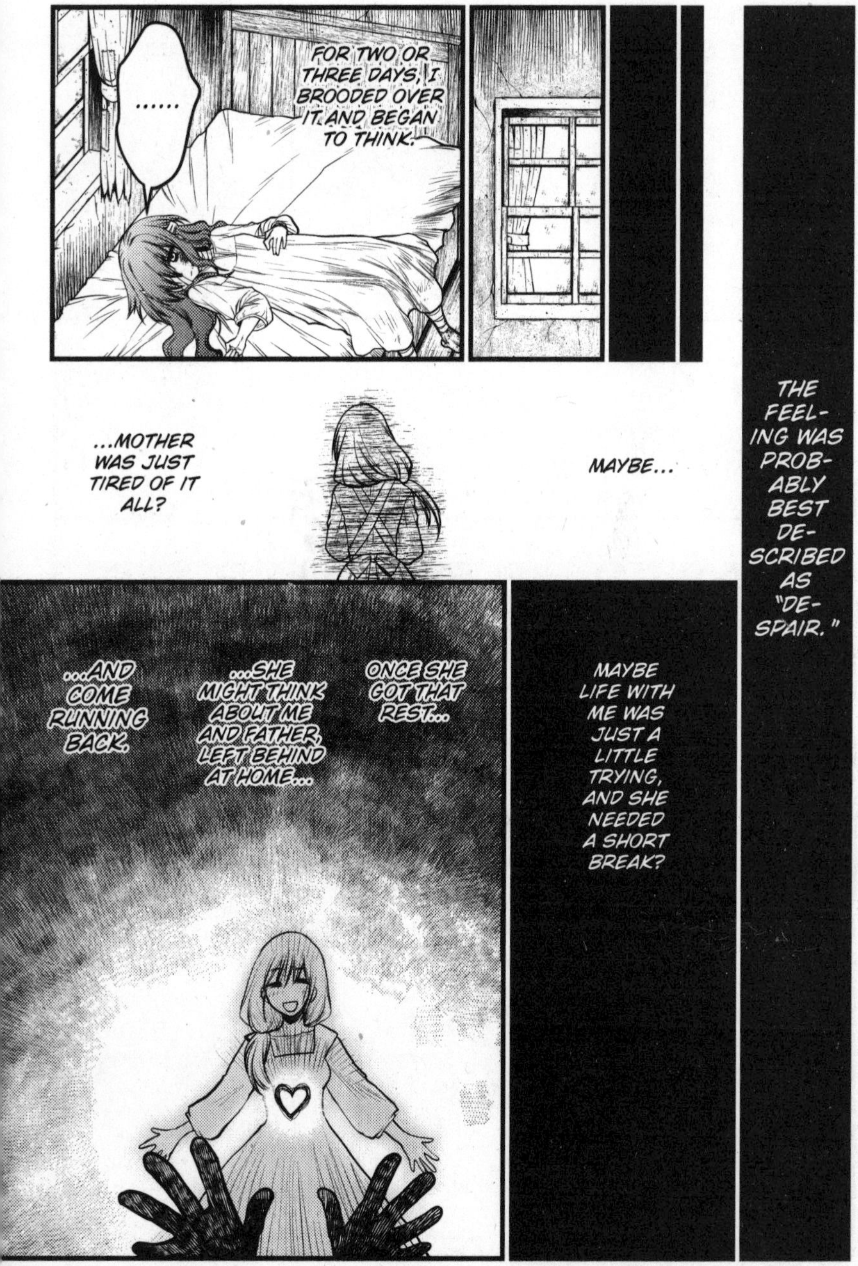
THE FEELING WAS PROBABLY BEST DESCRIBED AS "DESPAIR."
FOR TWO OR THREE DAYS, I BROODED OVER IT AND BEGAN TO THINK.
......
MAYBE...
...MOTHER WAS JUST TIRED OF IT ALL?
MAYBE LIFE WITH ME WAS JUST A LITTLE TRYING, AND SHE NEEDED A SHORT BREAK?
ONCE SHE GOT THAT REST...
...SHE MIGHT THINK ABOUT ME AND FATHER, LEFT BEHIND AT HOME...
...AND COME RUNNING BACK.

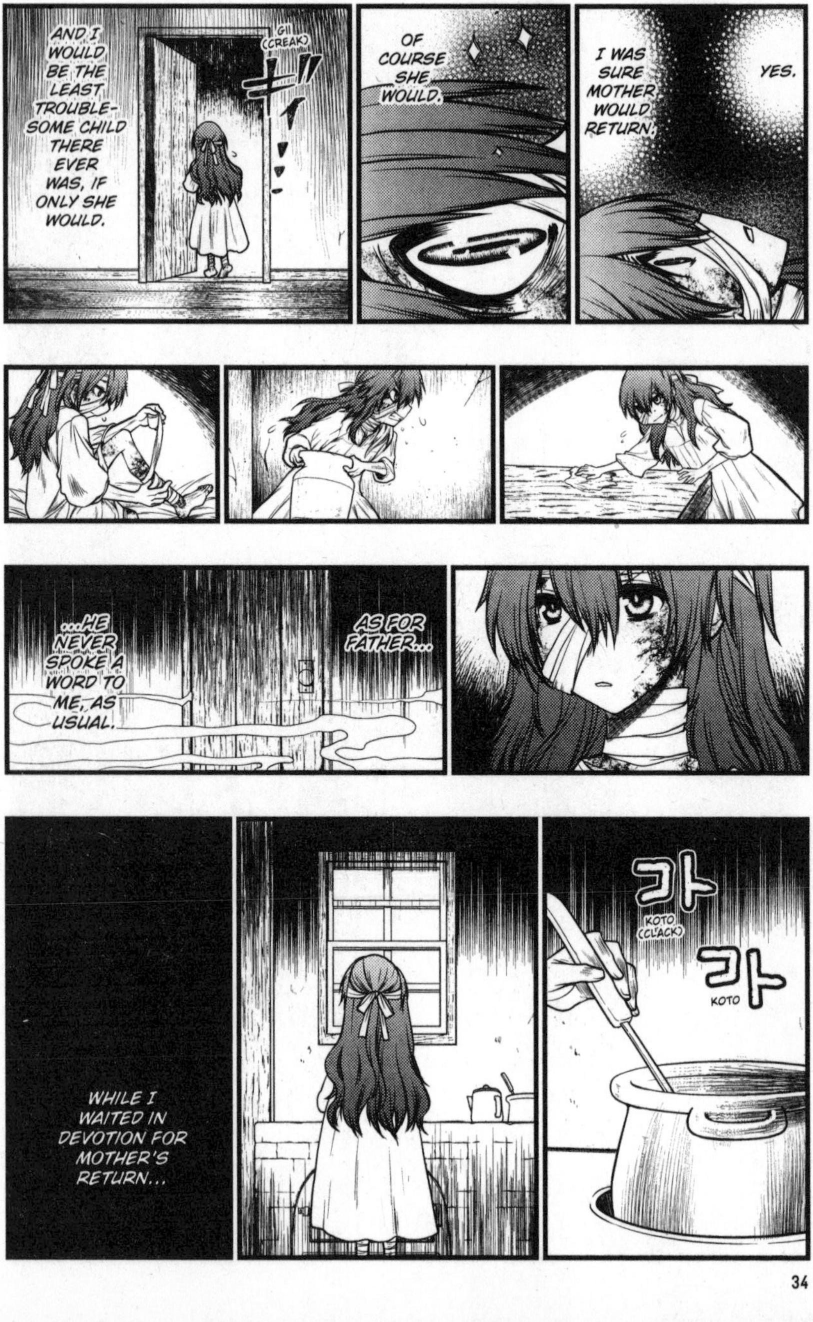
YES.
I WAS SURE MOTHER WOULD RETURN.
OF COURSE SHE WOULD.
GII (CREAK)
AND I WOULD BE THE LEAST TROUBLE-SOME CHILD THERE EVER WAS, IF ONLY SHE WOULD.
AS FOR FATHER...
...HE NEVER SPOKE A WORD TO ME, AS USUAL.
コト
KOTO (CLACK)
コト
KOTO
WHILE I WAITED IN DEVOTION FOR MOTHER'S RETURN...

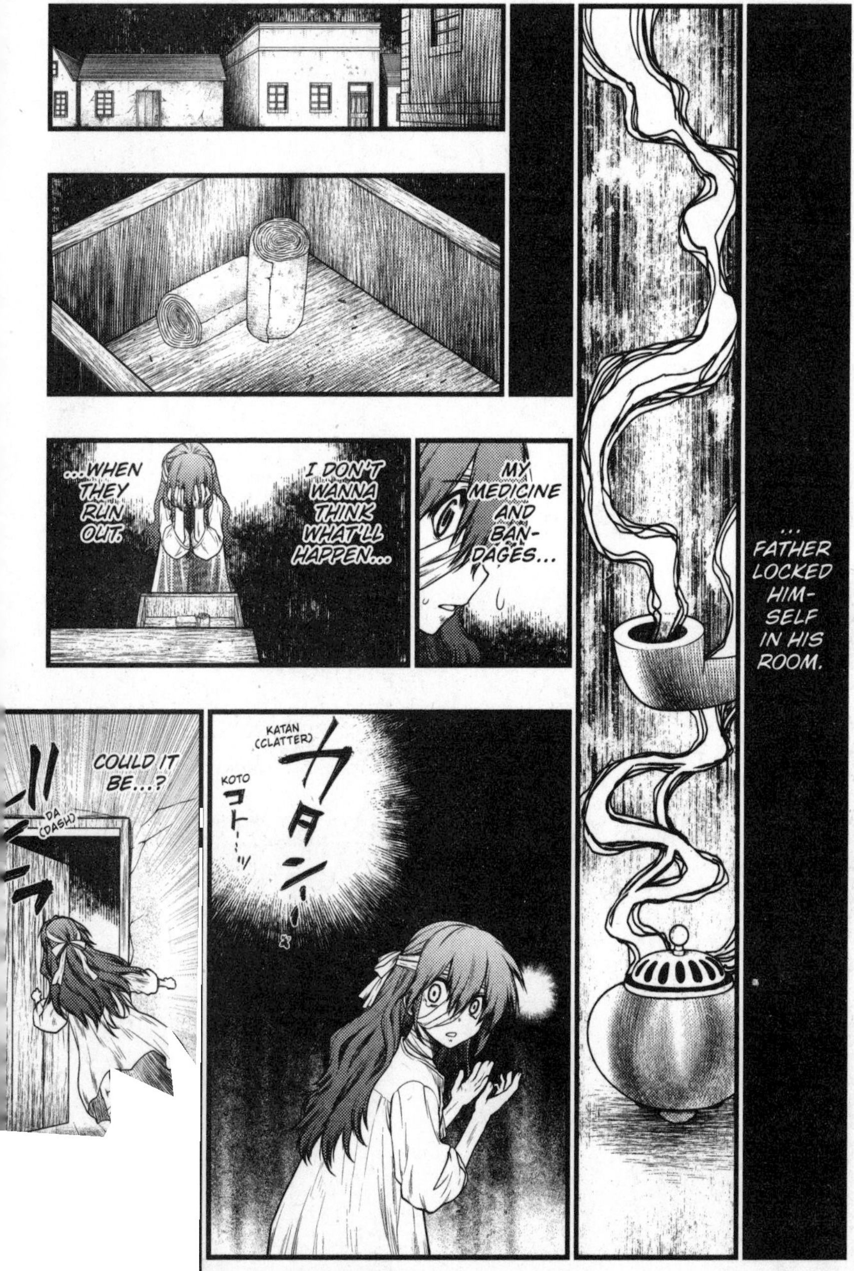
...FATHER LOCKED HIMSELF IN HIS ROOM.
MY MEDICINE AND BANDAGES...
I DON'T WANNA THINK WHAT'LL HAPPEN...
...WHEN THEY RUN OUT.
KATAN (CLATTER)
カタン
KOTO
コトー…ッ
COULD IT BE...?
DA (DASH)

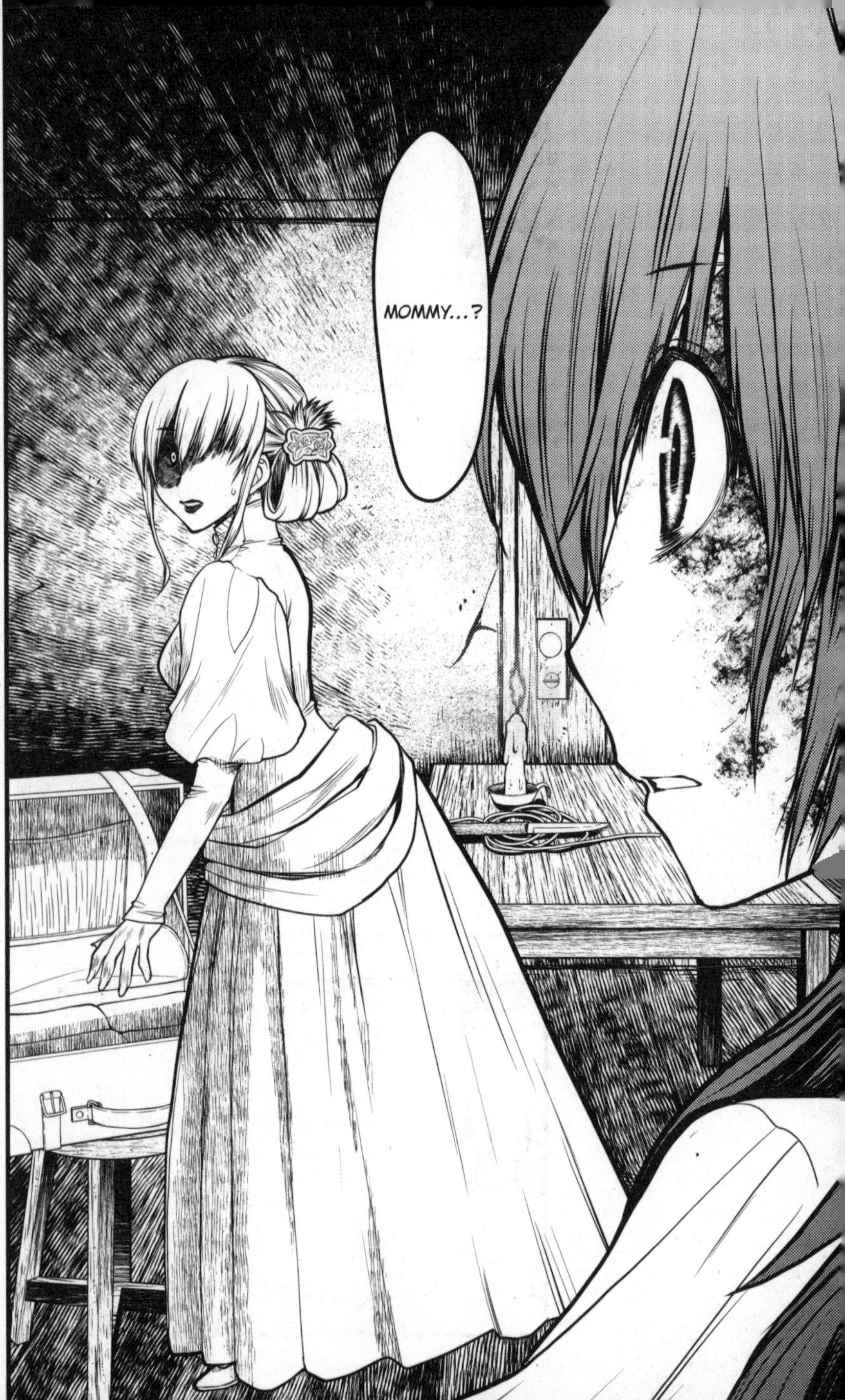
MOMMY...?

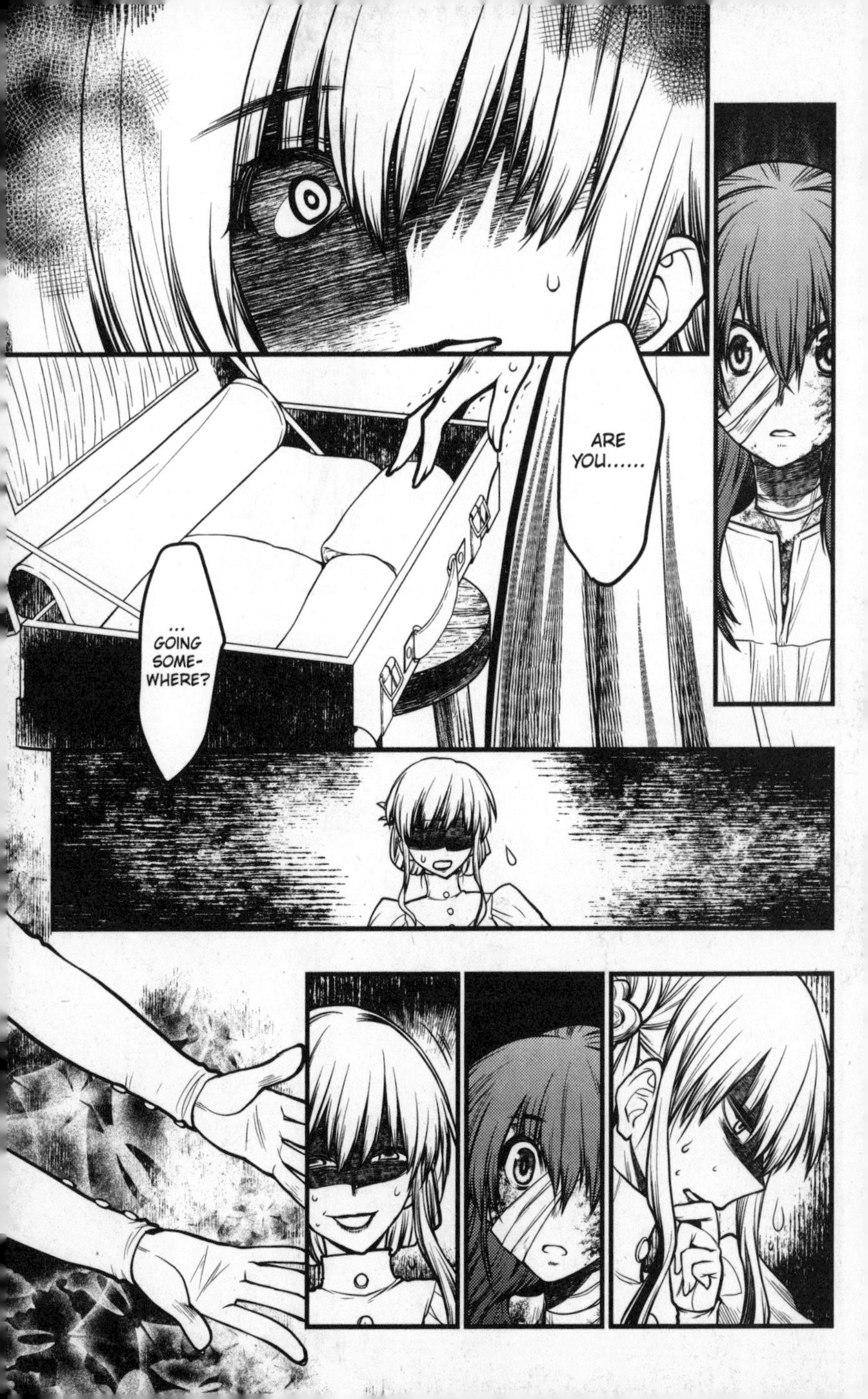
ARE YOU......
... GOING SOME-WHERE?

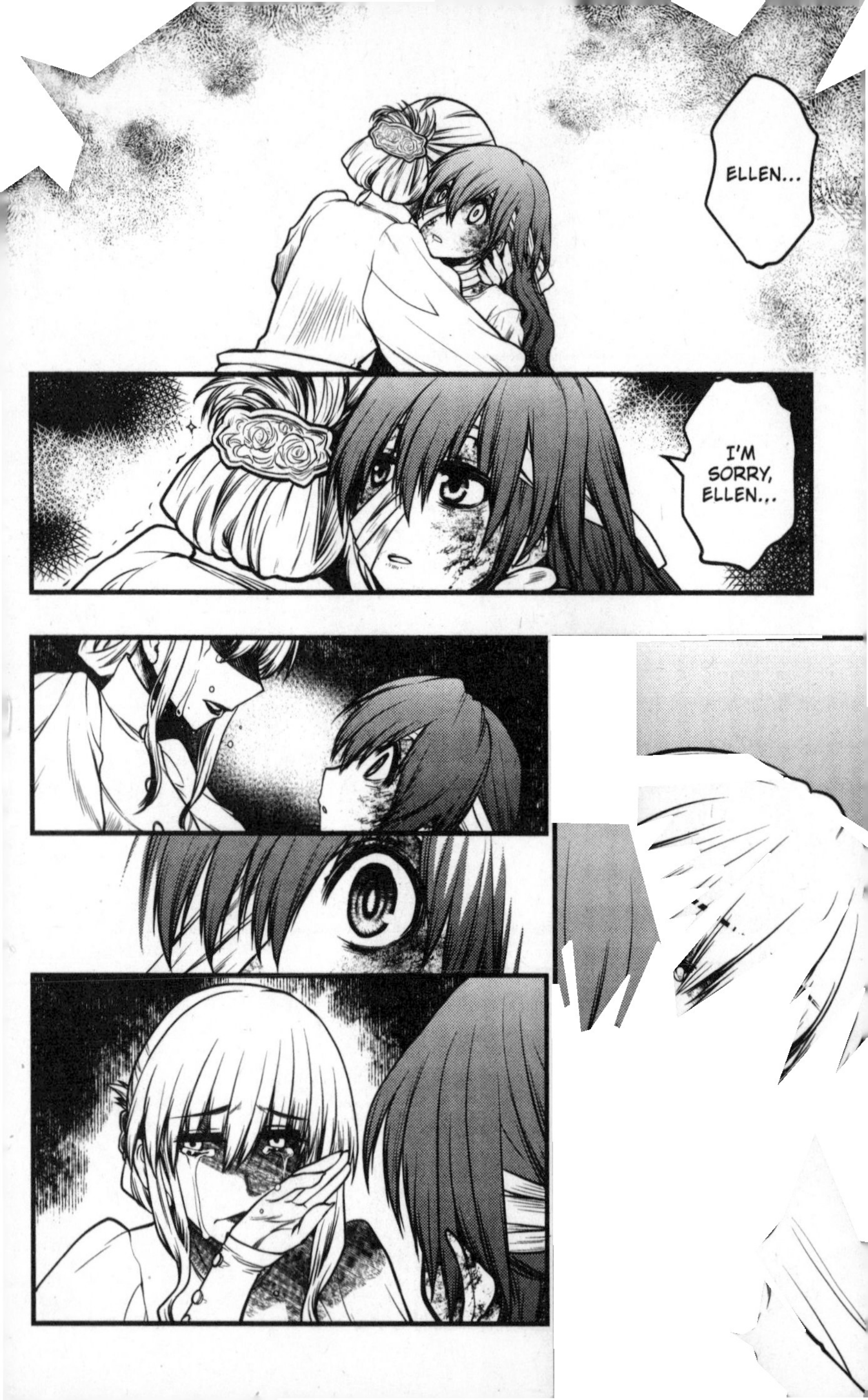
ELLEN...
I'M SORRY, ELLEN...

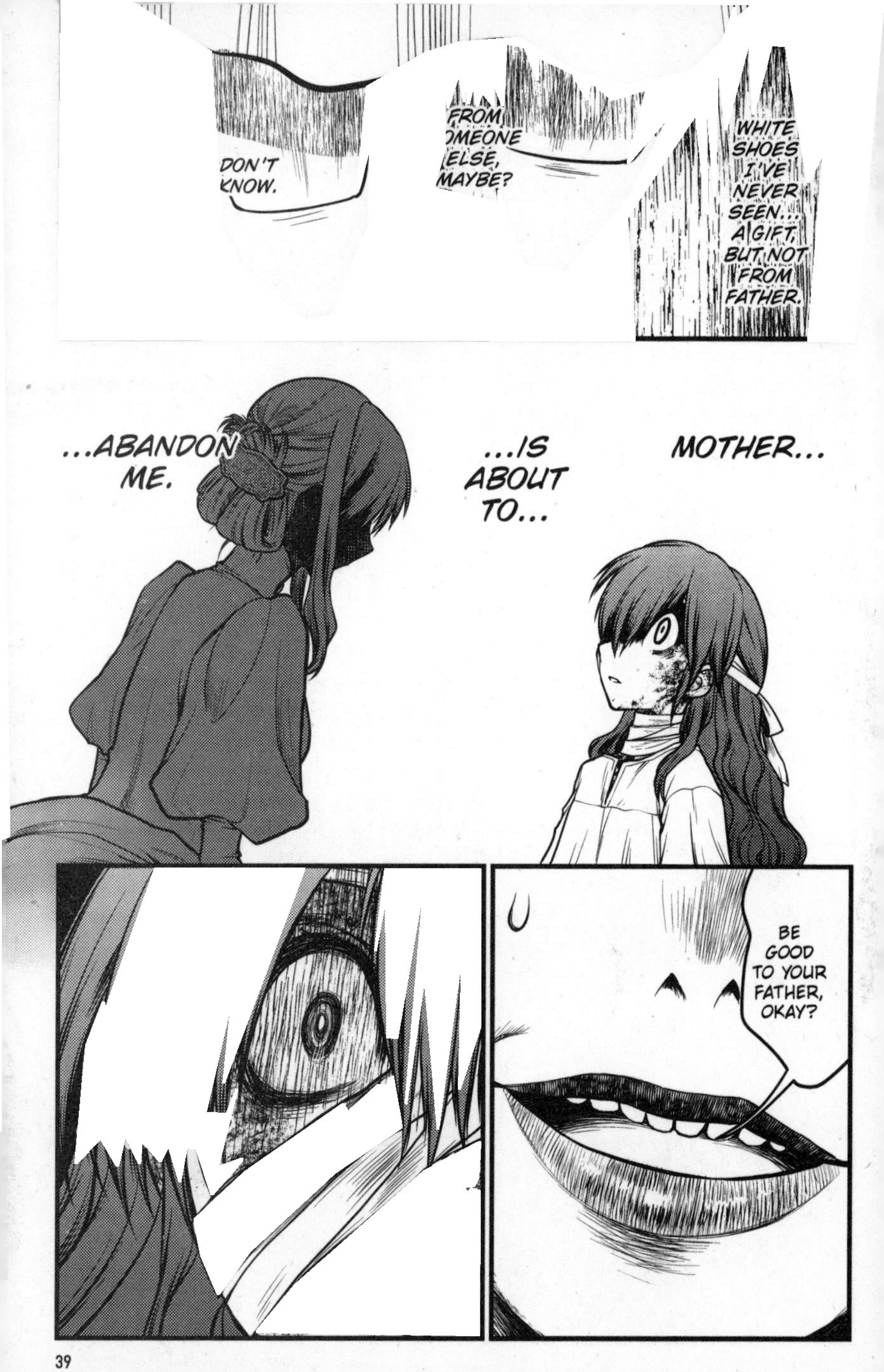
WHITE SHOES I'VE NEVER SEEN... A GIFT, BUT NOT FROM FATHER.
FROM OMEONE ELSE, MAYBE?
DON'T KNOW.
MOTHER...
...IS ABOUT TO...
...ABANDON ME.
BE GOOD TO YOUR FATHER, OKAY?

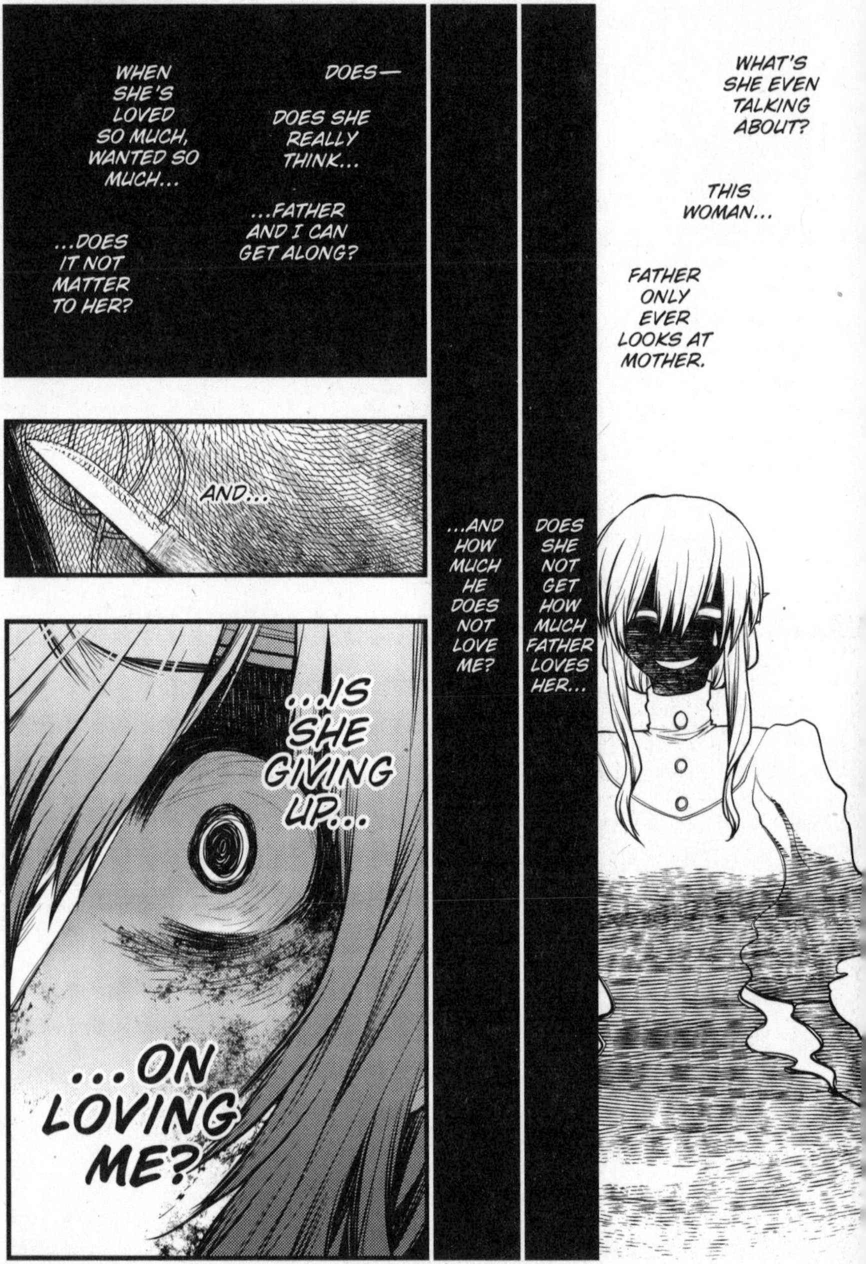
WHAT'S SHE EVEN TALKING ABOUT?
THIS WOMAN...
FATHER ONLY EVER LOOKS AT MOTHER.
DOES SHE NOT GET HOW MUCH FATHER LOVES HER...
...AND HOW MUCH HE DOES NOT LOVE ME?
DOES—
DOES SHE REALLY THINK...
...FATHER AND I CAN GET ALONG?
WHEN SHE'S LOVED SO MUCH, WANTED SO MUCH...
...DOES IT NOT MATTER TO HER?
AND...
...IS SHE GIVING UP...
...ON LOVING ME?

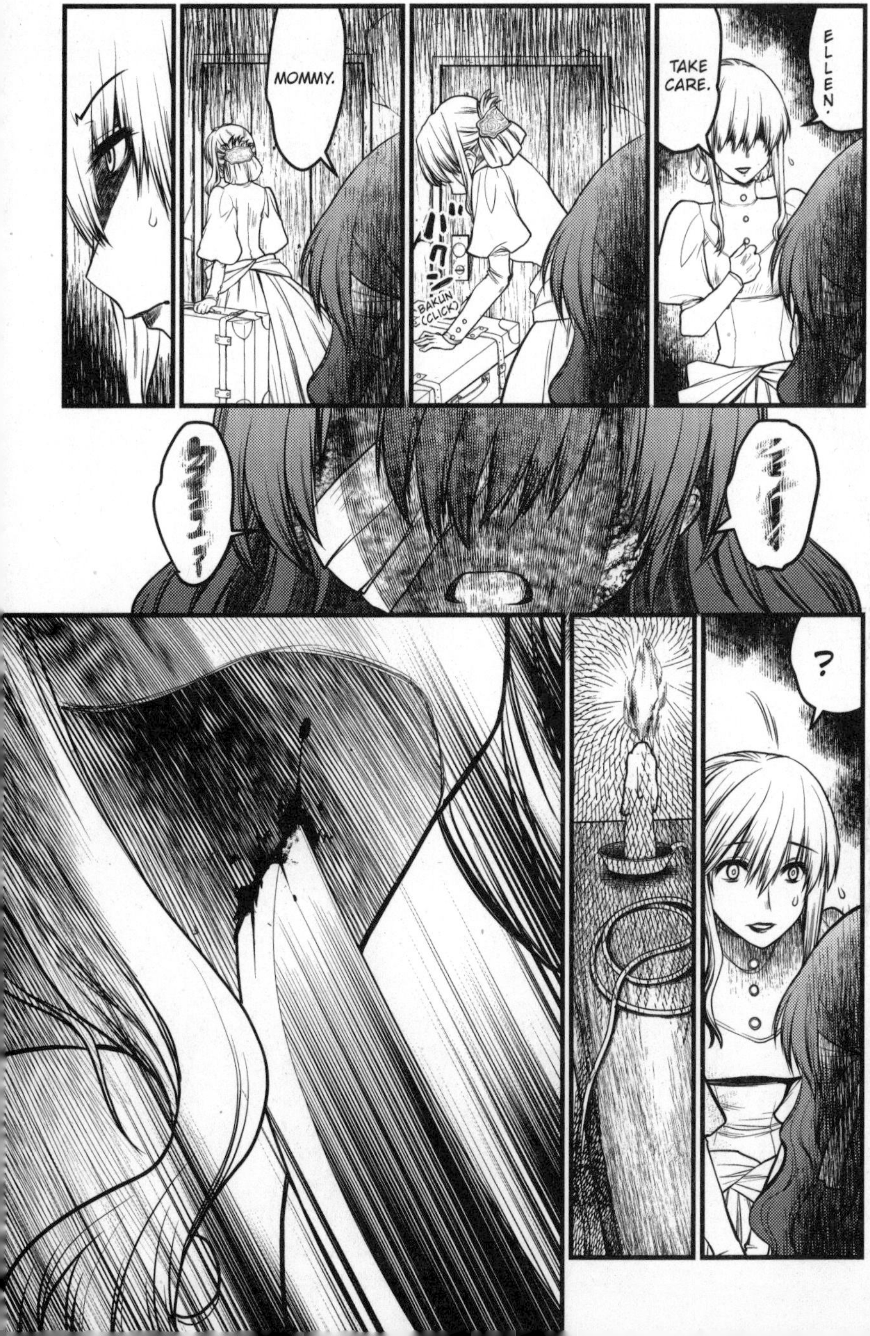
ELLEN.
TAKE CARE.
BAKUN (CLICK)
MOMMY.
?

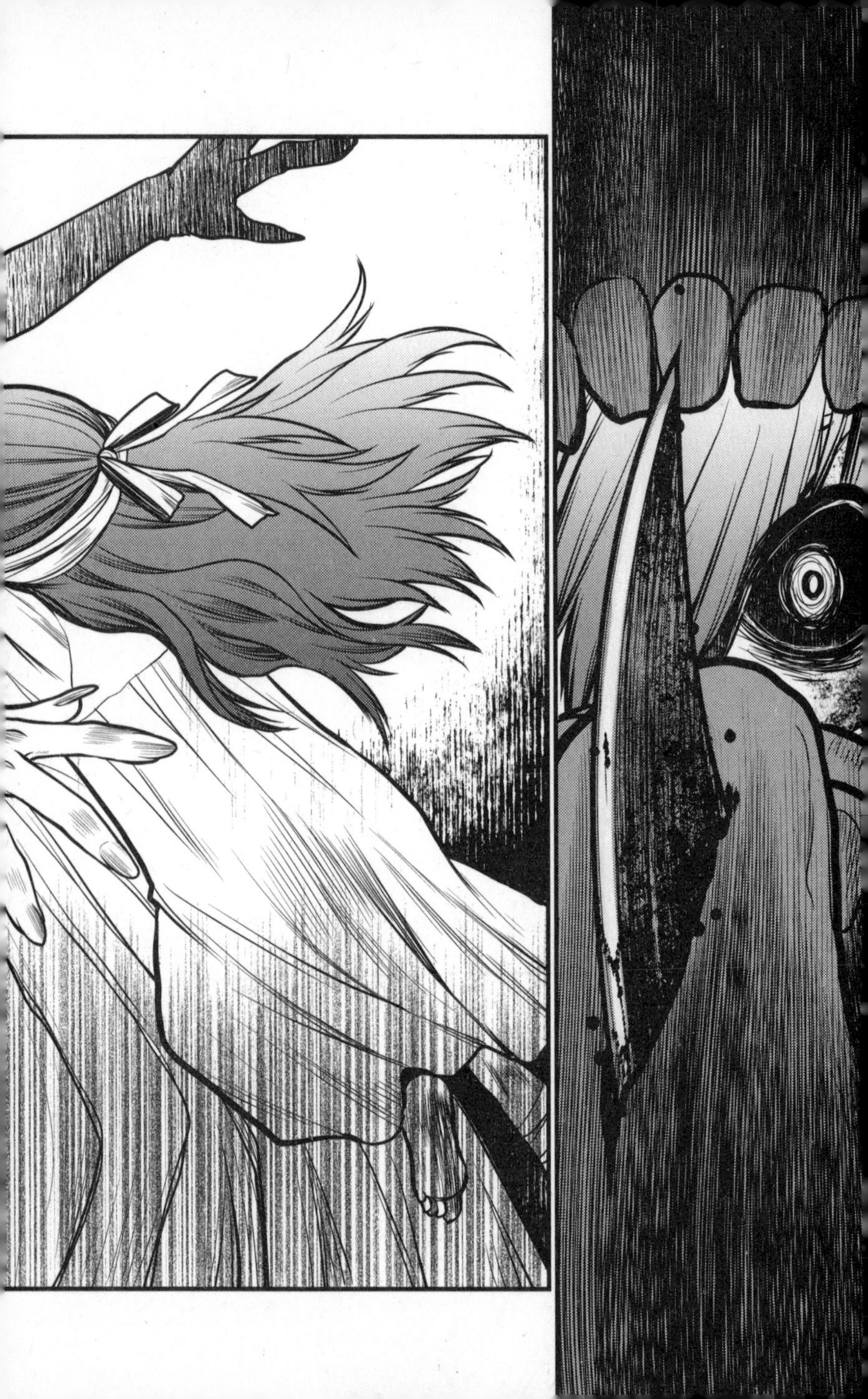

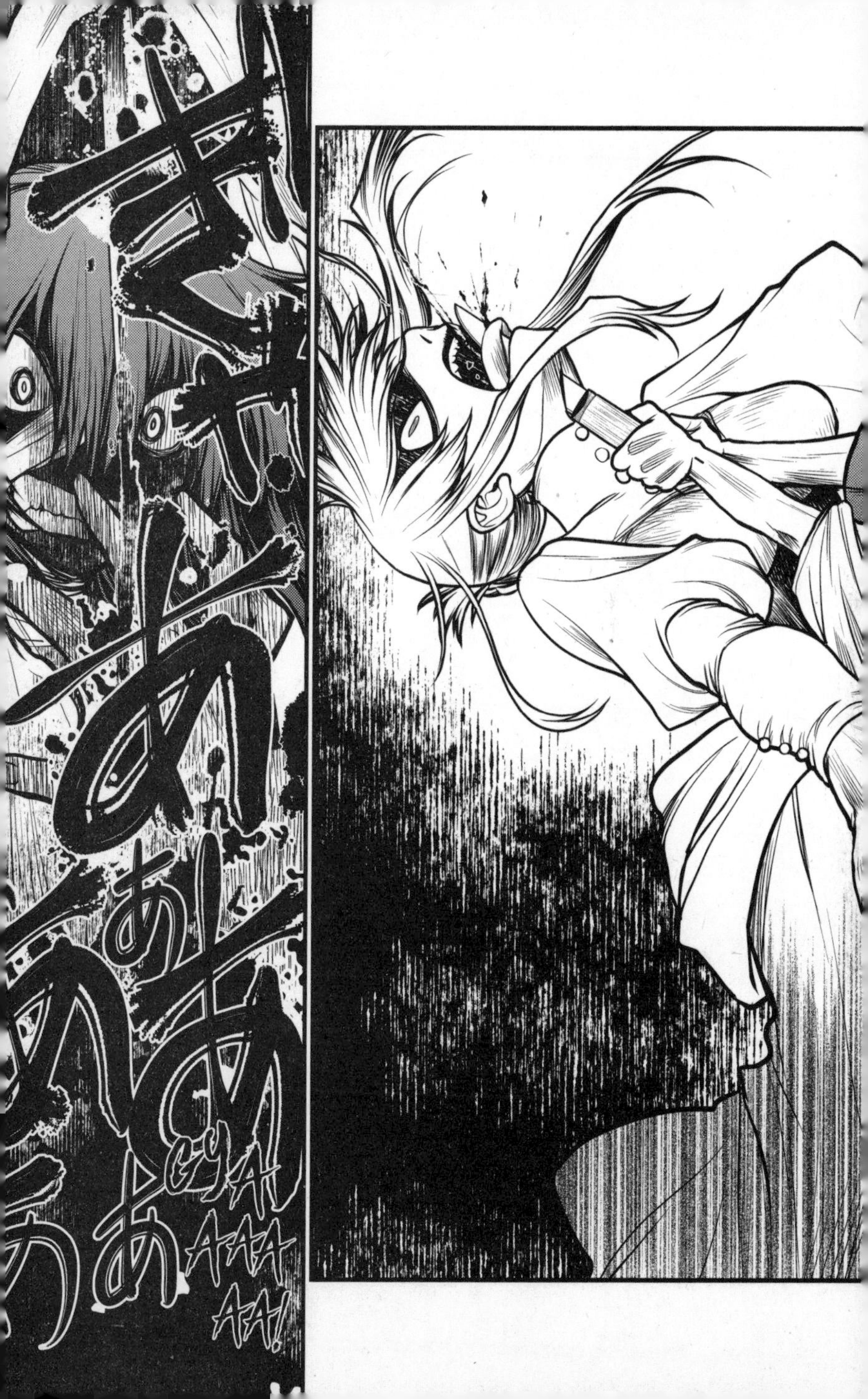
GYAAAAAA!

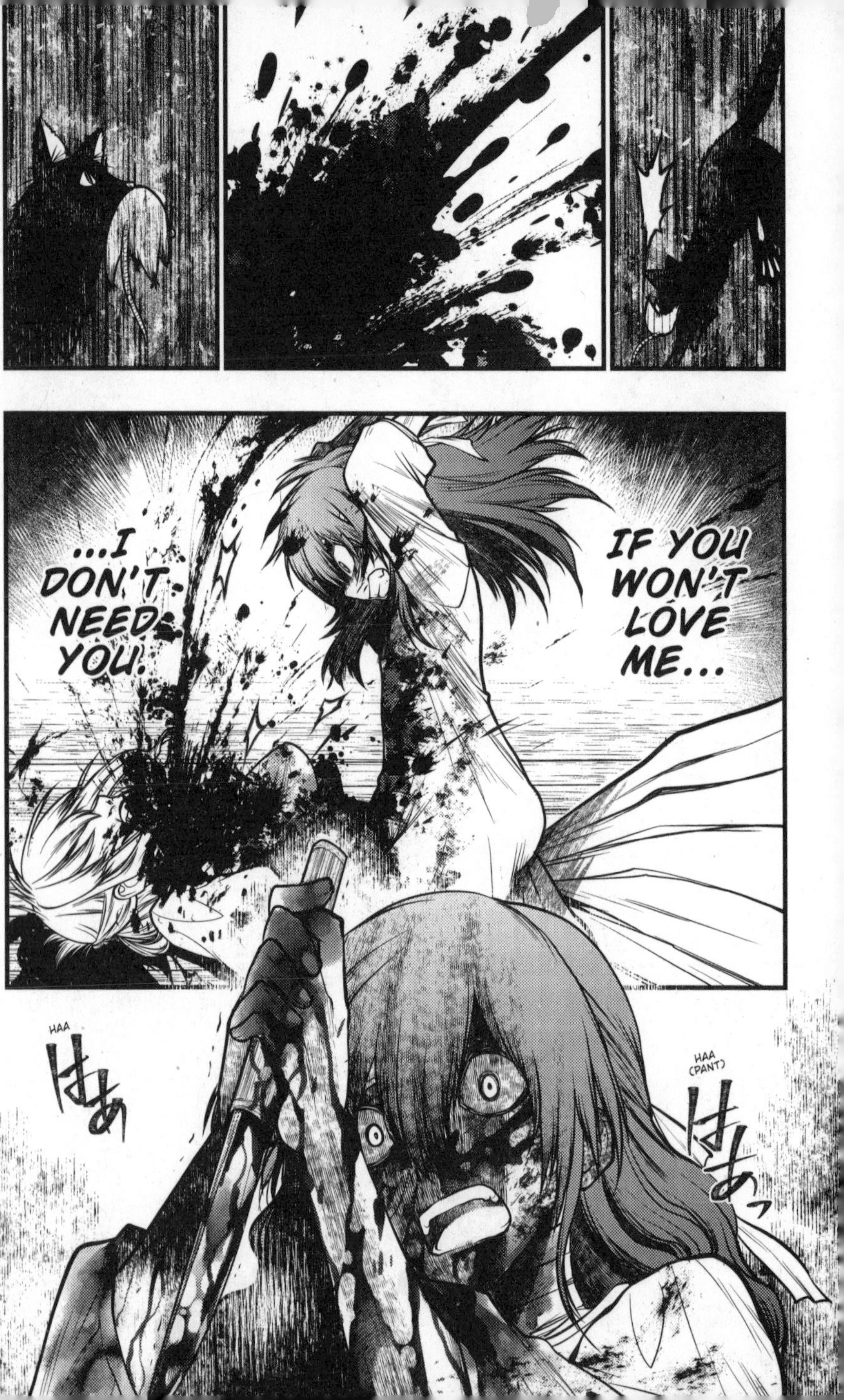
IF YOU WON'T LOVE ME...
...I DON'T NEED YOU.
HAA (PANT)
はあっ
HAA
はあ

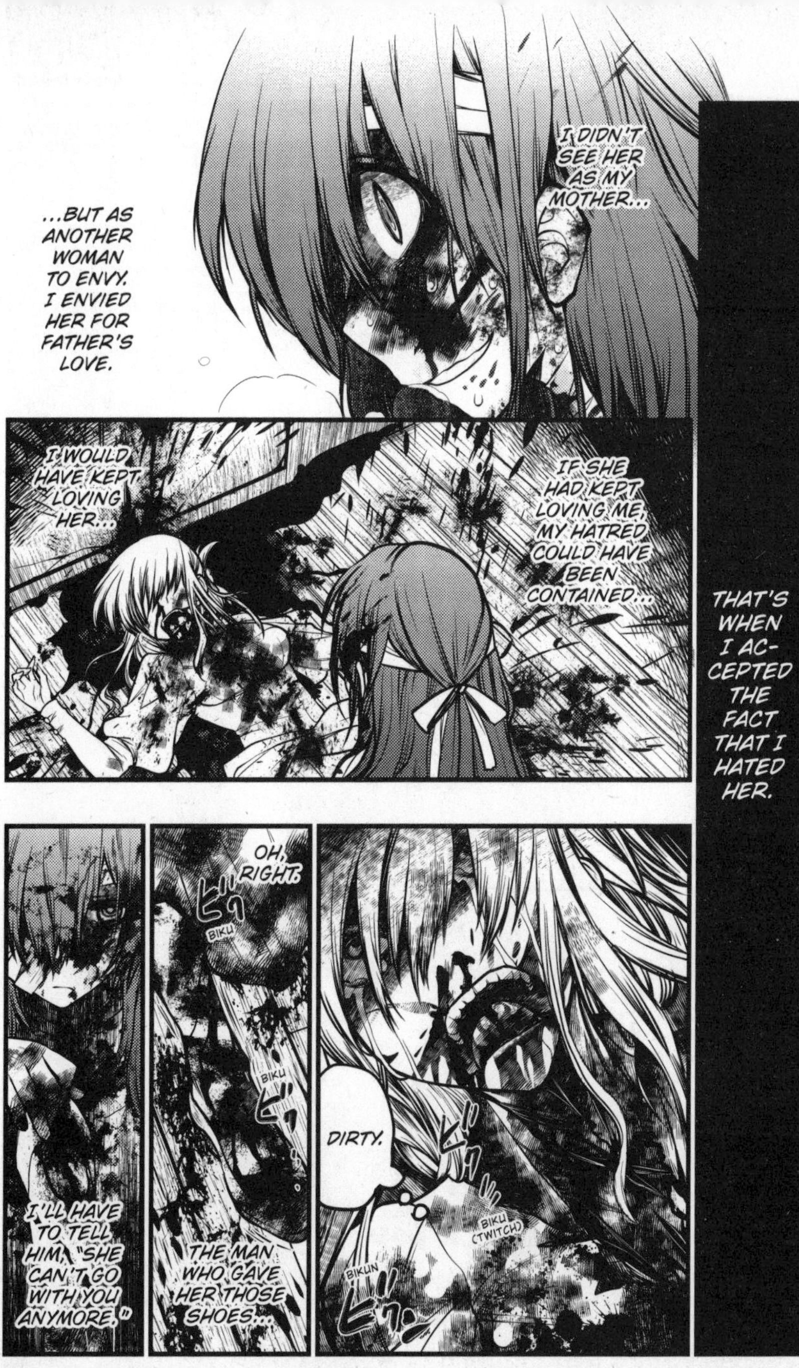
I DIDN'T SEE HER AS MY MOTHER...
...BUT AS ANOTHER WOMAN TO ENVY. I ENVIED HER FOR FATHER'S LOVE.
IF SHE HAD KEPT LOVING ME, MY HATRED COULD HAVE BEEN CONTAINED...
I WOULD HAVE KEPT LOVING HER...
THAT'S WHEN I AC-CEPTED THE FACT THAT I HATED HER.
DIRTY.
BIKU (TWITCH)
BIKUN
OH, RIGHT.
BIKU
BIKU
THE MAN WHO GAVE HER THOSE SHOES...
I'LL HAVE TO TELL HIM, "SHE CAN'T GO WITH YOU ANYMORE."

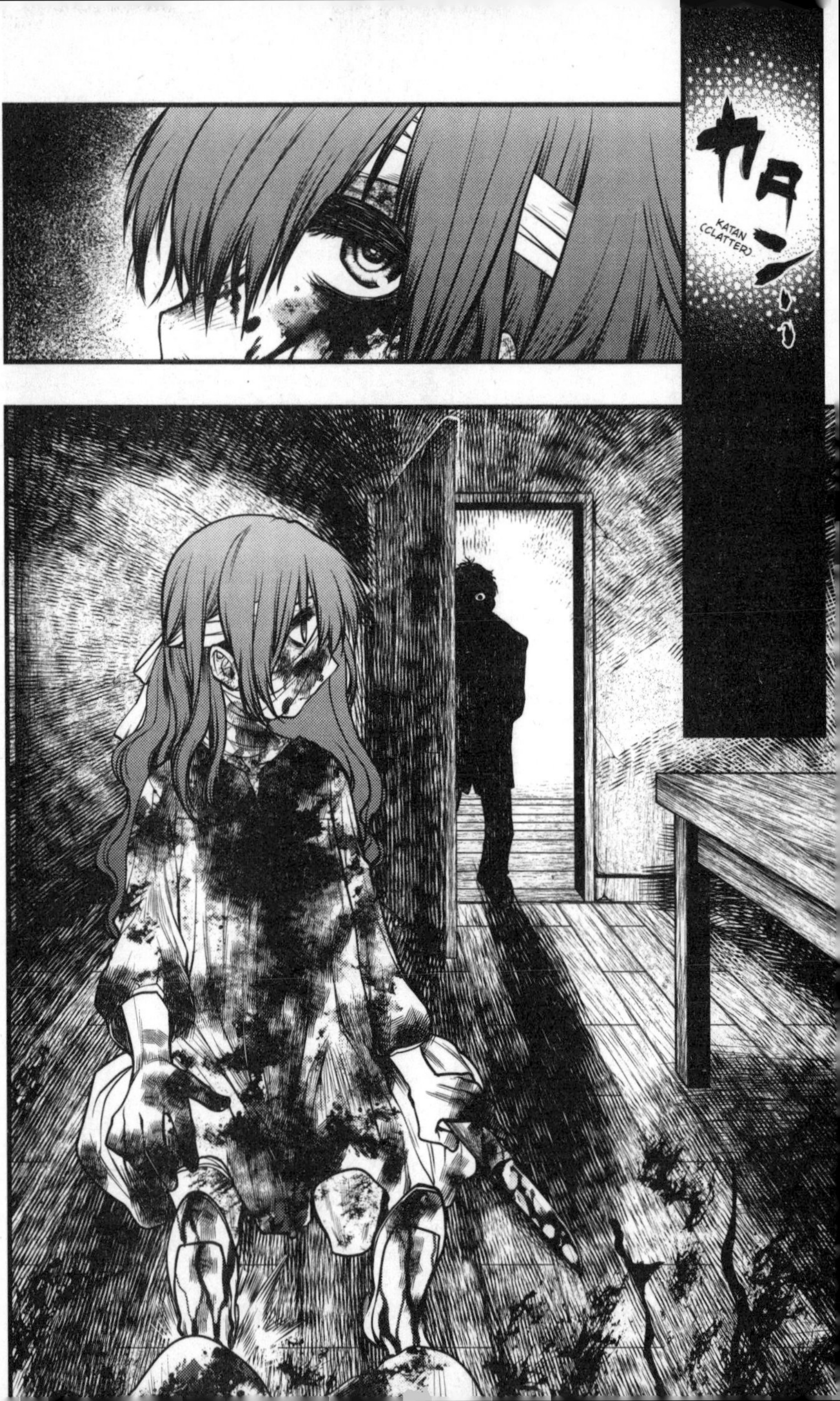
KATAN (CLATTER)

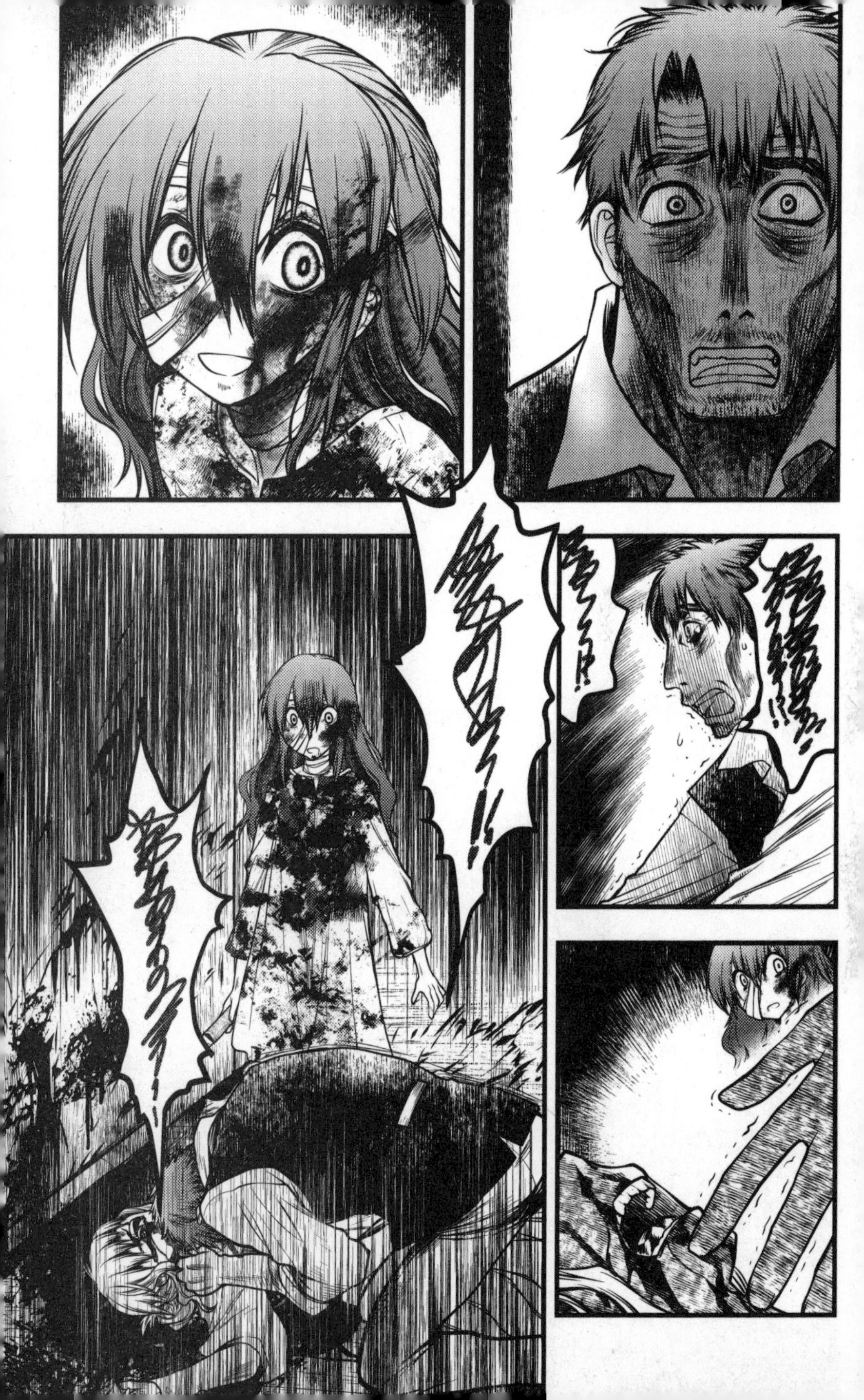

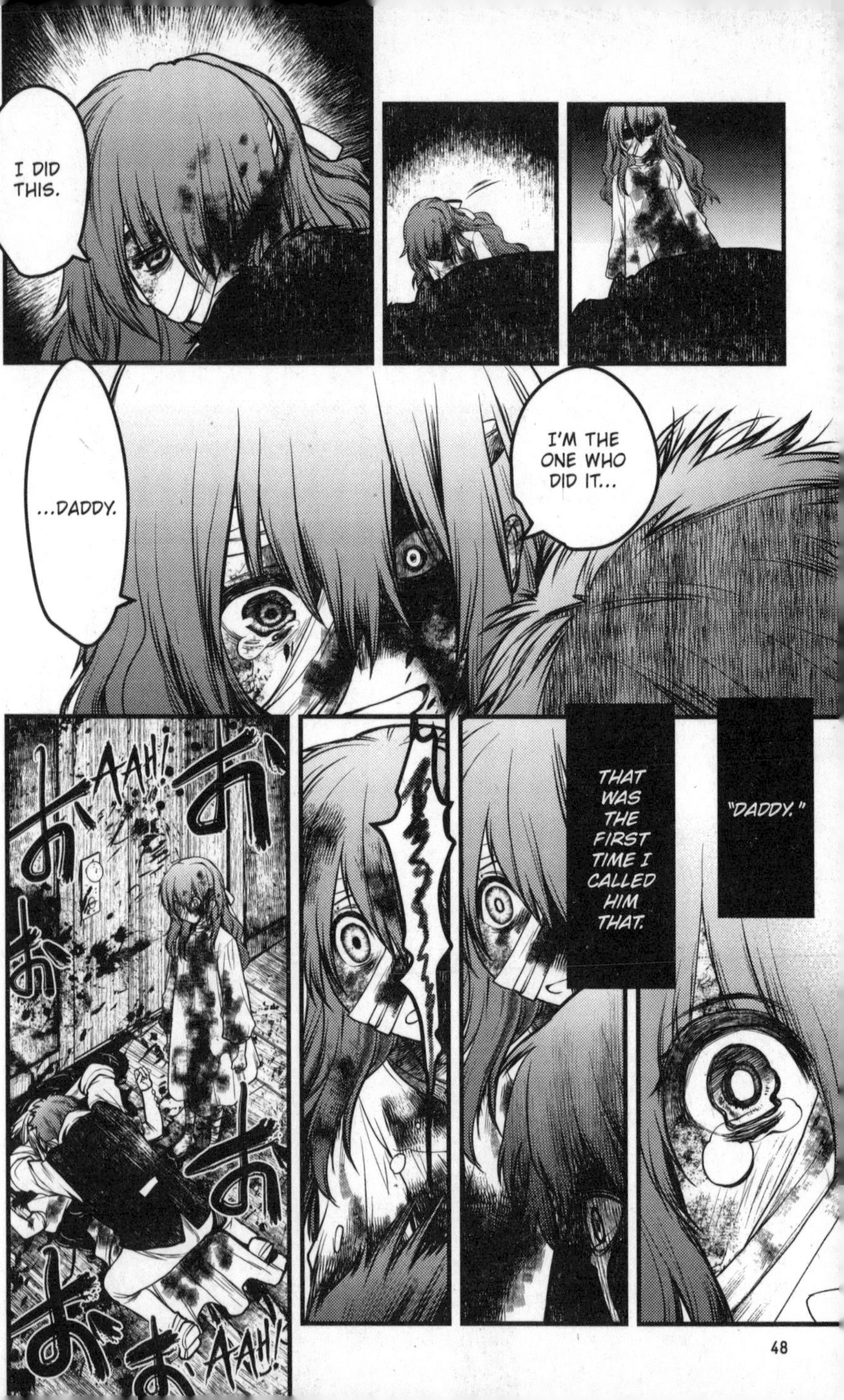
I DID THIS.
I'M THE ONE WHO DID IT...
...DADDY.
"DADDY."
THAT WAS THE FIRST TIME I CALLED HIM THAT.
AAH!
AAH!

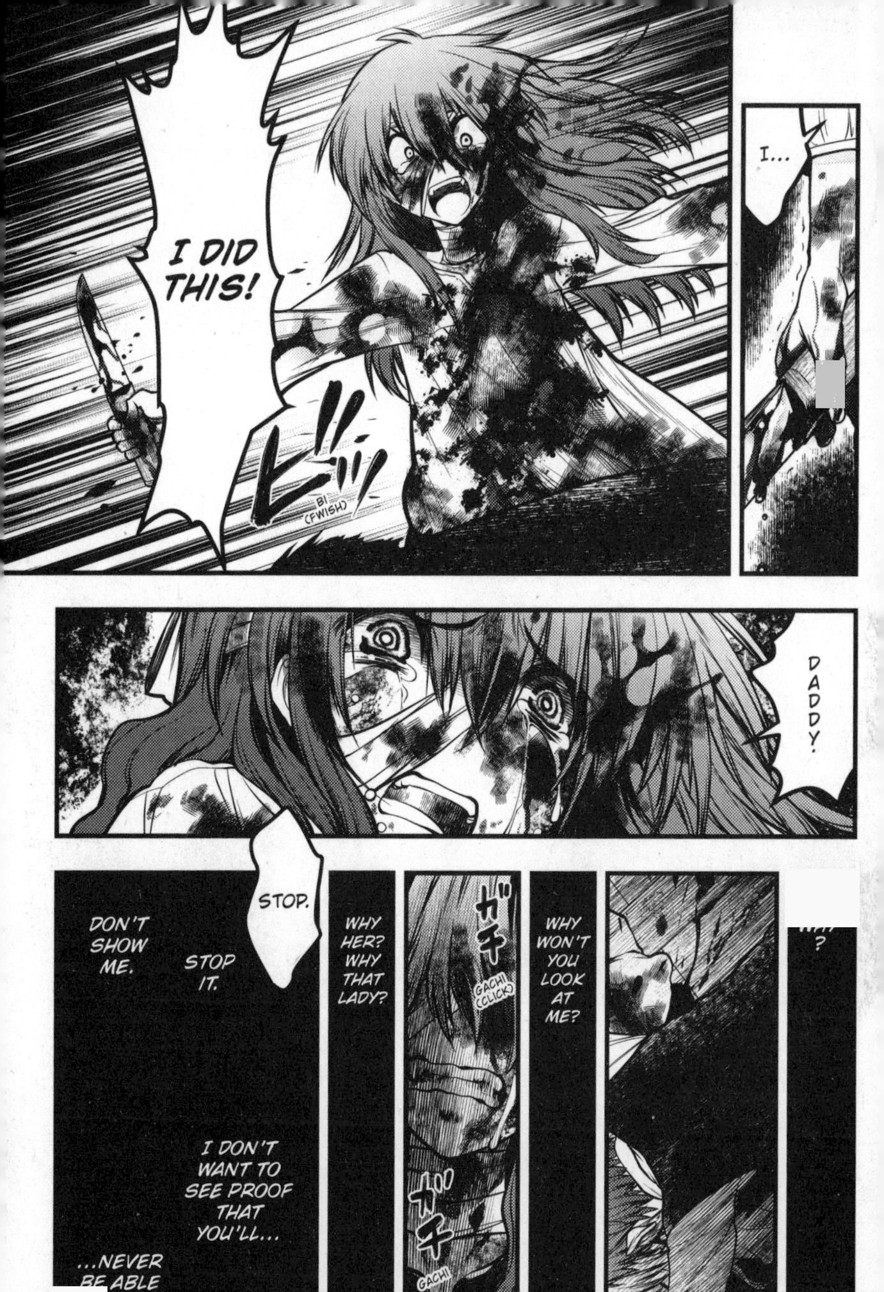
I...
I DID THIS!
BI (FWISH)
DADDY.
?
WHY WON'T YOU LOOK AT ME?
GACHI (CLICK)
GACHI
WHY HER? WHY THAT LADY?
STOP.
STOP IT.
DON'T SHOW ME.
I DON'T WANT TO SEE PROOF THAT YOU'LL...
...NEVER BE ABLE LOVE ME.

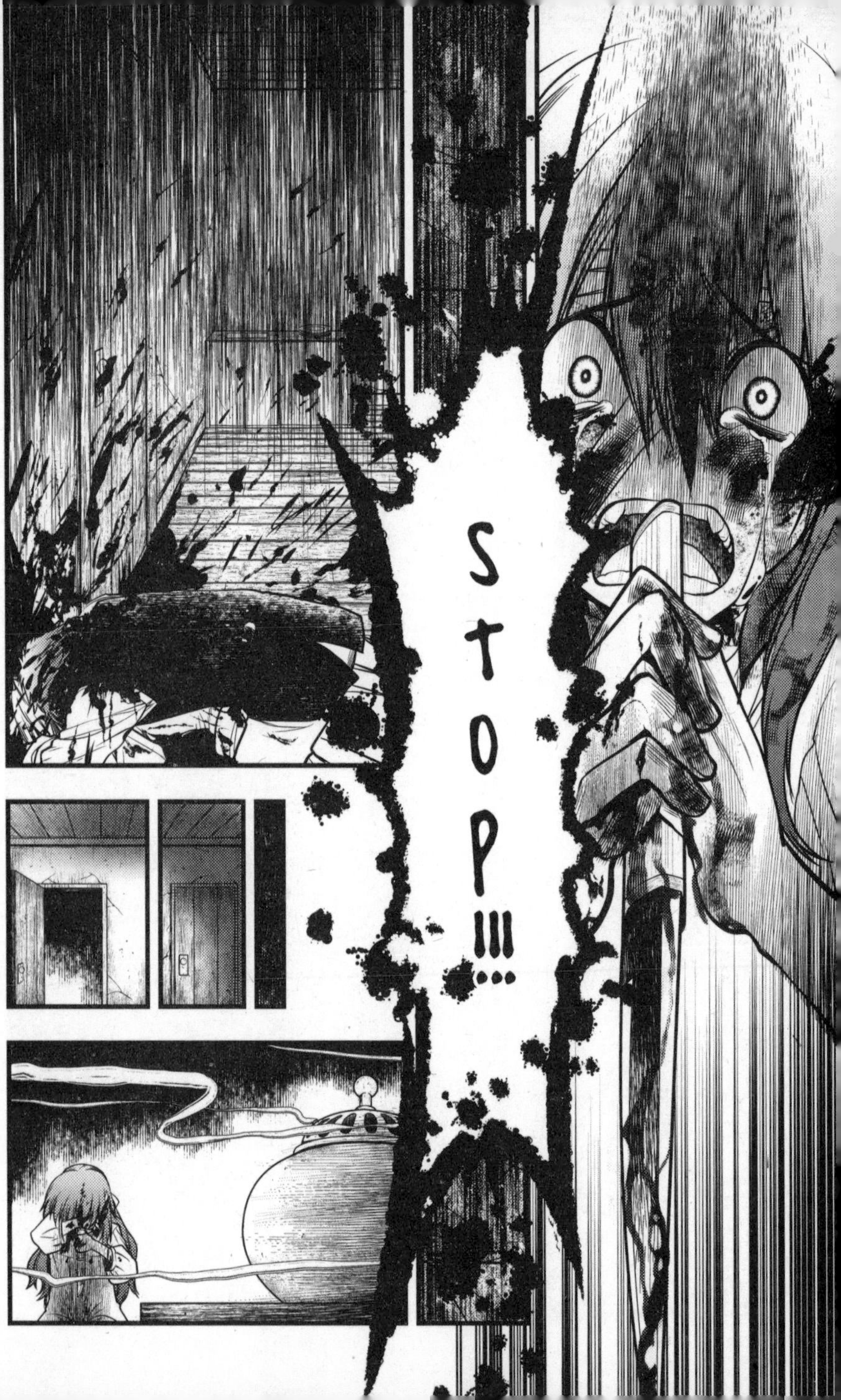
STOP!!!...

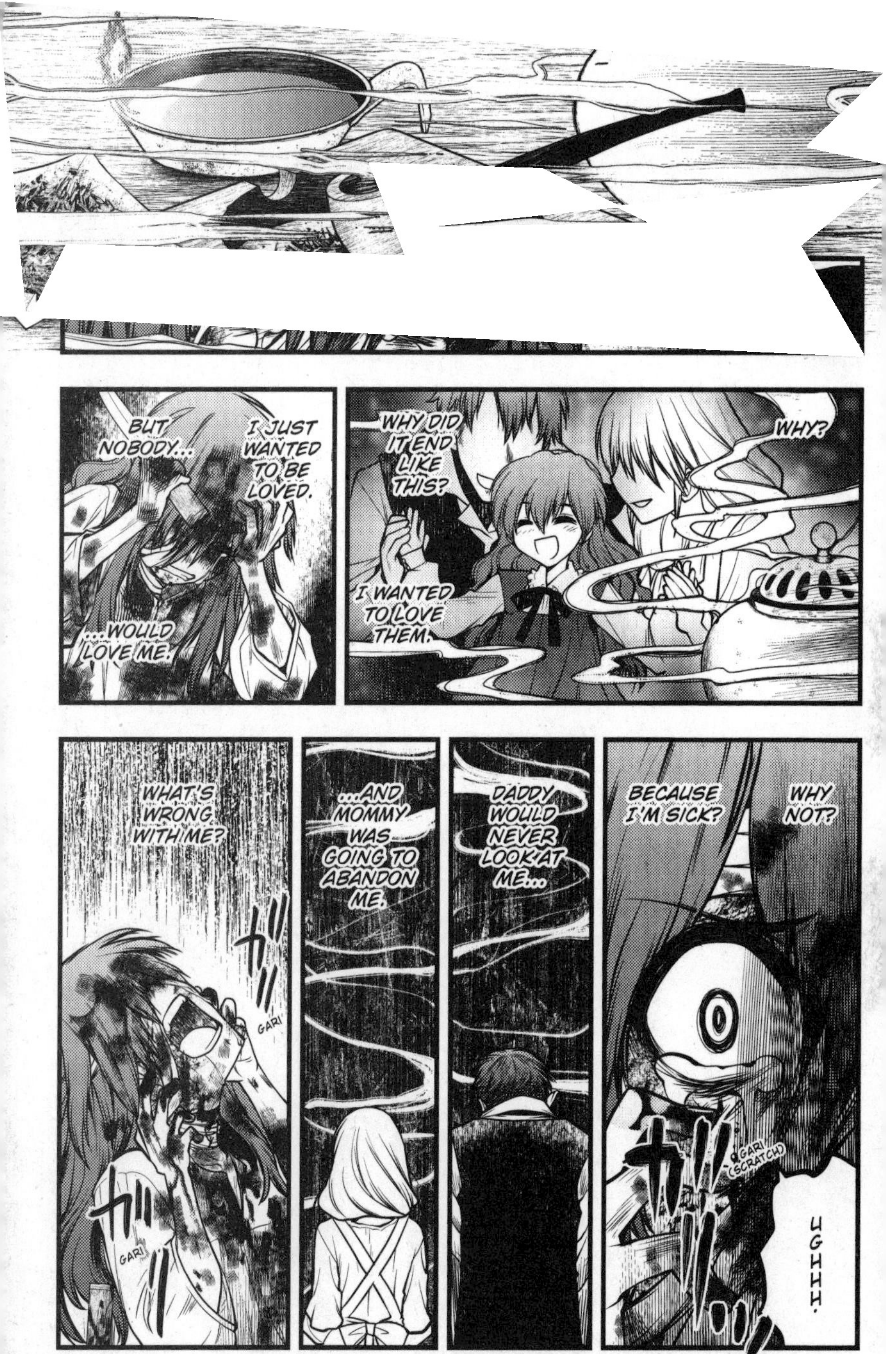
WHY?
WHY DID IT END LIKE THIS?
I WANTED TO LOVE THEM.
I JUST WANTED TO BE LOVED.
BUT NOBODY...
...WOULD LOVE ME.
WHY NOT?
BECAUSE I'M SICK?
GARI (SCRATCH)
UGHHH.
DADDY WOULD NEVER LOOK AT ME...
...AND MOMMY WAS GOING TO ABANDON ME.
WHAT'S WRONG WITH ME?
GARI
GARI

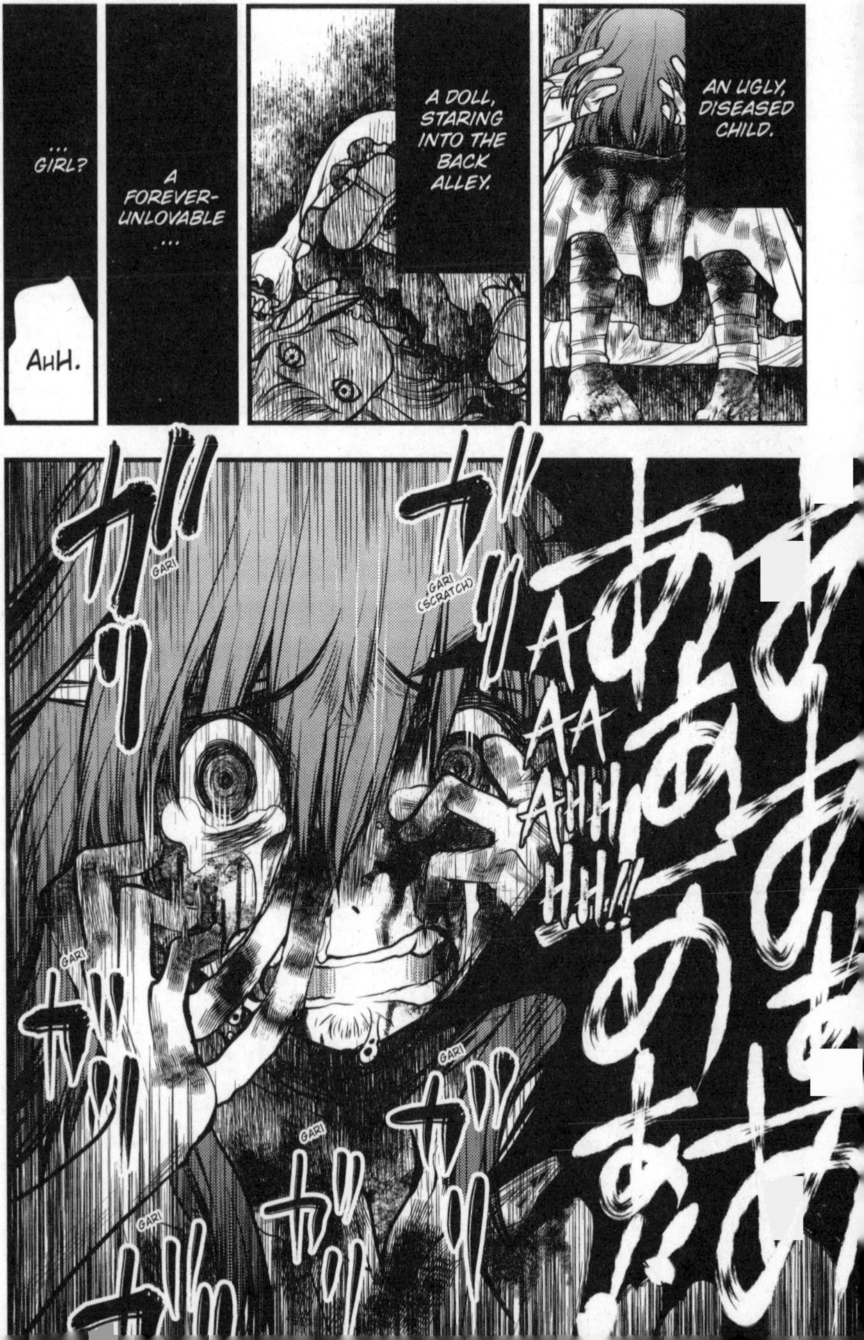
AN UGLY, DISEASED CHILD.
A DOLL, STARING INTO THE BACK ALLEY.
A FOREVER-UNLOVABLE ...
... GIRL?
AHH.
GARI (SCRATCH)
AAAAHHHHH!!
GARI
GARI
GARI
GARI
GARI

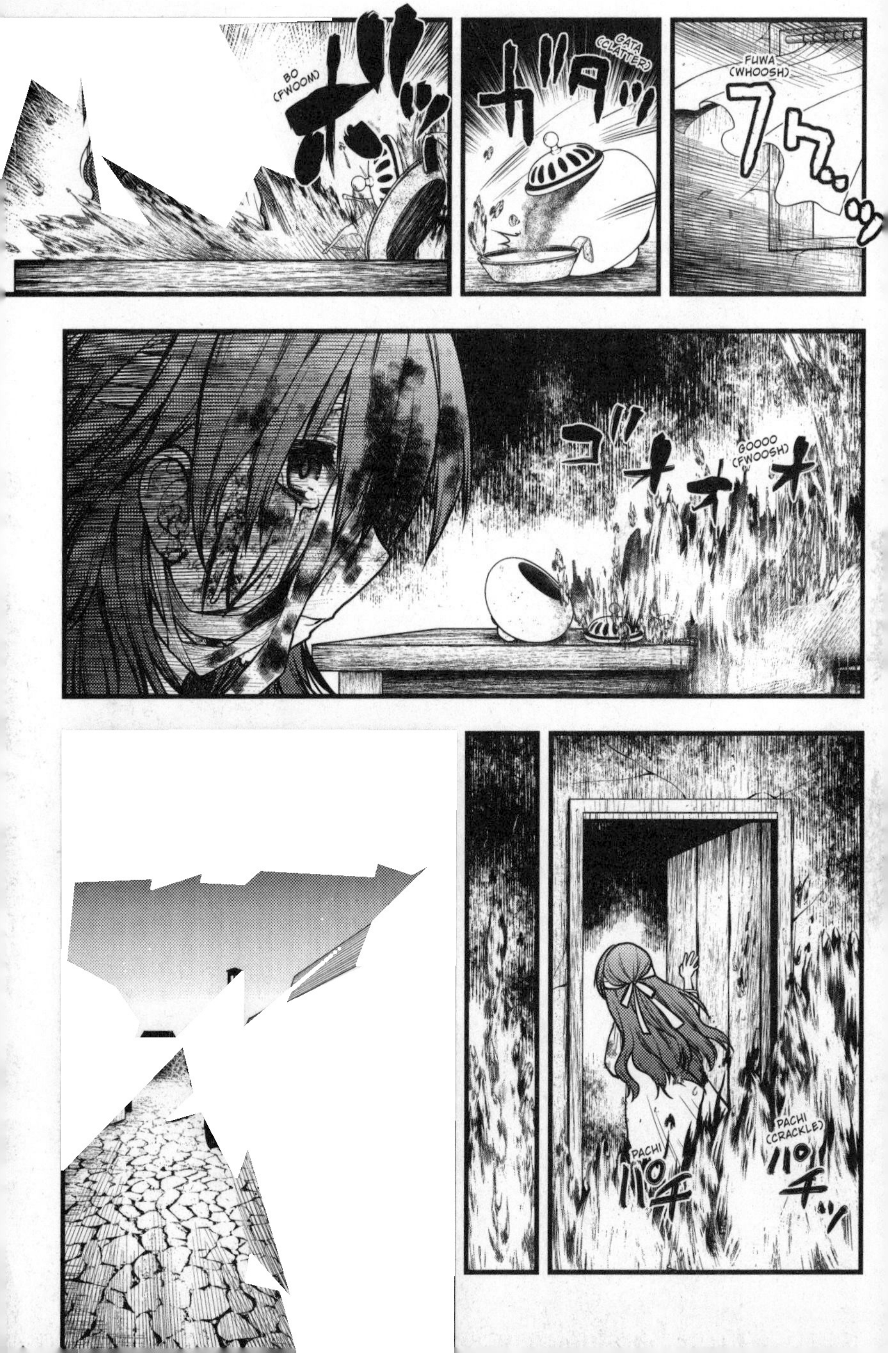
FUWA
(WHOOSH)
GATA
(CLATTER)
BO
(FWOOM)
GOOOO
(FWOOSH)
PACHI
(CRACKLE)
PACHI

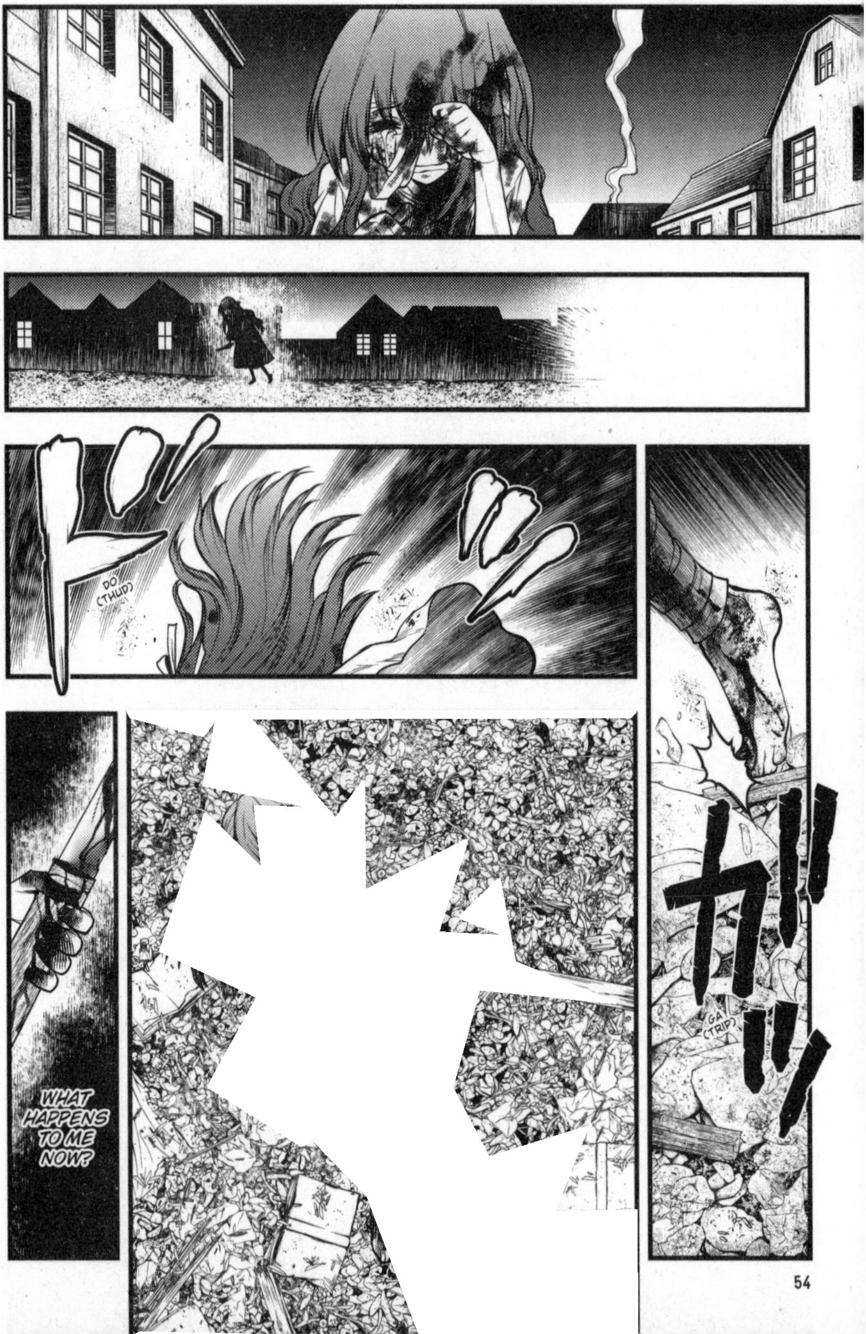
GA (TRIP)
DO (THUD)
WHAT HAPPENS TO ME NOW?

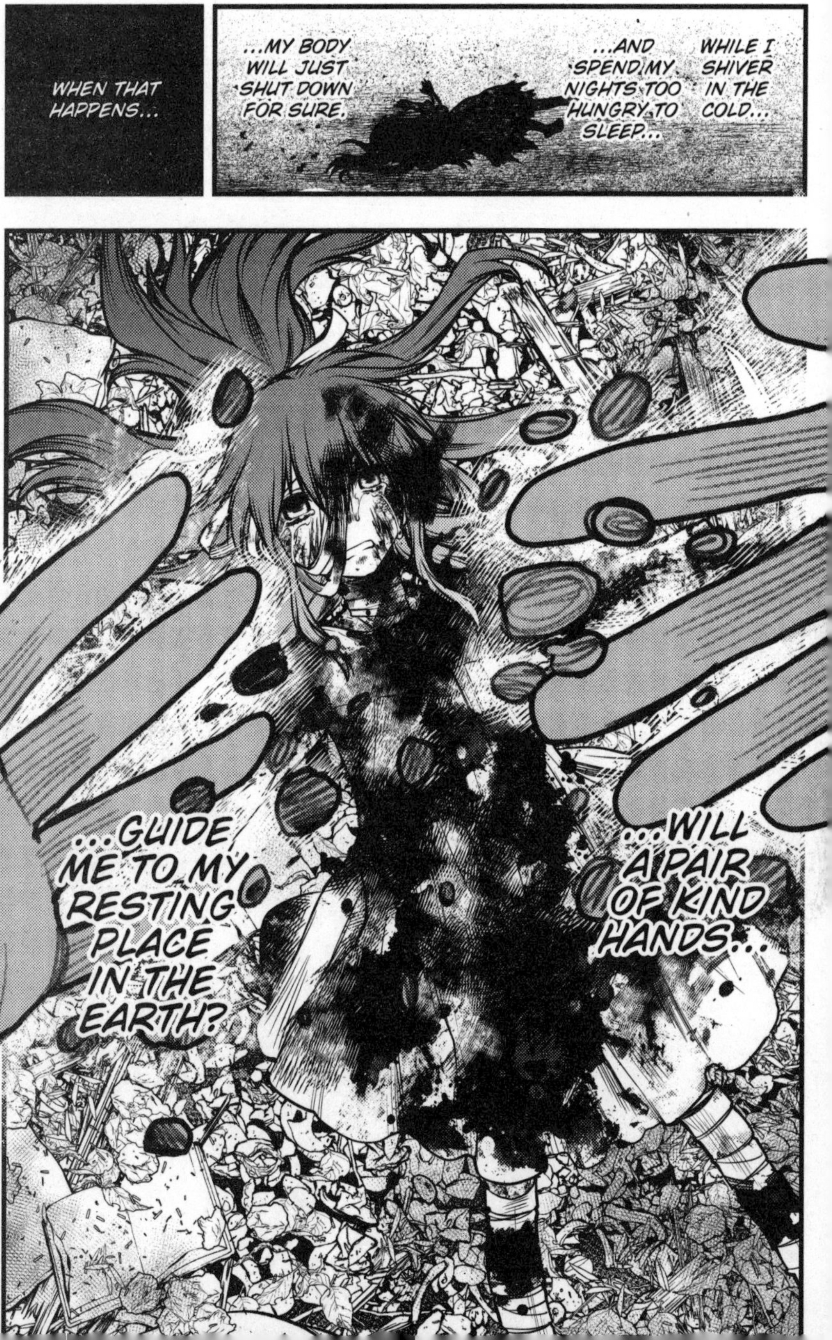
WHILE I SHIVER IN THE COLD...
...AND SPEND MY NIGHTS TOO HUNGRY TO SLEEP...
...MY BODY WILL JUST SHUT DOWN FOR SURE.
WHEN THAT HAPPENS...
...WILL A PAIR OF KIND HANDS...
...GUIDE ME TO MY RESTING PLACE IN THE EARTH?

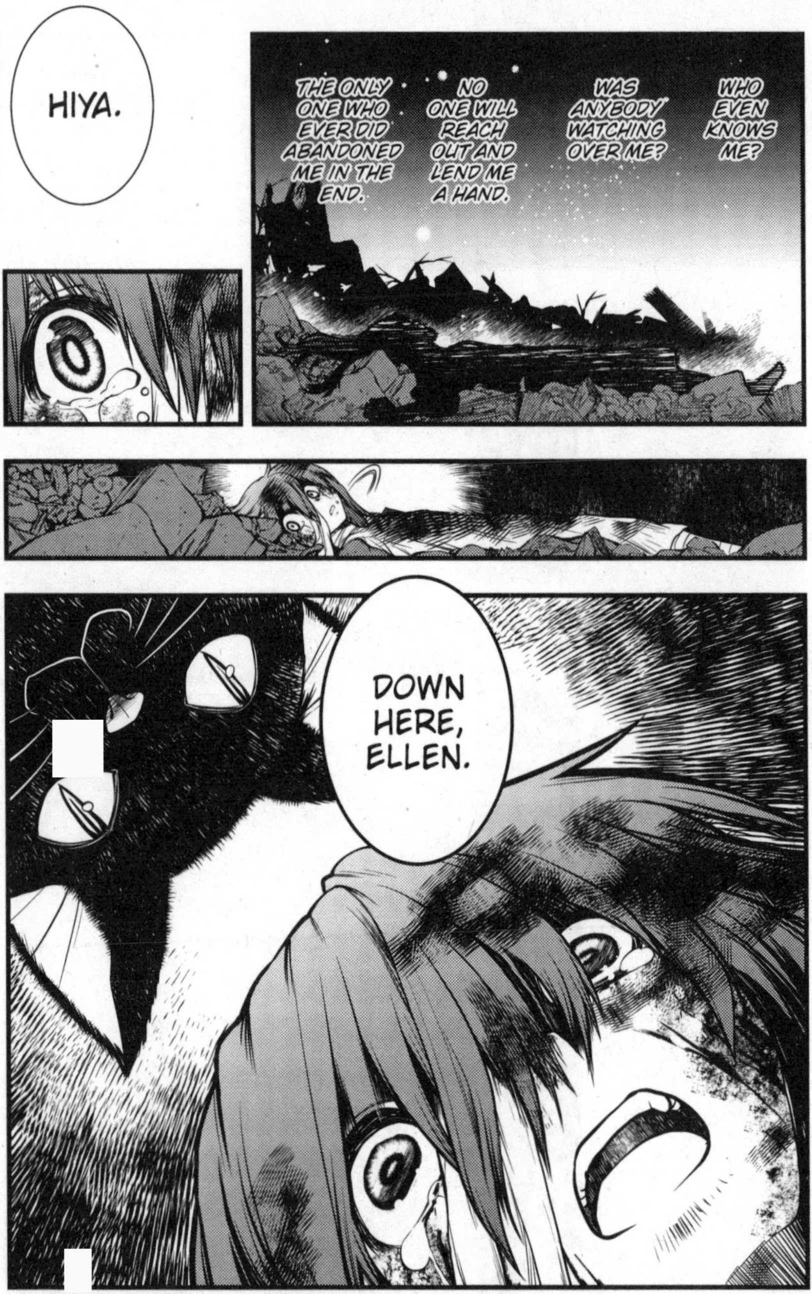
WHO EVEN KNOWS ME?
WAS ANYBODY WATCHING OVER ME?
NO ONE WILL REACH OUT AND LEND ME A HAND.
THE ONLY ONE WHO EVER DID ABANDONED ME IN THE END.
HIYA.
DOWN HERE, ELLEN.

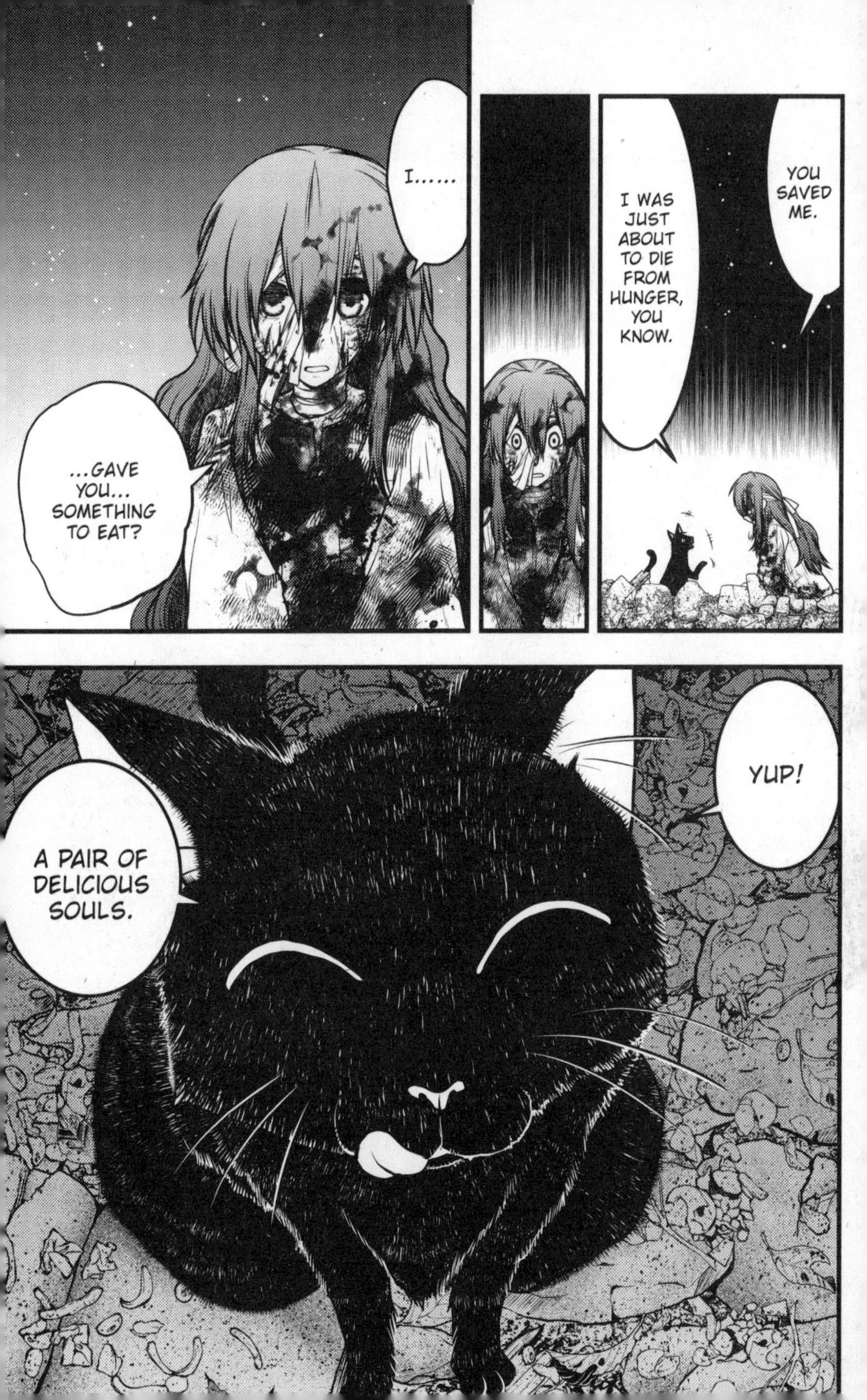
YOU SAVED ME.
I WAS JUST ABOUT TO DIE FROM HUNGER, YOU KNOW.
I……
…GAVE YOU… SOMETHING TO EAT?
YUP!
A PAIR OF DELICIOUS SOULS.

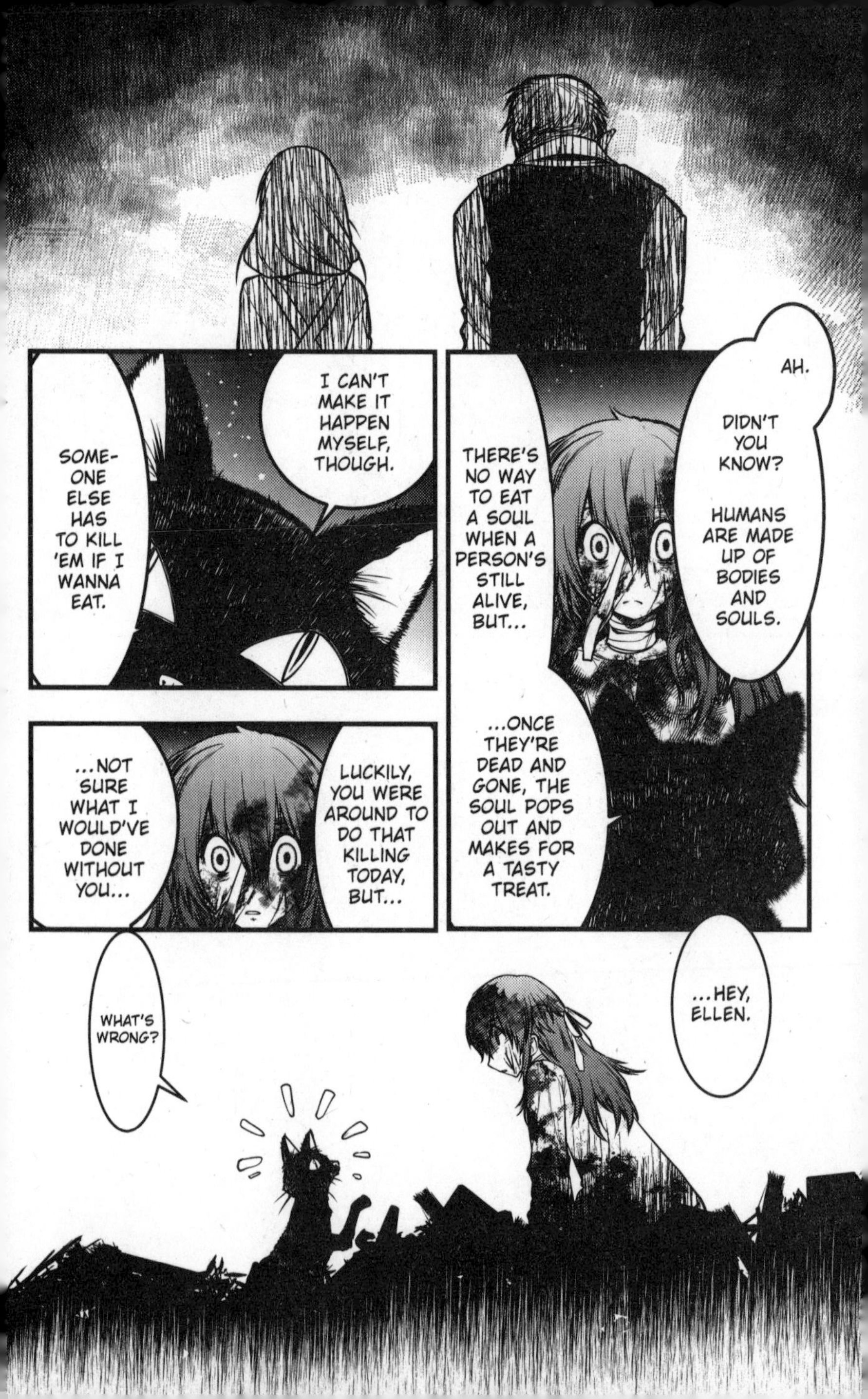
AH.
DIDN'T YOU KNOW?
HUMANS ARE MADE UP OF BODIES AND SOULS.
THERE'S NO WAY TO EAT A SOUL WHEN A PERSON'S STILL ALIVE, BUT...
...ONCE THEY'RE DEAD AND GONE, THE SOUL POPS OUT AND MAKES FOR A TASTY TREAT.
I CAN'T MAKE IT HAPPEN MYSELF, THOUGH.
SOME-ONE ELSE HAS TO KILL 'EM IF I WANNA EAT.
LUCKILY, YOU WERE AROUND TO DO THAT KILLING TODAY, BUT...
...NOT SURE WHAT I WOULD'VE DONE WITHOUT YOU...
...HEY, ELLEN.
WHAT'S WRONG?

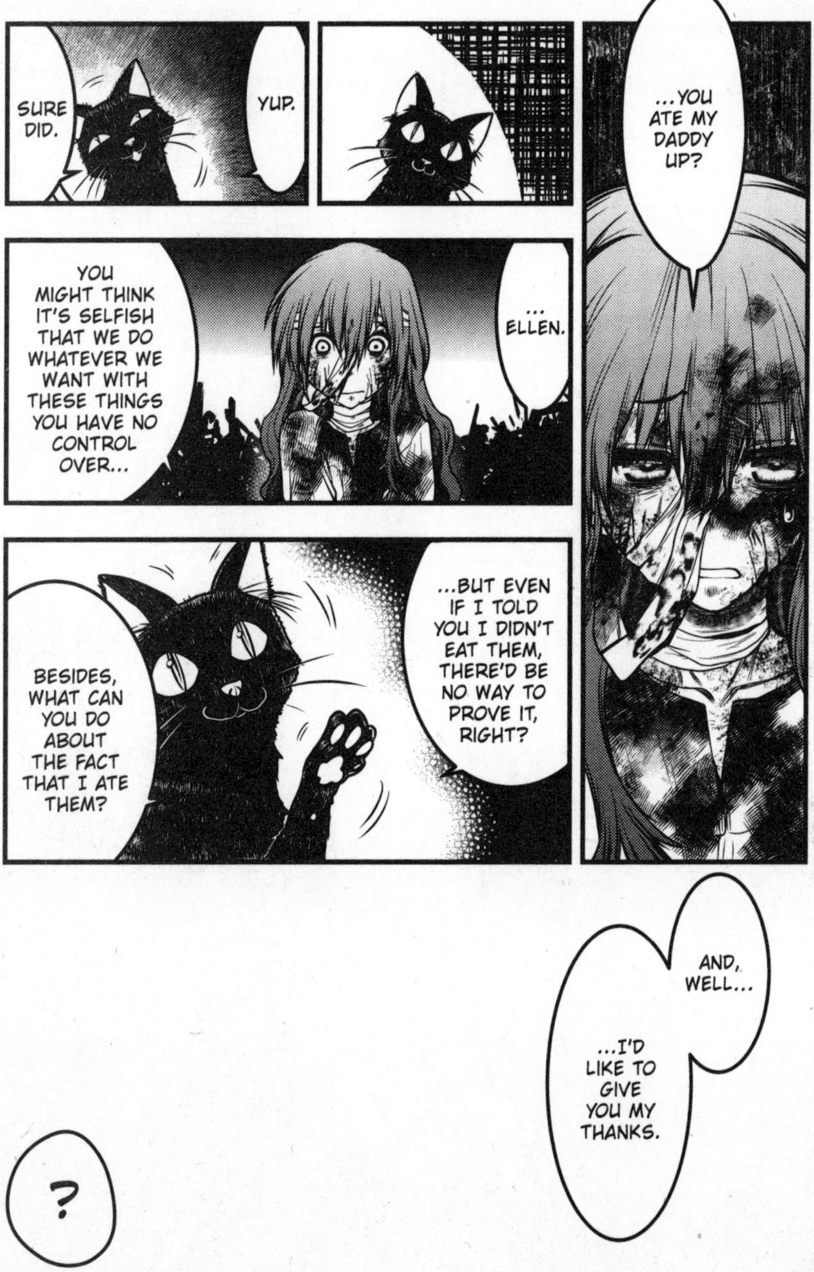
...YOU ATE MY DADDY UP?
YUP.
SURE DID.
... ELLEN.
YOU MIGHT THINK IT'S SELFISH THAT WE DO WHATEVER WE WANT WITH THESE THINGS YOU HAVE NO CONTROL OVER...
...BUT EVEN IF I TOLD YOU I DIDN'T EAT THEM, THERE'D BE NO WAY TO PROVE IT, RIGHT?
BESIDES, WHAT CAN YOU DO ABOUT THE FACT THAT I ATE THEM?
AND, WELL...
...I'D LIKE TO GIVE YOU MY THANKS.
?

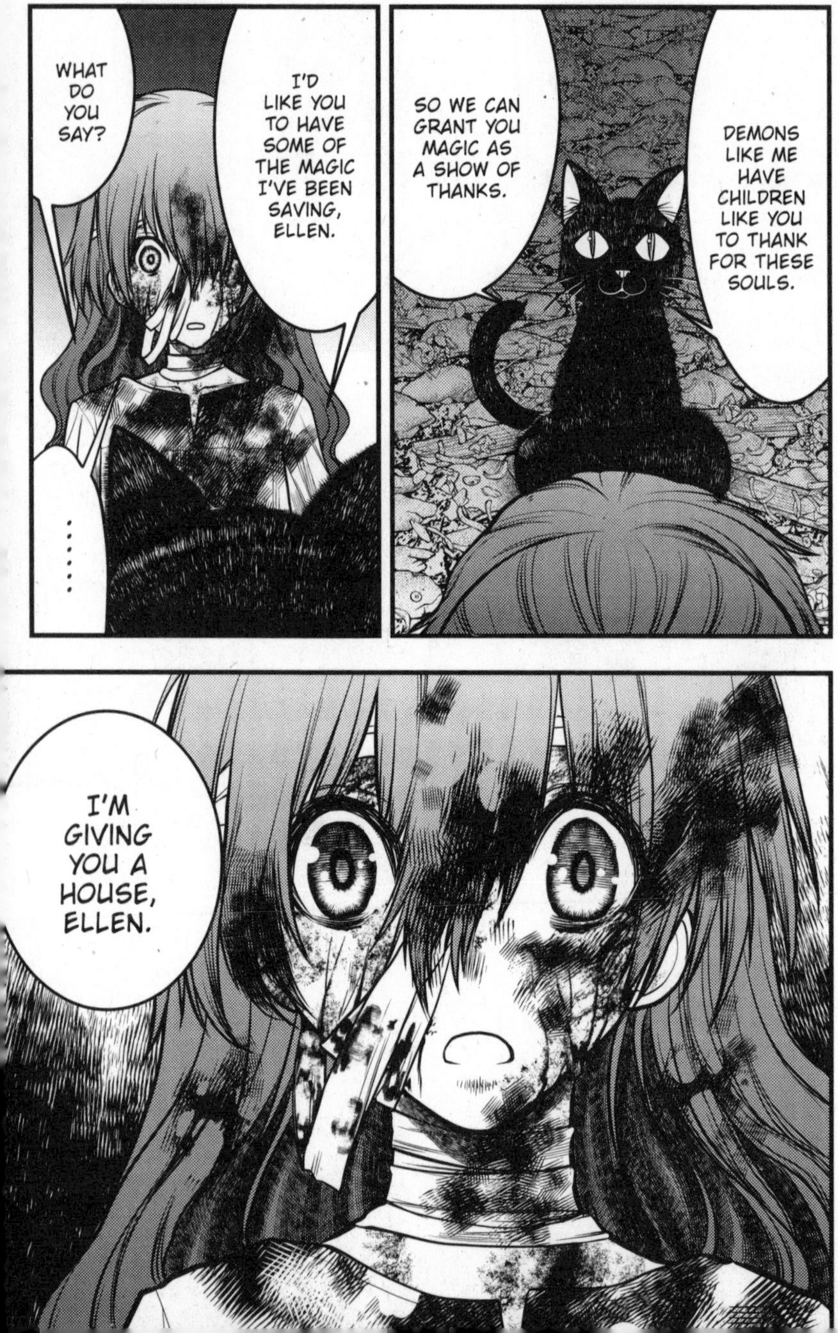
DEMONS LIKE ME HAVE CHILDREN LIKE YOU TO THANK FOR THESE SOULS.
SO WE CAN GRANT YOU MAGIC AS A SHOW OF THANKS.
I'D LIKE YOU TO HAVE SOME OF THE MAGIC I'VE BEEN SAVING, ELLEN.
WHAT DO YOU SAY?
......
I'M GIVING YOU A HOUSE, ELLEN.

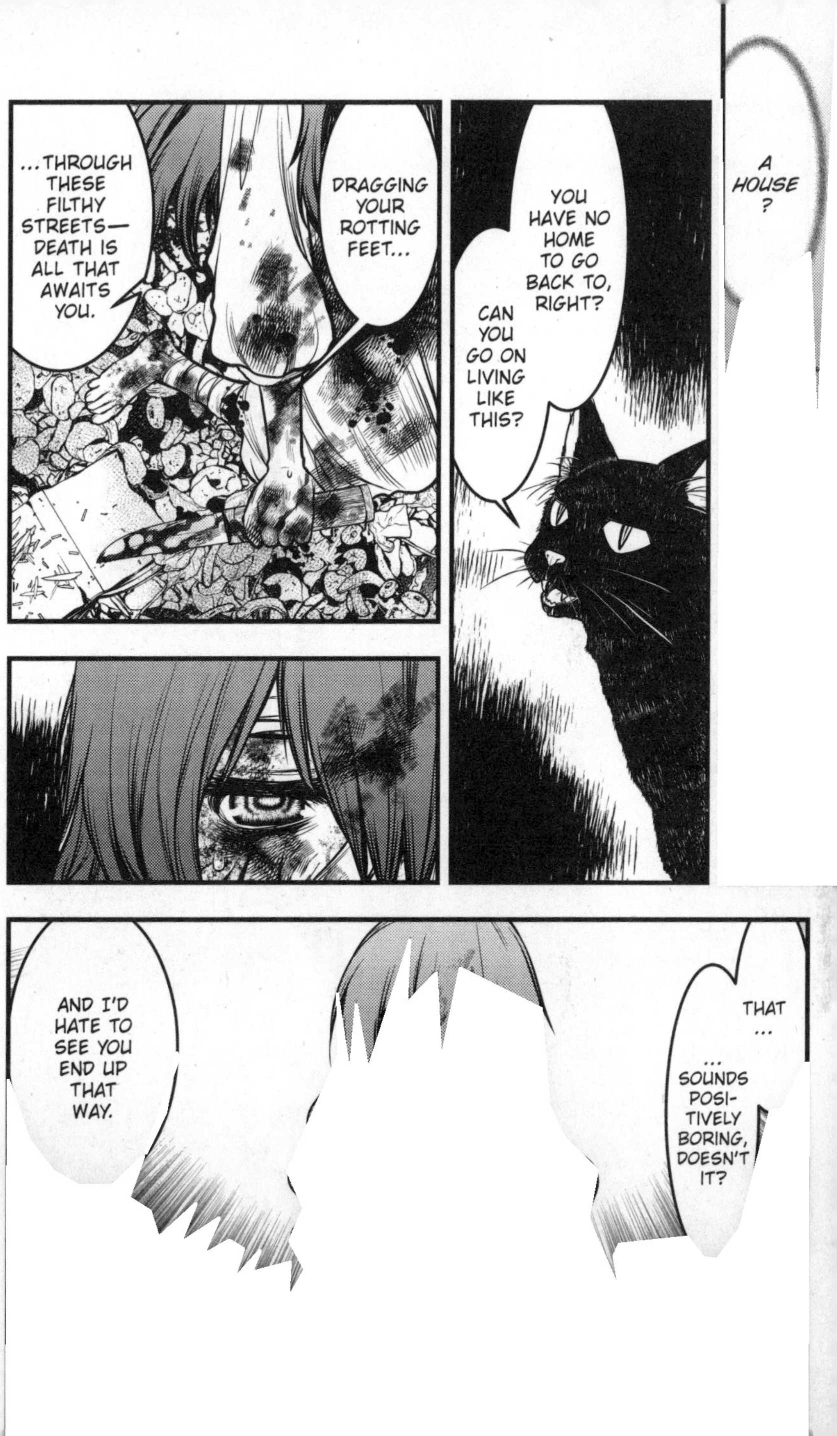
A HOUSE?
YOU HAVE NO HOME TO GO BACK TO, RIGHT?
CAN YOU GO ON LIVING LIKE THIS?
DRAGGING YOUR ROTTING FEET...
...THROUGH THESE FILTHY STREETS—DEATH IS ALL THAT AWAITS YOU.
THAT...
...SOUNDS POSI-TIVELY BORING, DOESN'T IT?
AND I'D HATE TO SEE YOU END UP THAT WAY.

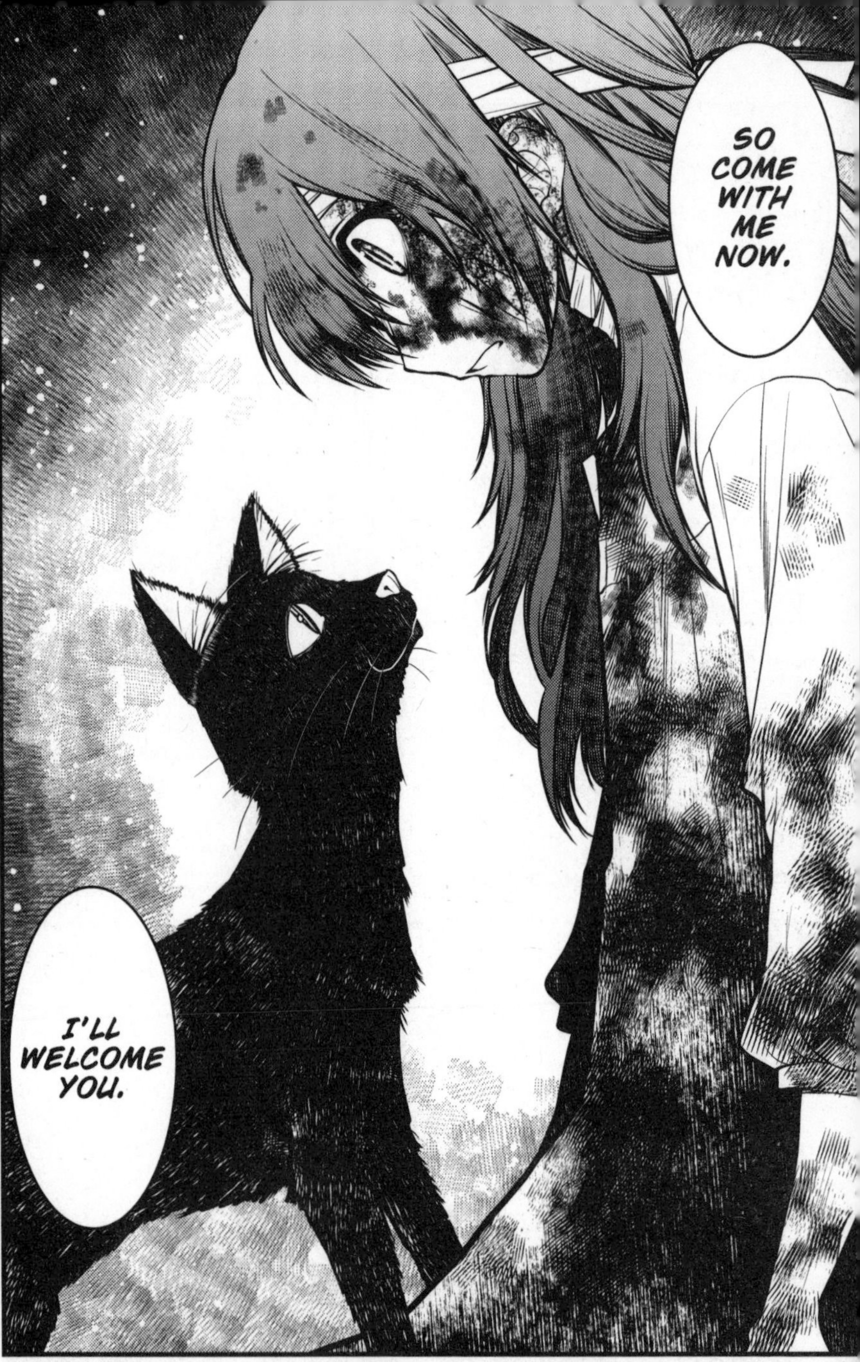
SO COME WITH ME NOW.
I'LL WELCOME YOU.

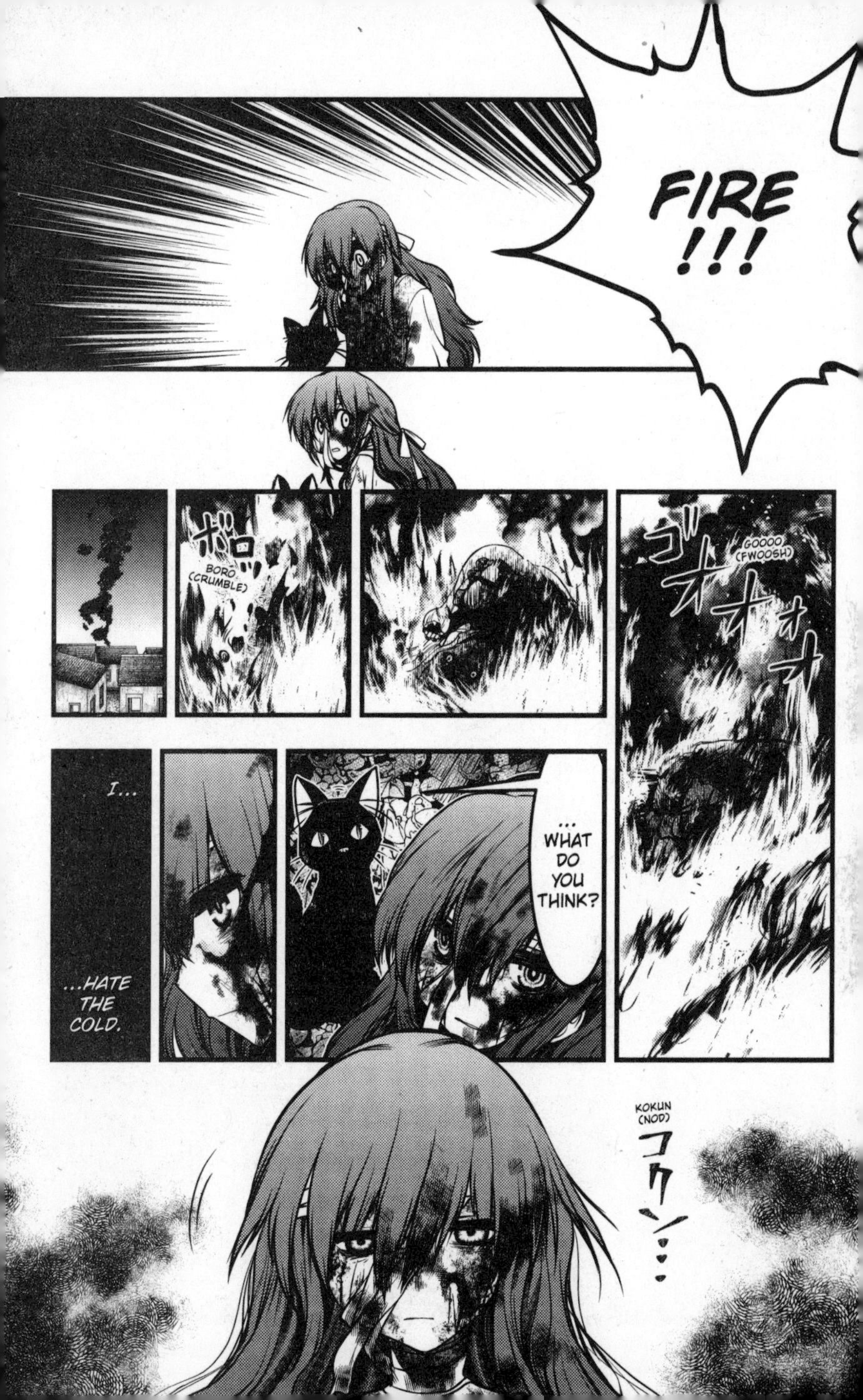
FIRE !!!
ゴオオオオ
GOOOO (FWOOSH)
ボロ
BORO (CRUMBLE)
... WHAT DO YOU THINK?
I...
...HATE THE COLD.
コクン...
KOKUN (NOD)

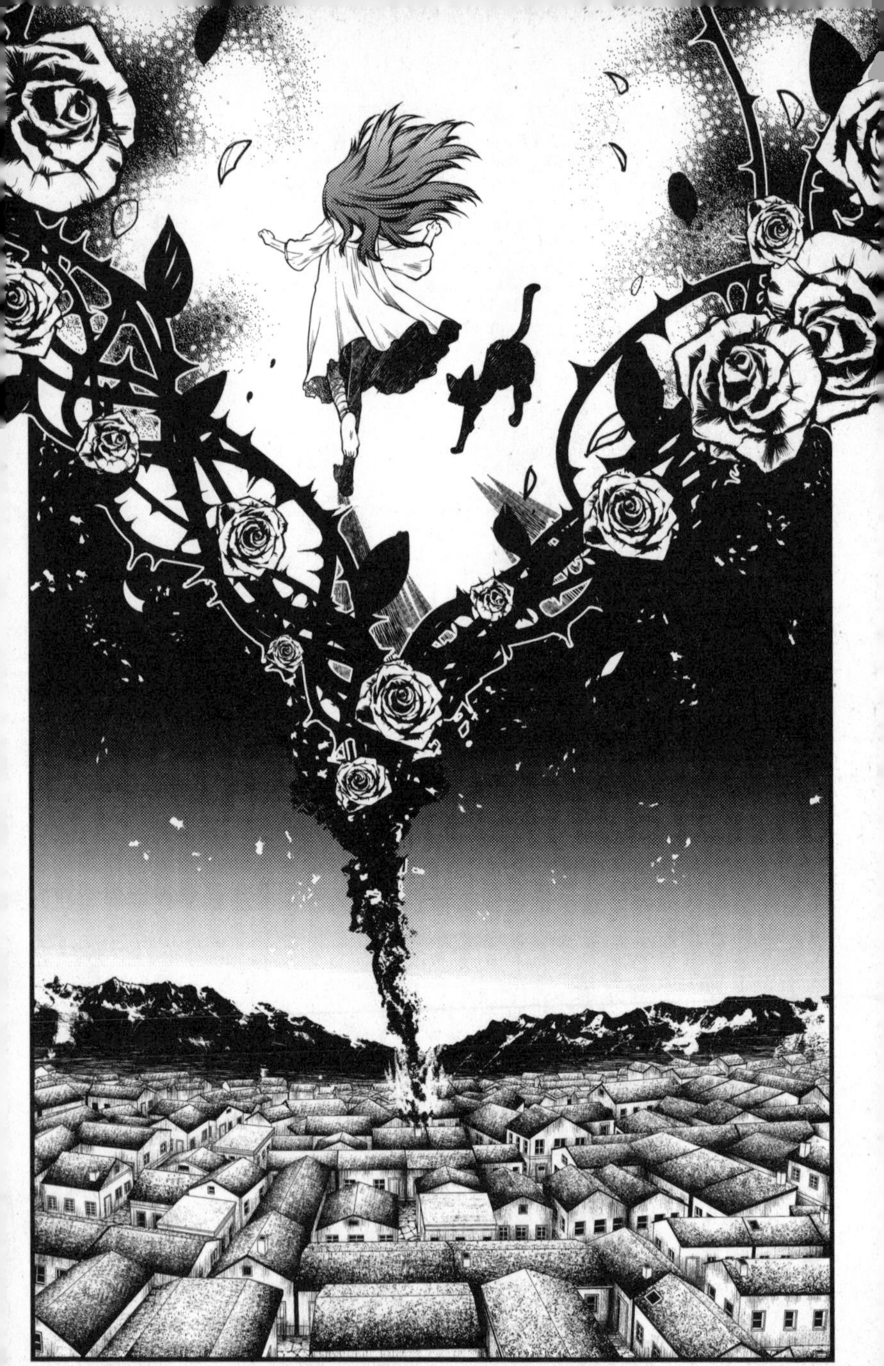

THE WITCH'S HOUSE

The Diary of Ellen

THE WITCH'S HOUSE
The Diary of Ellen

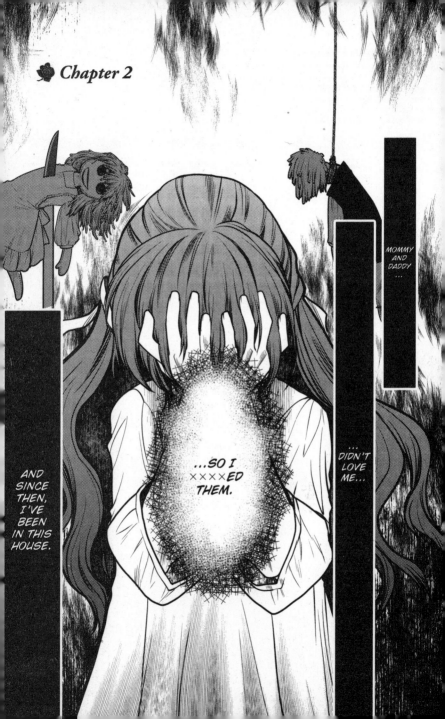

Chapter 2

MOMMY AND DADDY...

...DIDN'T LOVE ME...

...SO I ××××ED THEM.

AND SINCE THEN, I'VE BEEN IN THIS HOUSE.

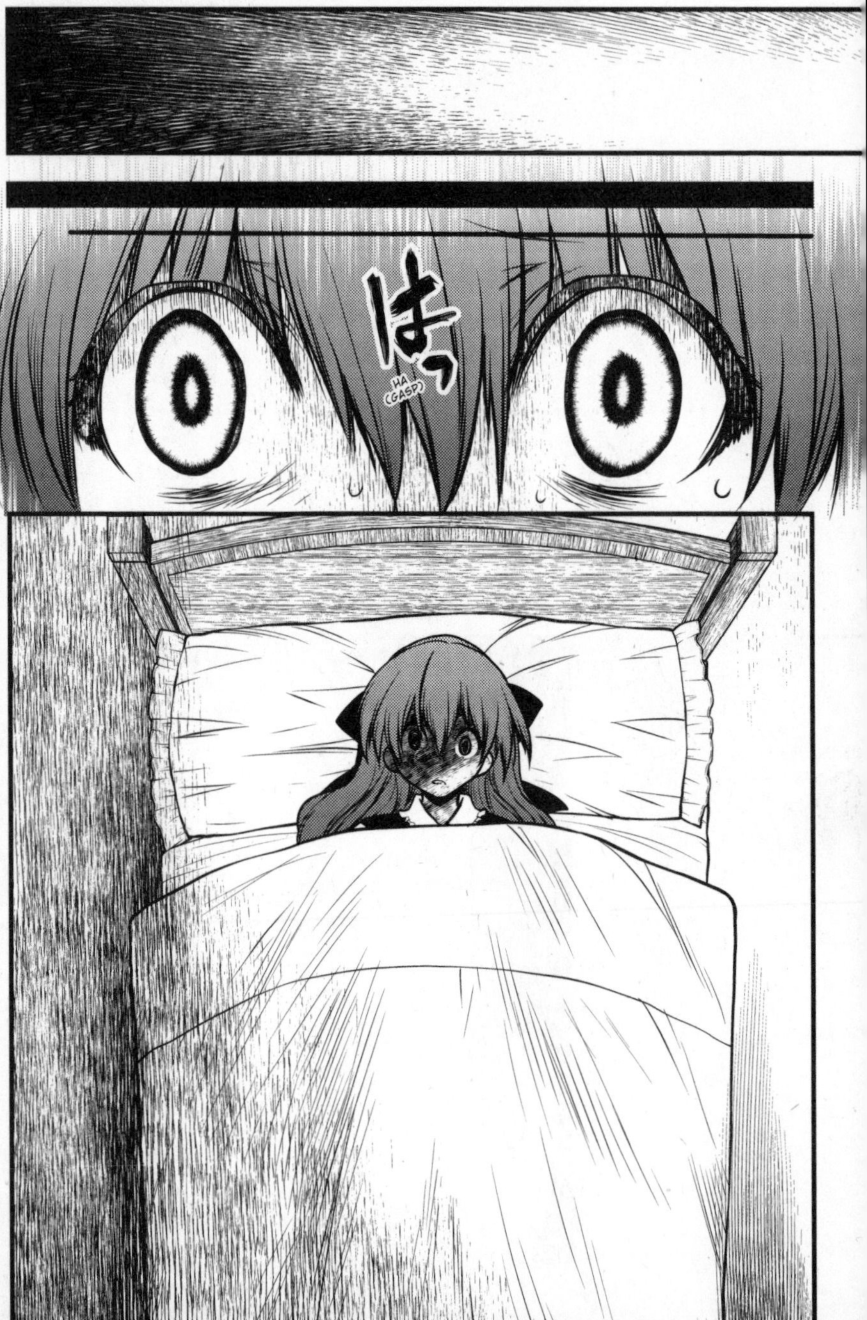
はっ
HA (GASP)

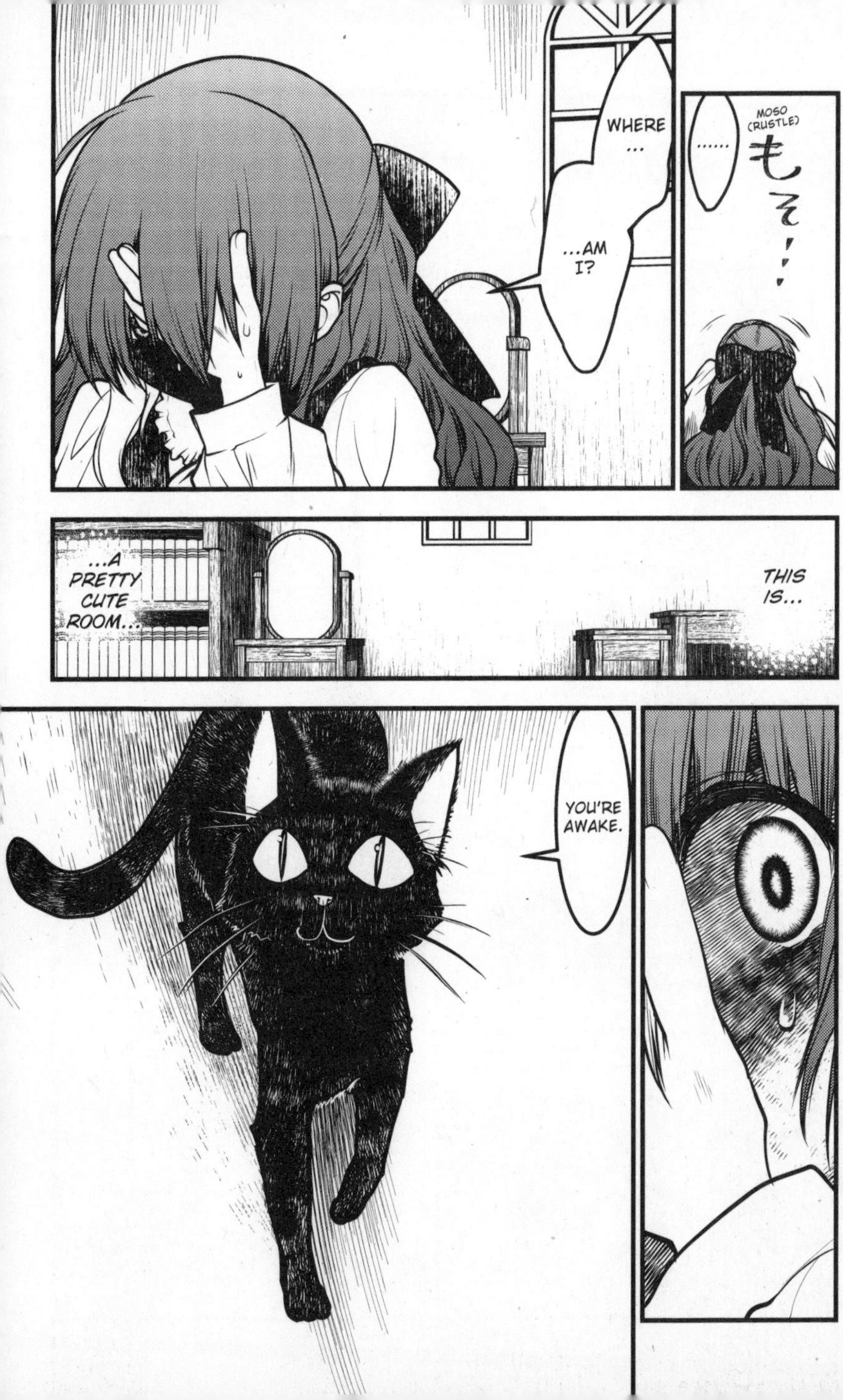
......
MOSO (RUSTLE)
もそ!!
WHERE...
...AM I?
THIS IS...
...A PRETTY CUTE ROOM...
YOU'RE AWAKE.

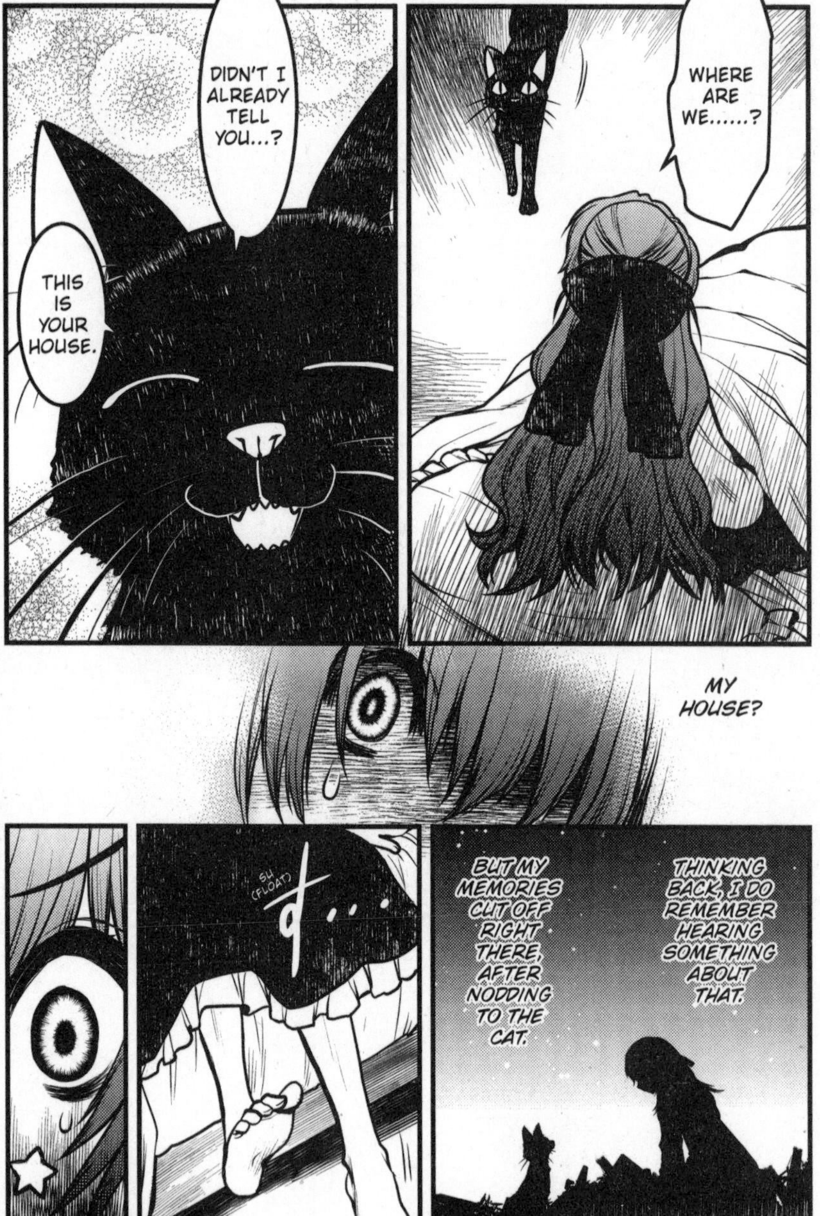
WHERE ARE WE......?
DIDN'T I ALREADY TELL YOU...?
THIS IS YOUR HOUSE.
MY HOUSE?
THINKING BACK, I DO REMEMBER HEARING SOMETHING ABOUT THAT.
BUT MY MEMORIES CUT OFF RIGHT THERE, AFTER NODDING TO THE CAT.
SU (FLOAT)
...

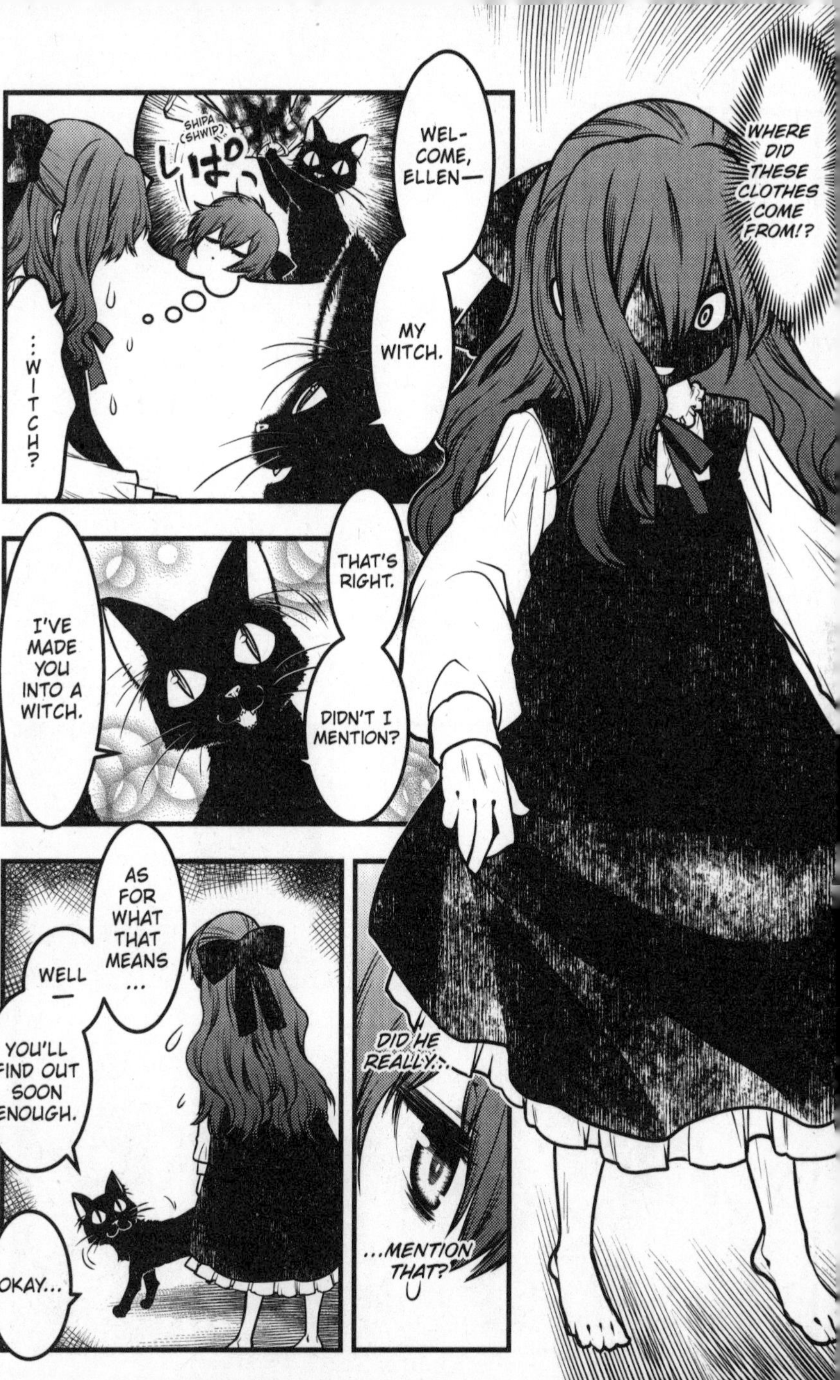
WHERE DID THESE CLOTHES COME FROM!?
WEL-COME, ELLEN—
MY WITCH.
SHIPA (SHWIP)
しぱっ
...WITCH?
THAT'S RIGHT.
DIDN'T I MENTION?
I'VE MADE YOU INTO A WITCH.
DID HE REALLY...
...MENTION THAT?
AS FOR WHAT THAT MEANS...
WELL—
YOU'LL FIND OUT SOON ENOUGH.
OKAY...

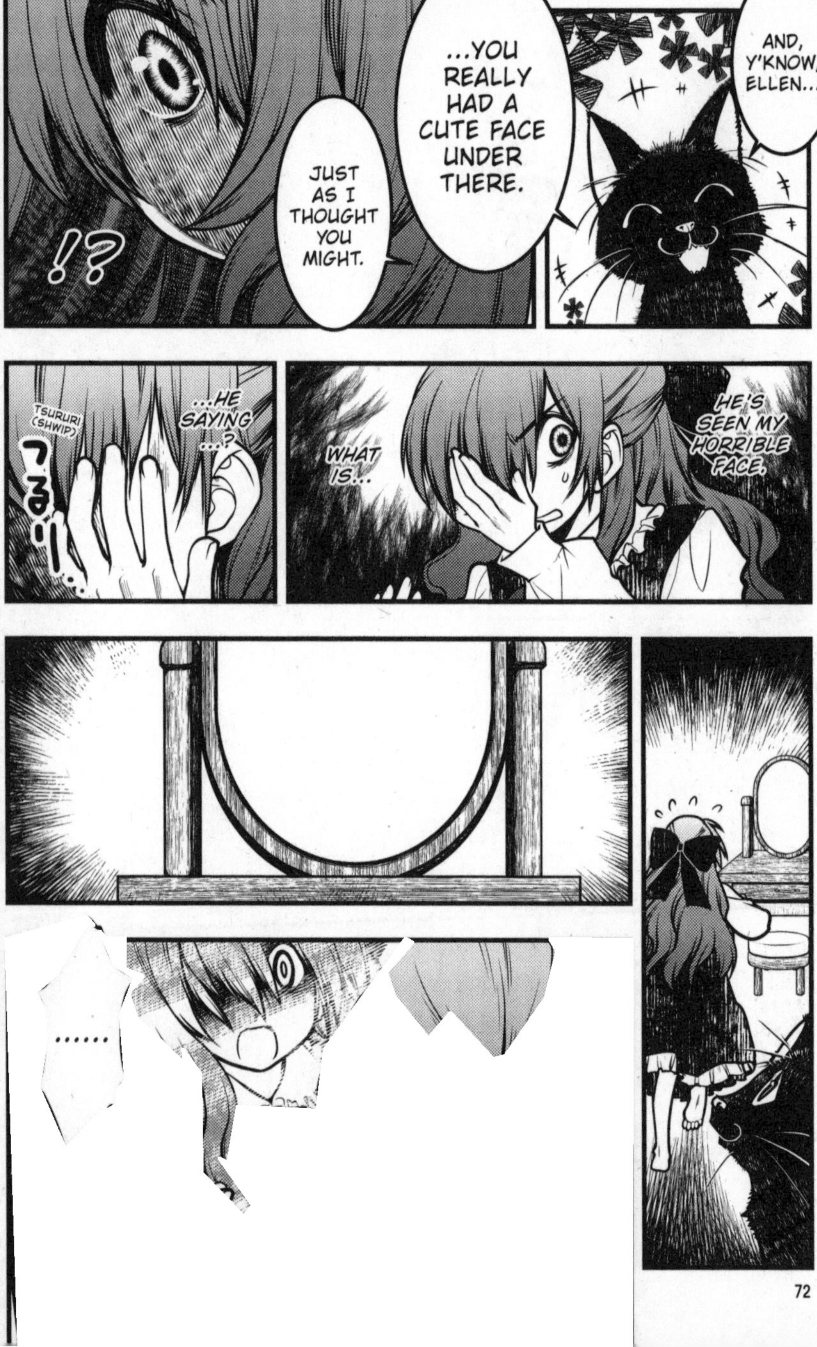
AND, Y'KNOW, ELLEN...
...YOU REALLY HAD A CUTE FACE UNDER THERE.
JUST AS I THOUGHT YOU MIGHT.
!?
HE'S SEEN MY HORRIBLE FACE.
WHAT IS...
...HE SAYING...?
TSURURI (SHWIP)
......

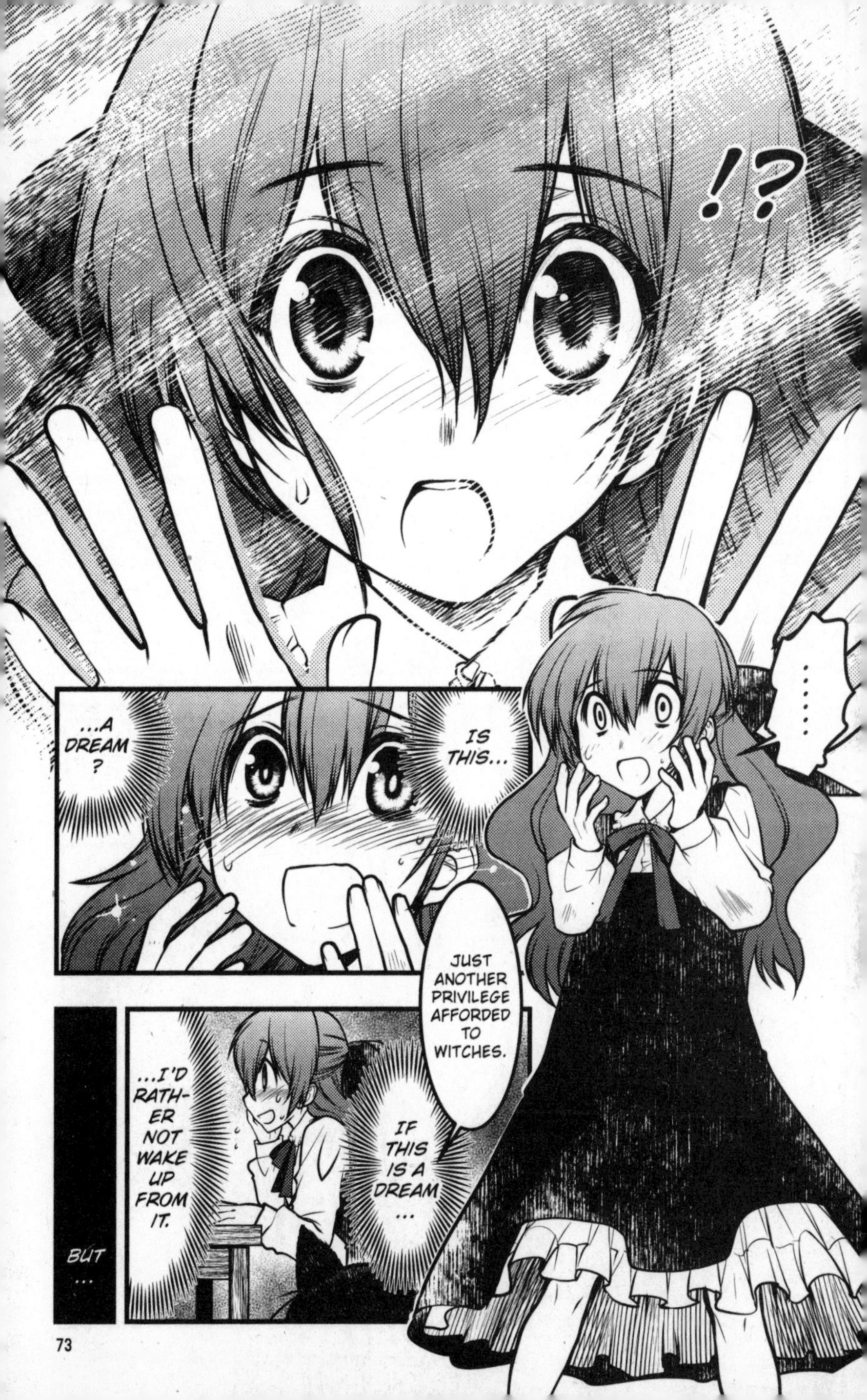
!?
......
IS THIS...
...A DREAM?
JUST ANOTHER PRIVILEGE AFFORDED TO WITCHES.
IF THIS IS A DREAM...
...I'D RATH-ER NOT WAKE UP FROM IT.
BUT...

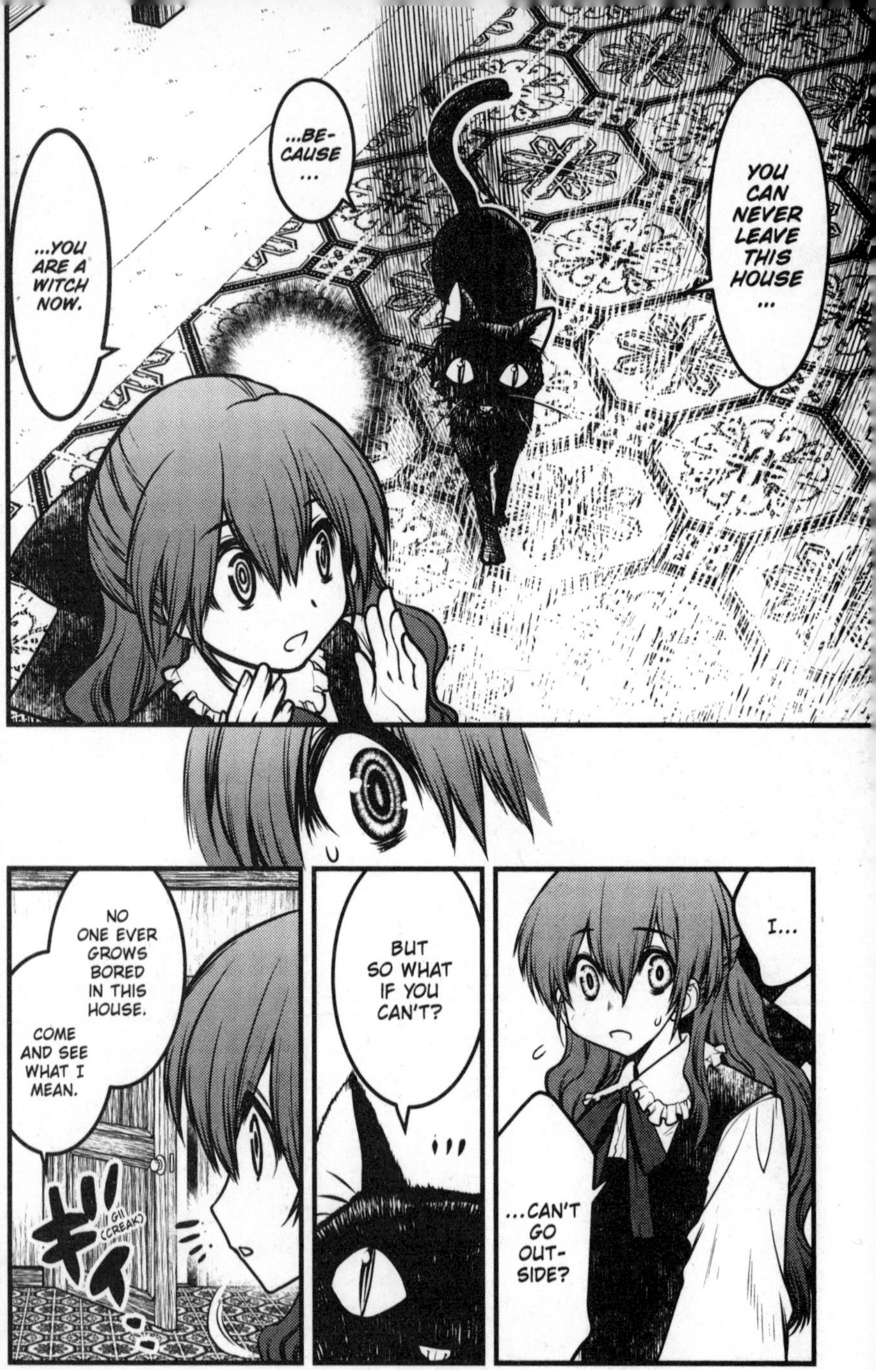
YOU CAN NEVER LEAVE THIS HOUSE...
...BE-CAUSE...
...YOU ARE A WITCH NOW.
I...
...CAN'T GO OUT-SIDE?
BUT SO WHAT IF YOU CAN'T?
NO ONE EVER GROWS BORED IN THIS HOUSE.
COME AND SEE WHAT I MEAN.
GII (CREAK)

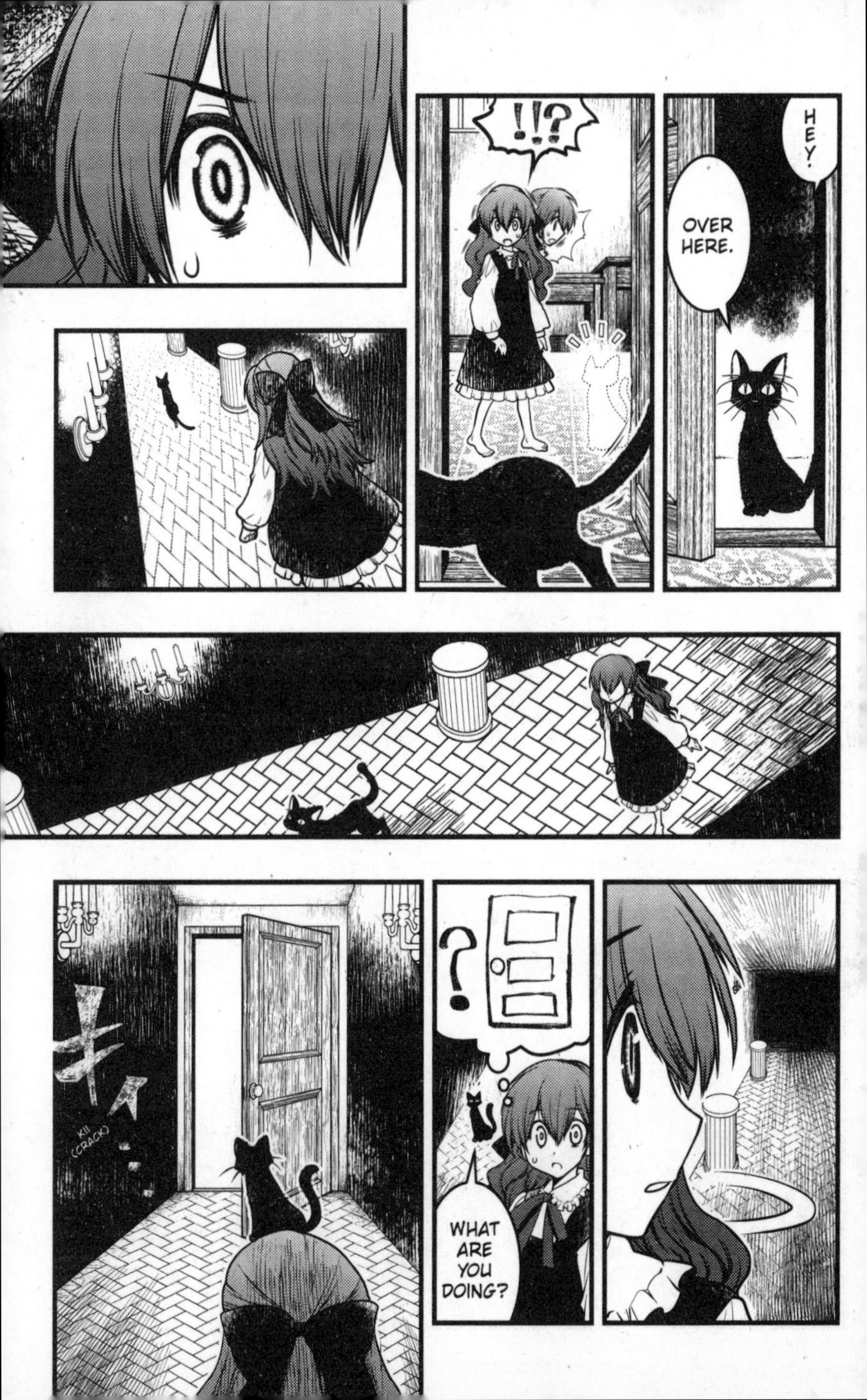

HEY.
OVER HERE.
!!?
?
WHAT ARE YOU DOING?
KII (CRACK)

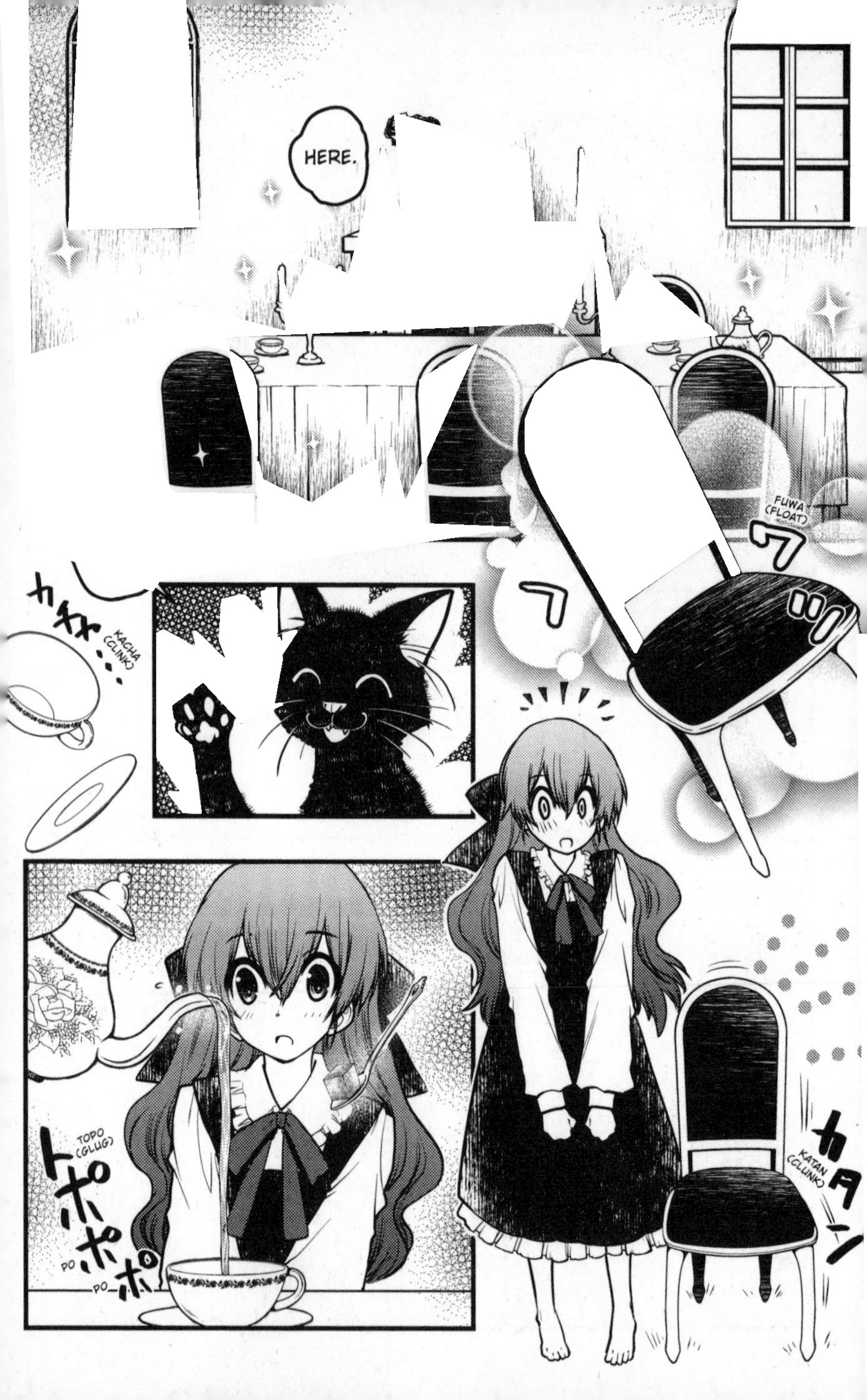
HERE.
FUWA (FLOAT)
KATAN (CLUNK)
KACHA (CLINK)
TOPO (GLUG)
PO
PO

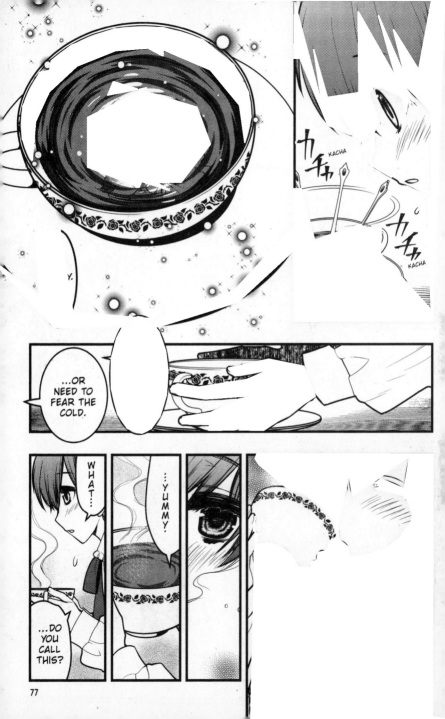

KACHA

KACHA

...OR NEED TO FEAR THE COLD.

WHAT...

...YUMMY.

...DO YOU CALL THIS?

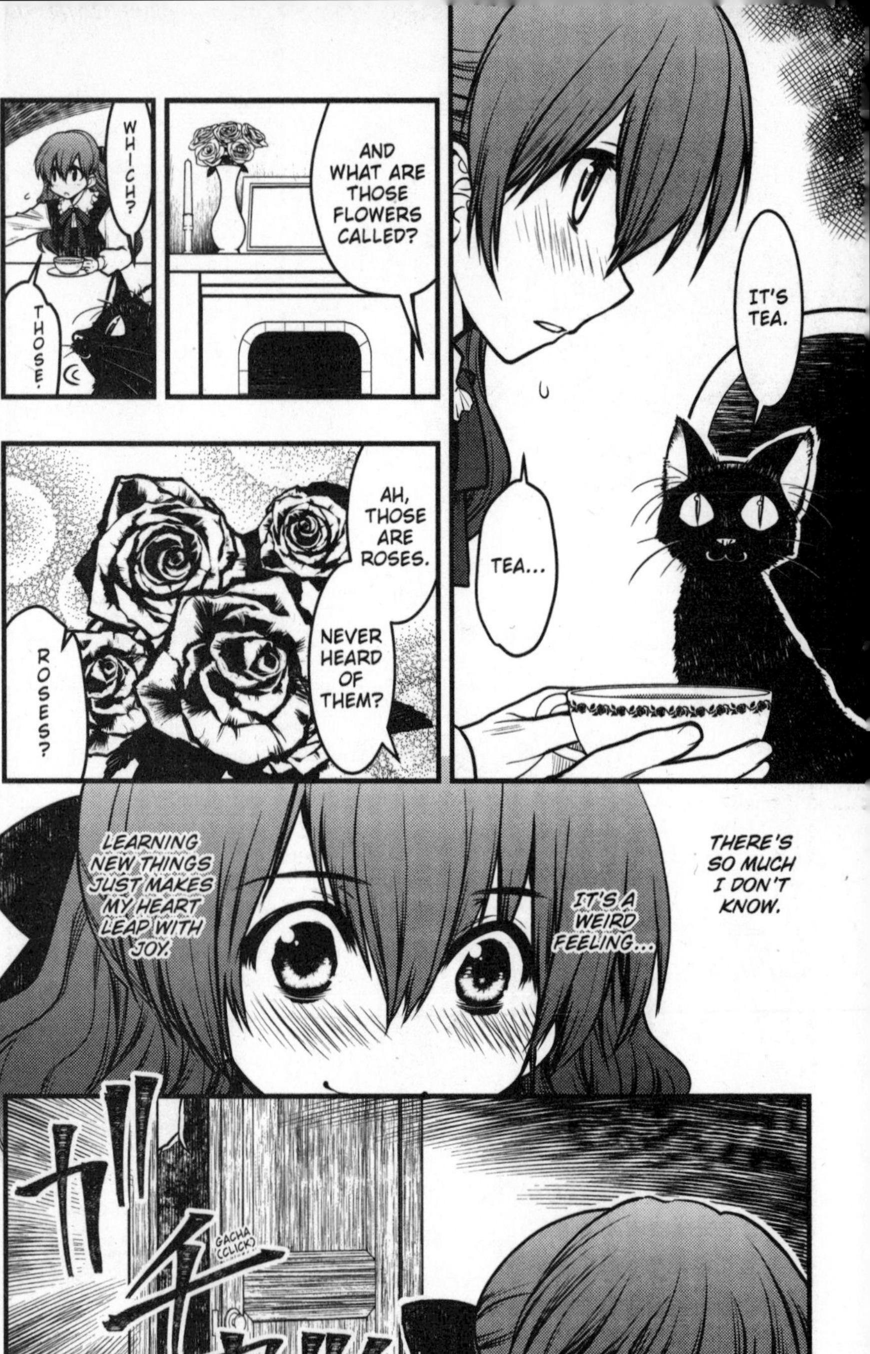
IT'S TEA.
TEA...
AND WHAT ARE THOSE FLOWERS CALLED?
WHICH?
THOSE.
AH, THOSE ARE ROSES.
NEVER HEARD OF THEM?
ROSES?
THERE'S SO MUCH I DON'T KNOW.
IT'S A WEIRD FEELING...
LEARNING NEW THINGS JUST MAKES MY HEART LEAP WITH JOY.
GACHA (CLICK)

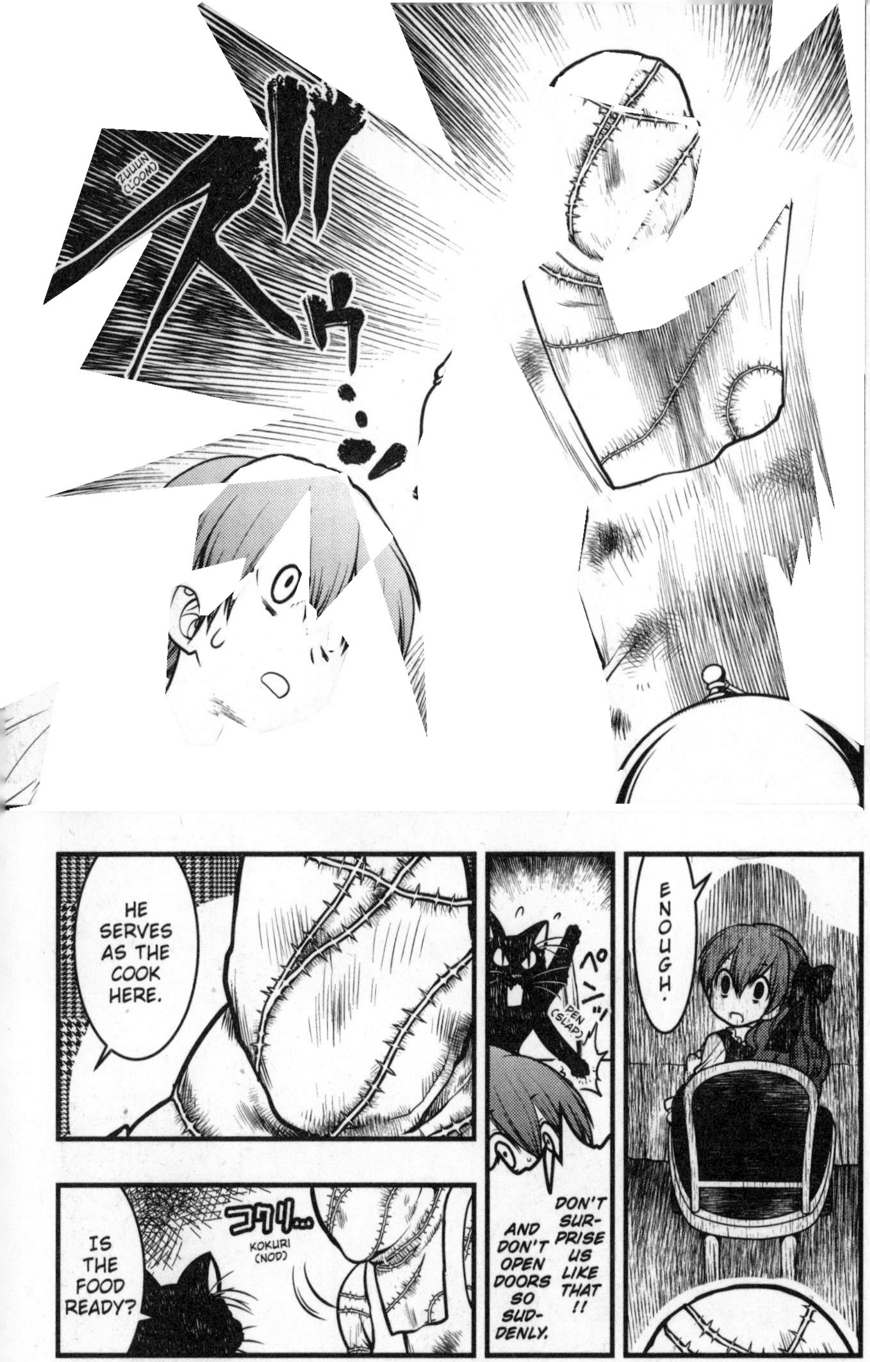
ZUUUN (LOOM)
ENOUGH.
PEN (SLAP)
DON'T SURPRISE US LIKE THAT!!
AND DON'T OPEN DOORS SO SUDDENLY.
HE SERVES AS THE COOK HERE.
KOKURI (NOD)
IS THE FOOD READY?

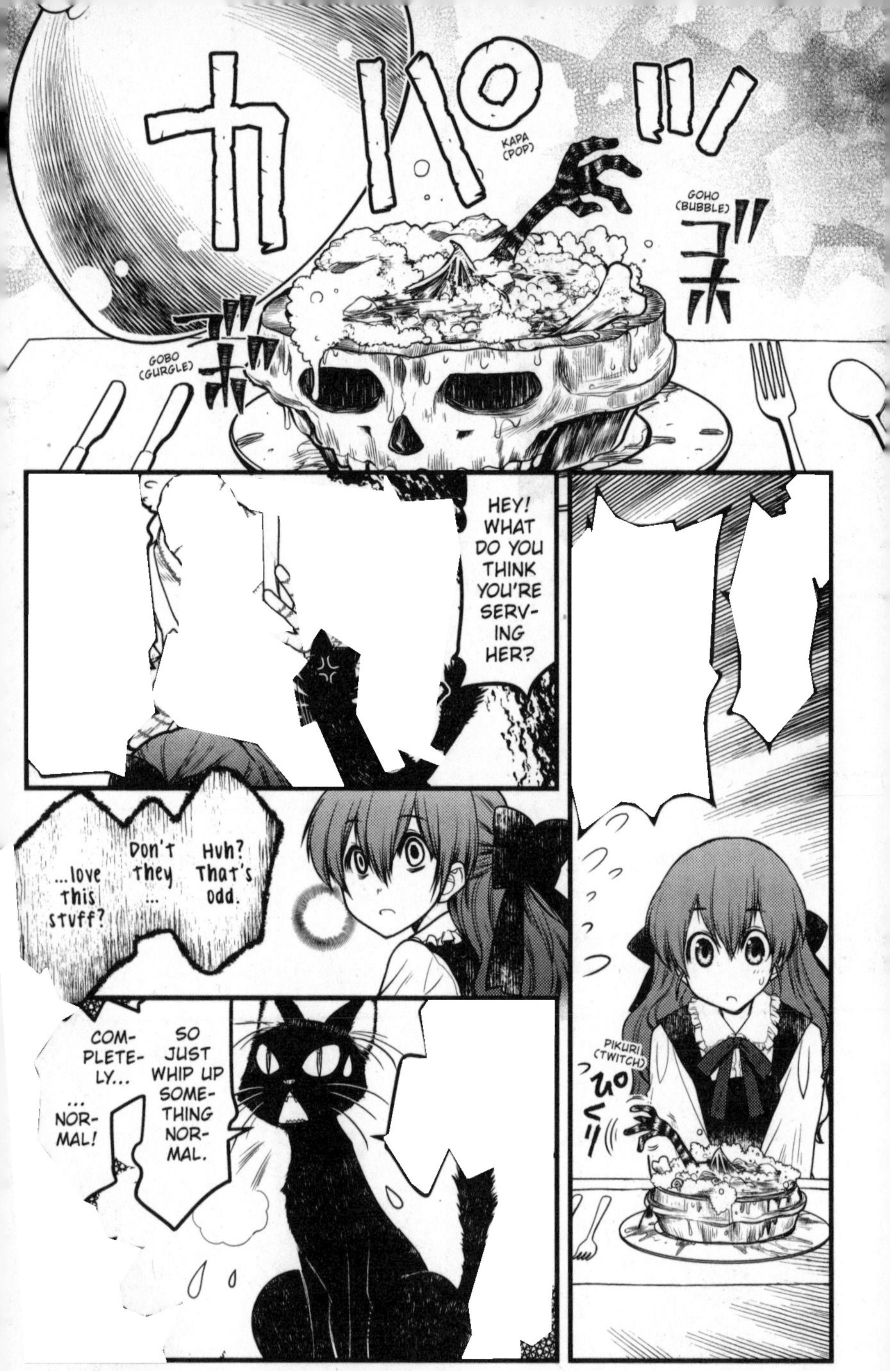

GOHO (BUBBLE)
KAPA (POP)
GOBO (GURGLE)
PIKURI (TWITCH)
HEY! WHAT DO YOU THINK YOU'RE SERV-ING HER?
Huh? That's odd.
Don't they ...
...love this stuff?
SO JUST WHIP UP SOME-THING NOR-MAL.
COM-PLETE-LY...
...NOR-MAL!

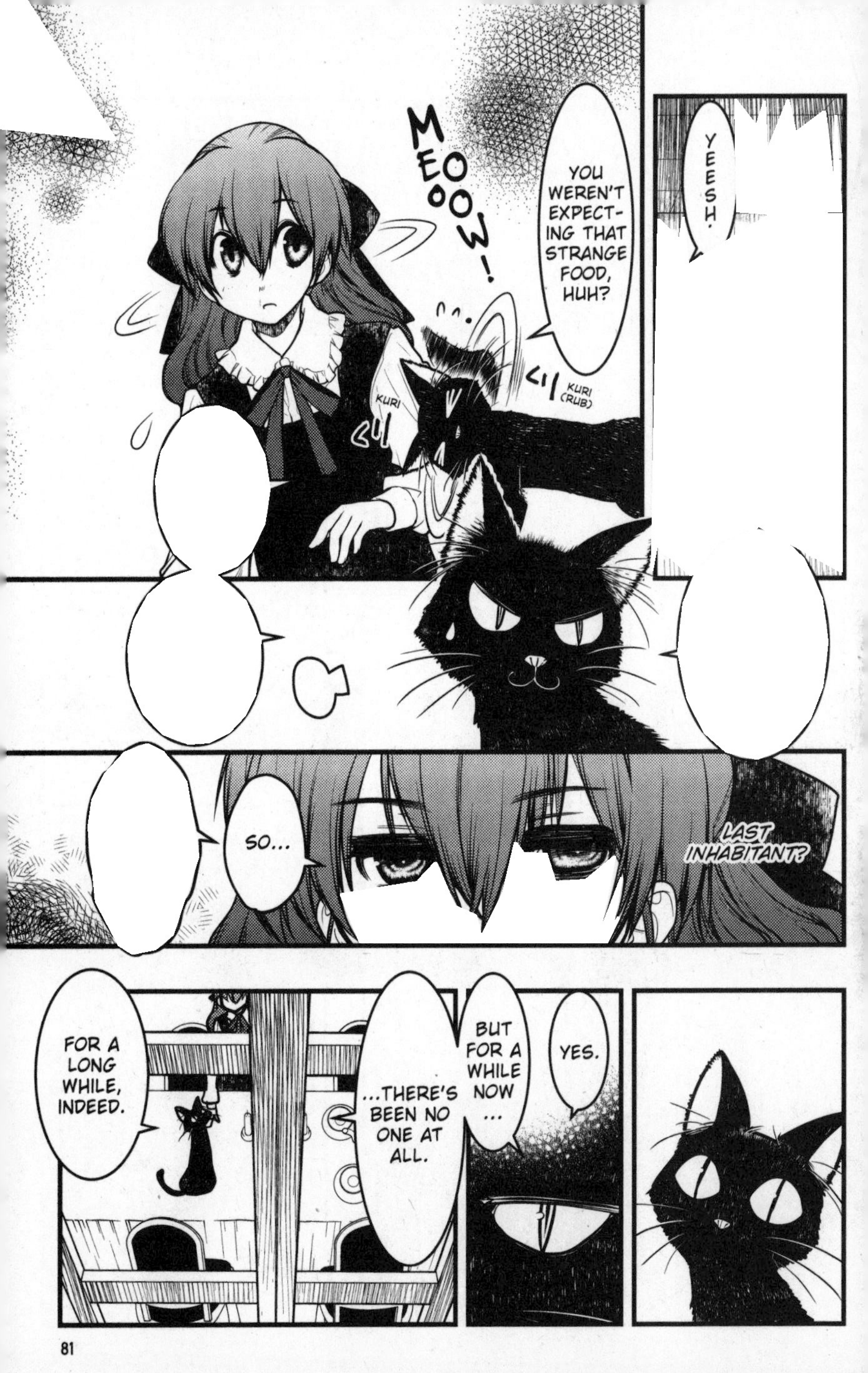
YEESH.
YOU WEREN'T EXPECTING THAT STRANGE FOOD, HUH?
MEOOOW!
KURI (RUB)
KURI
SO...
LAST INHABITANT?
YES.
BUT FOR A WHILE NOW...
...THERE'S BEEN NO ONE AT ALL.
FOR A LONG WHILE, INDEED.

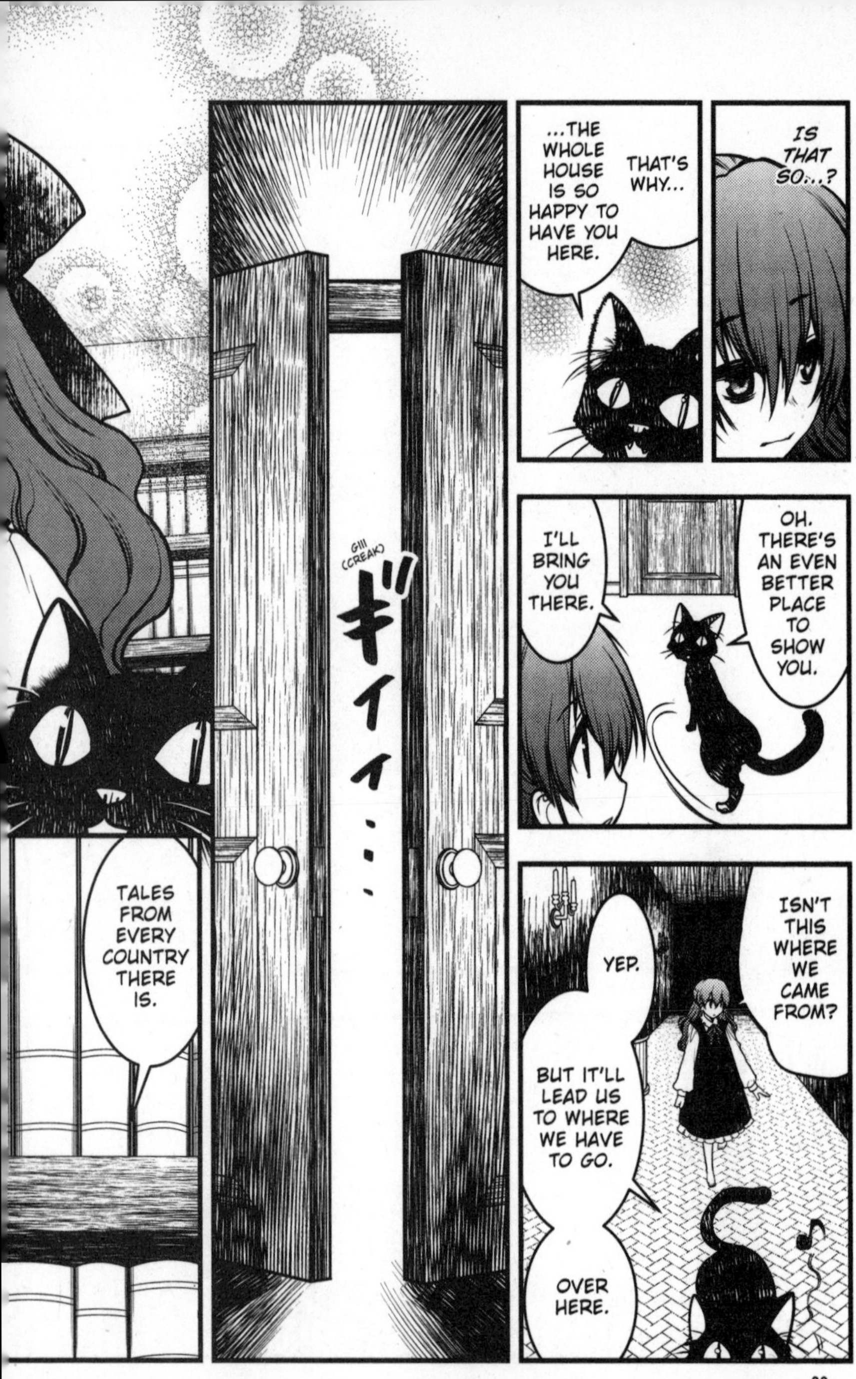
IS THAT SO...?
THAT'S WHY...
...THE WHOLE HOUSE IS SO HAPPY TO HAVE YOU HERE.
OH. THERE'S AN EVEN BETTER PLACE TO SHOW YOU.
I'LL BRING YOU THERE.
ISN'T THIS WHERE WE CAME FROM?
YEP.
BUT IT'LL LEAD US TO WHERE WE HAVE TO GO.
OVER HERE.
GIII (CREAK)
ギィィ…
TALES FROM EVERY COUNTRY THERE IS.

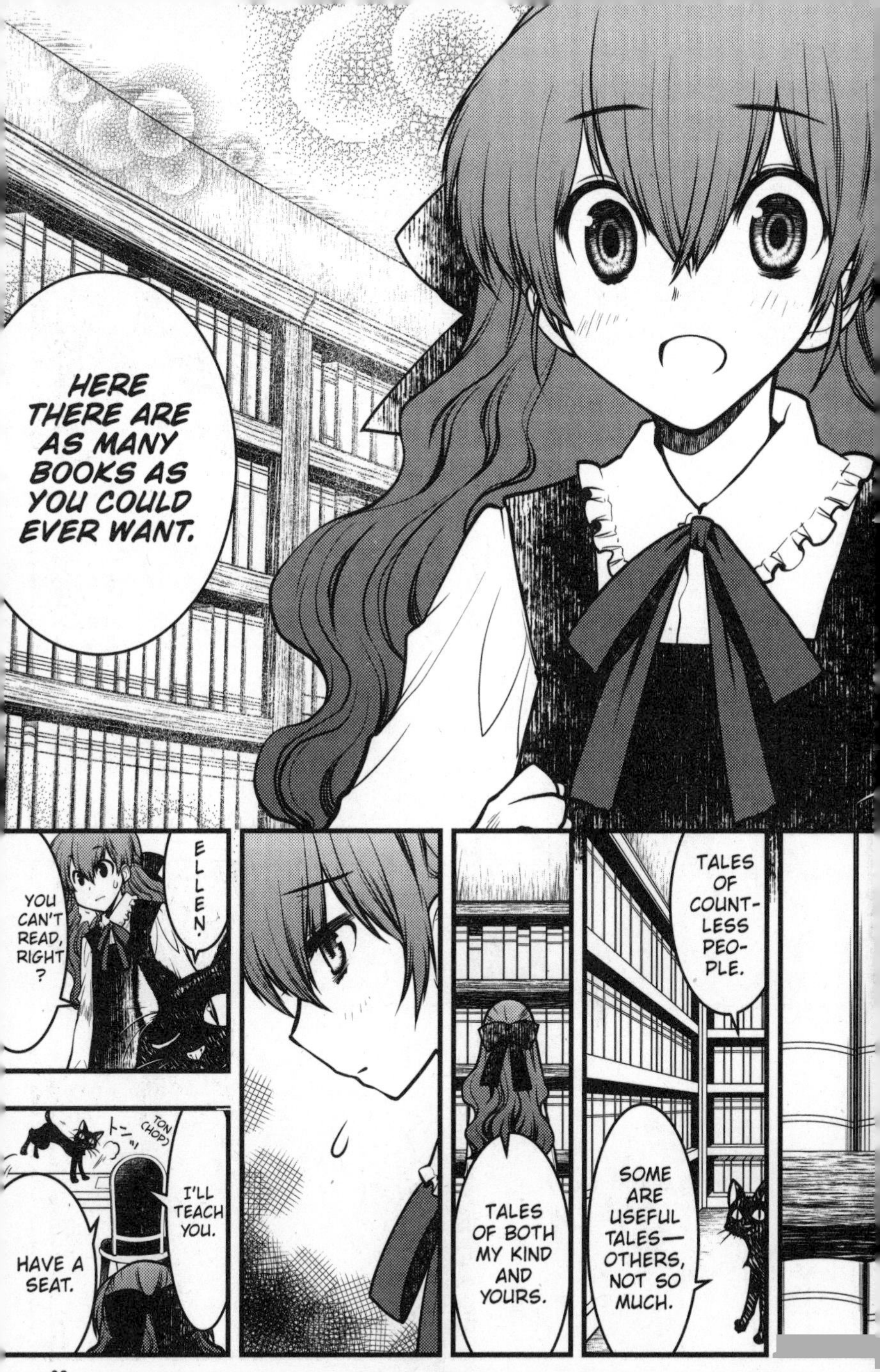
HERE THERE ARE AS MANY BOOKS AS YOU COULD EVER WANT.
TALES OF COUNT-LESS PEO-PLE.
SOME ARE USEFUL TALES—OTHERS, NOT SO MUCH.
TALES OF BOTH MY KIND AND YOURS.
ELLEN.
YOU CAN'T READ, RIGHT?
TON (CHOP)
I'LL TEACH YOU.
HAVE A SEAT.

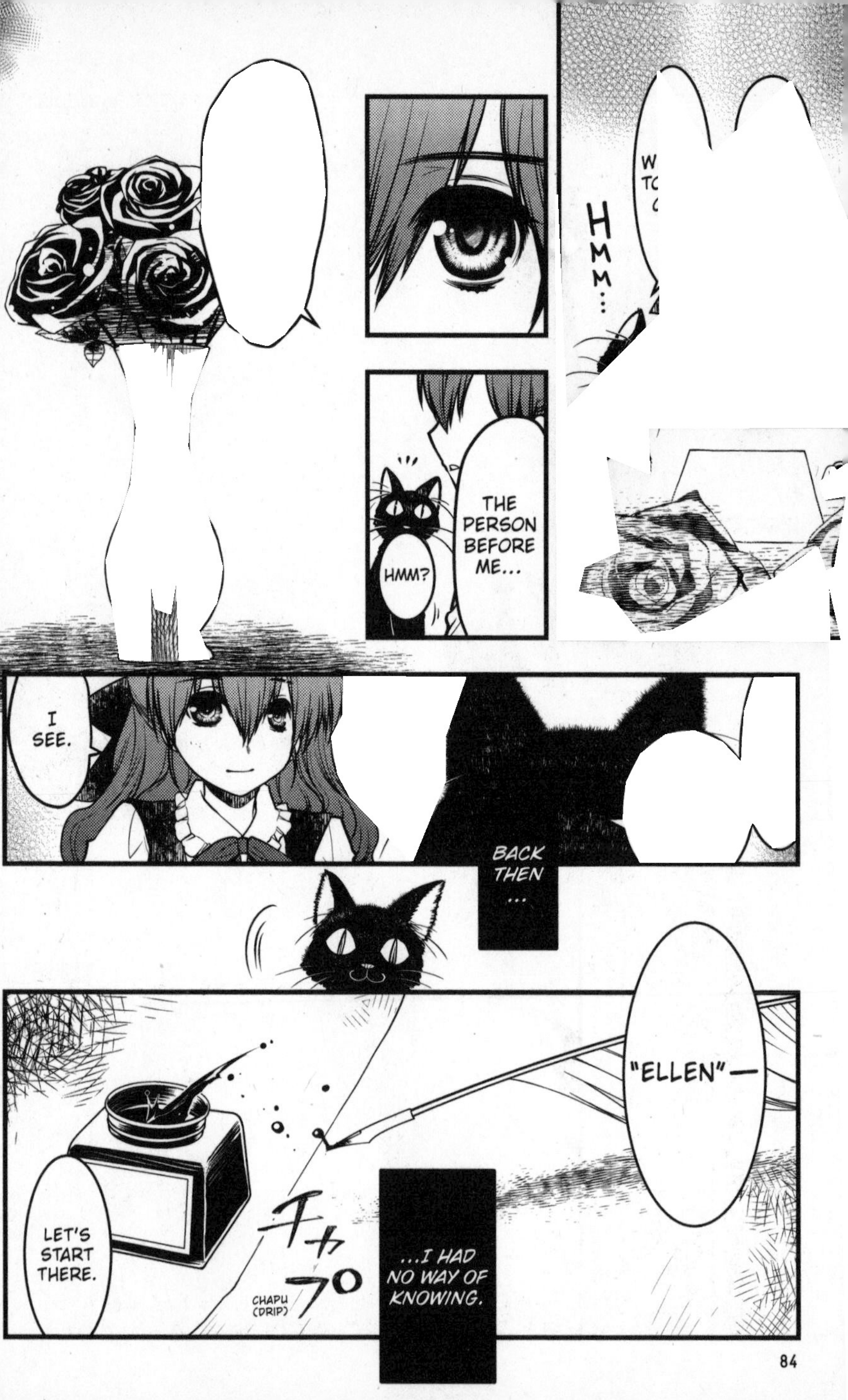
HMM...
THE PERSON BEFORE ME...
HMM?
I SEE.
BACK THEN...
"ELLEN"—
...I HAD NO WAY OF KNOWING.
CHAPU (DRIP)
LET'S START THERE.

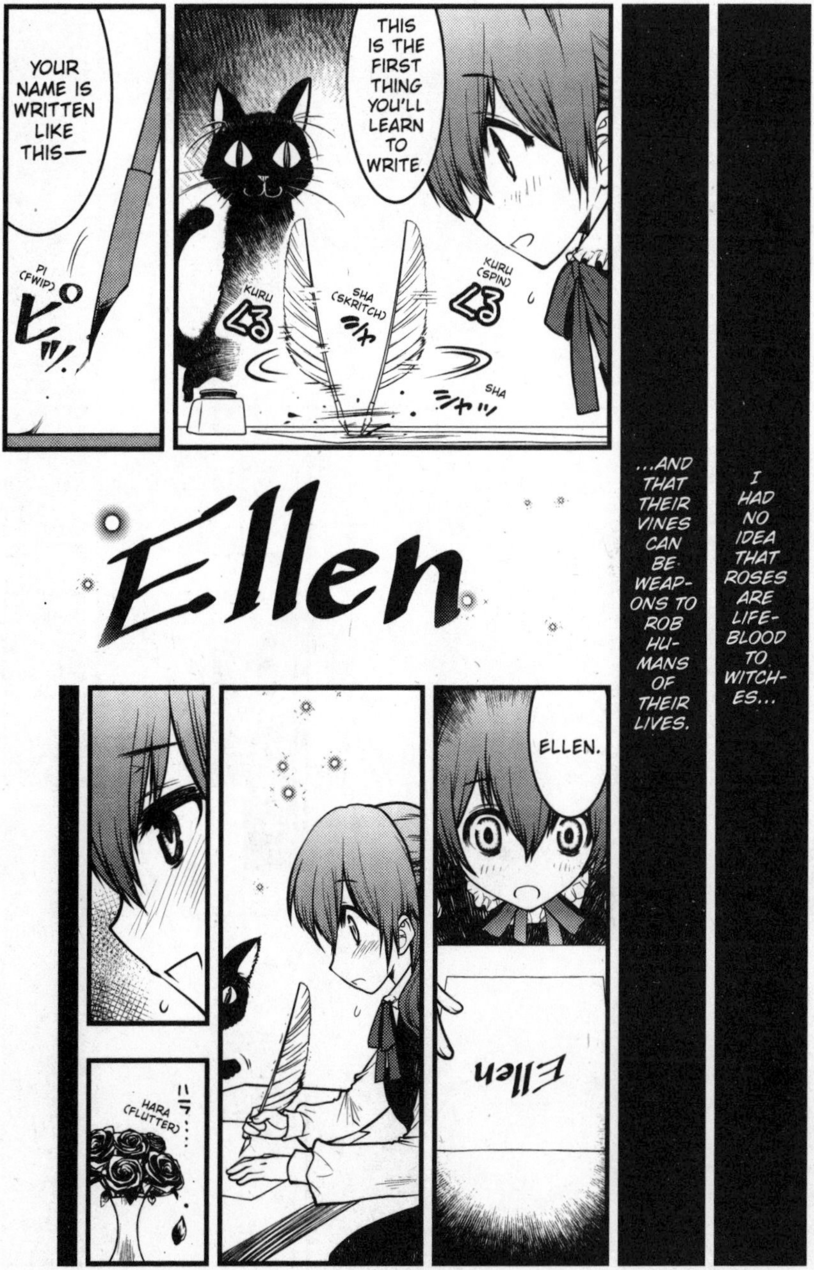
I HAD NO IDEA THAT ROSES ARE LIFE-BLOOD TO WITCH-ES...
...AND THAT THEIR VINES CAN BE WEAP-ONS TO ROB HU-MANS OF THEIR LIVES.
THIS IS THE FIRST THING YOU'LL LEARN TO WRITE.
KURU (SPIN)
SHA (SKRITCH)
KURU
SHA
YOUR NAME IS WRITTEN LIKE THIS—
PI (FWIP)
Ellen
ELLEN.
Ellen
HARA (FLUTTER)

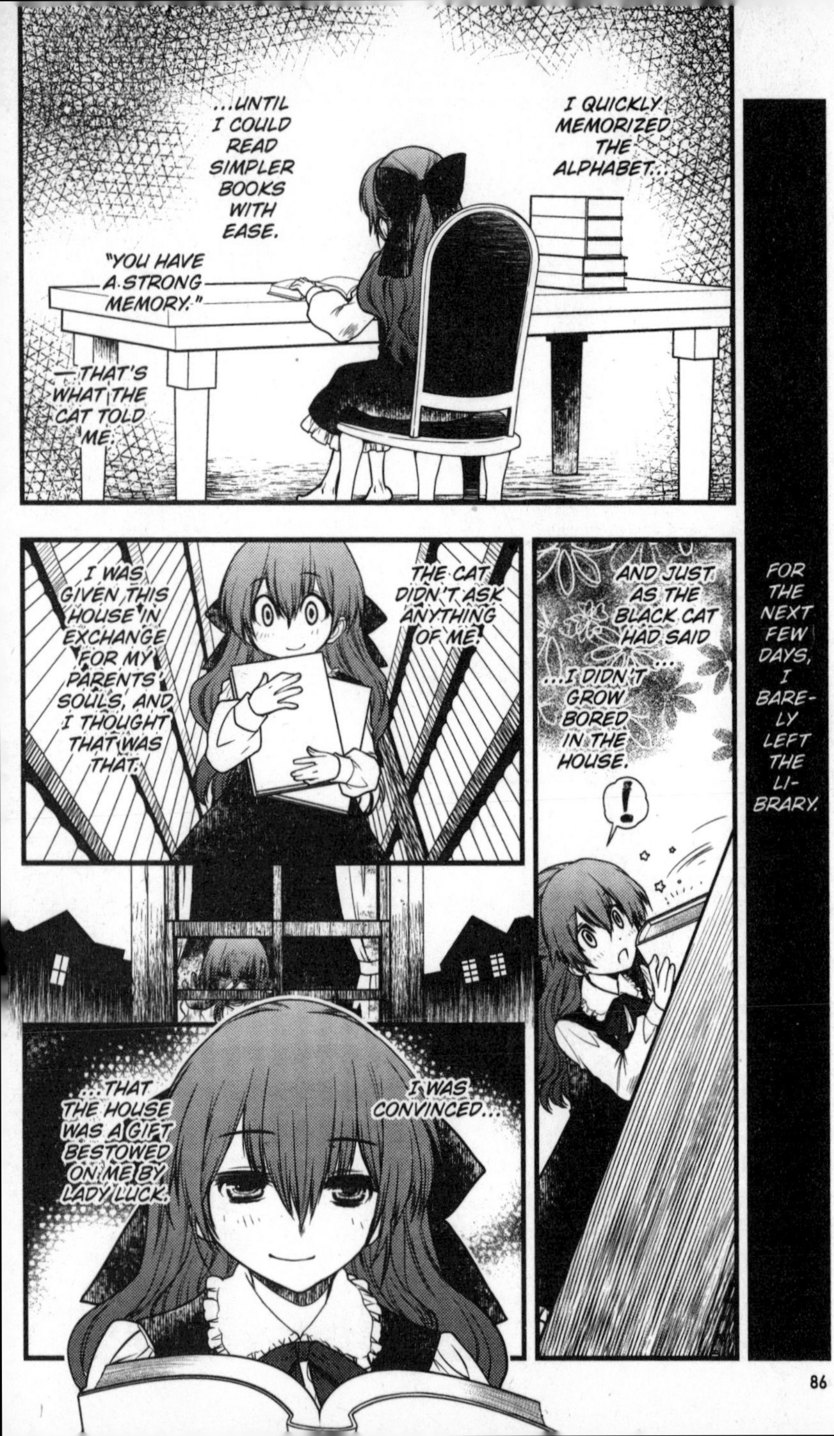
FOR THE NEXT FEW DAYS, I BARELY LEFT THE LIBRARY.
I QUICKLY MEMORIZED THE ALPHABET...
...UNTIL I COULD READ SIMPLER BOOKS WITH EASE.
"YOU HAVE A STRONG MEMORY."
—THAT'S WHAT THE CAT TOLD ME.
AND JUST AS THE BLACK CAT HAD SAID...
...I DIDN'T GROW BORED IN THE HOUSE.
!
THE CAT DIDN'T ASK ANYTHING OF ME.
I WAS GIVEN THIS HOUSE IN EXCHANGE FOR MY PARENTS' SOULS, AND I THOUGHT THAT WAS THAT.
I WAS CONVINCED...
...THAT THE HOUSE WAS A GIFT BESTOWED ON ME BY LADY LUCK.

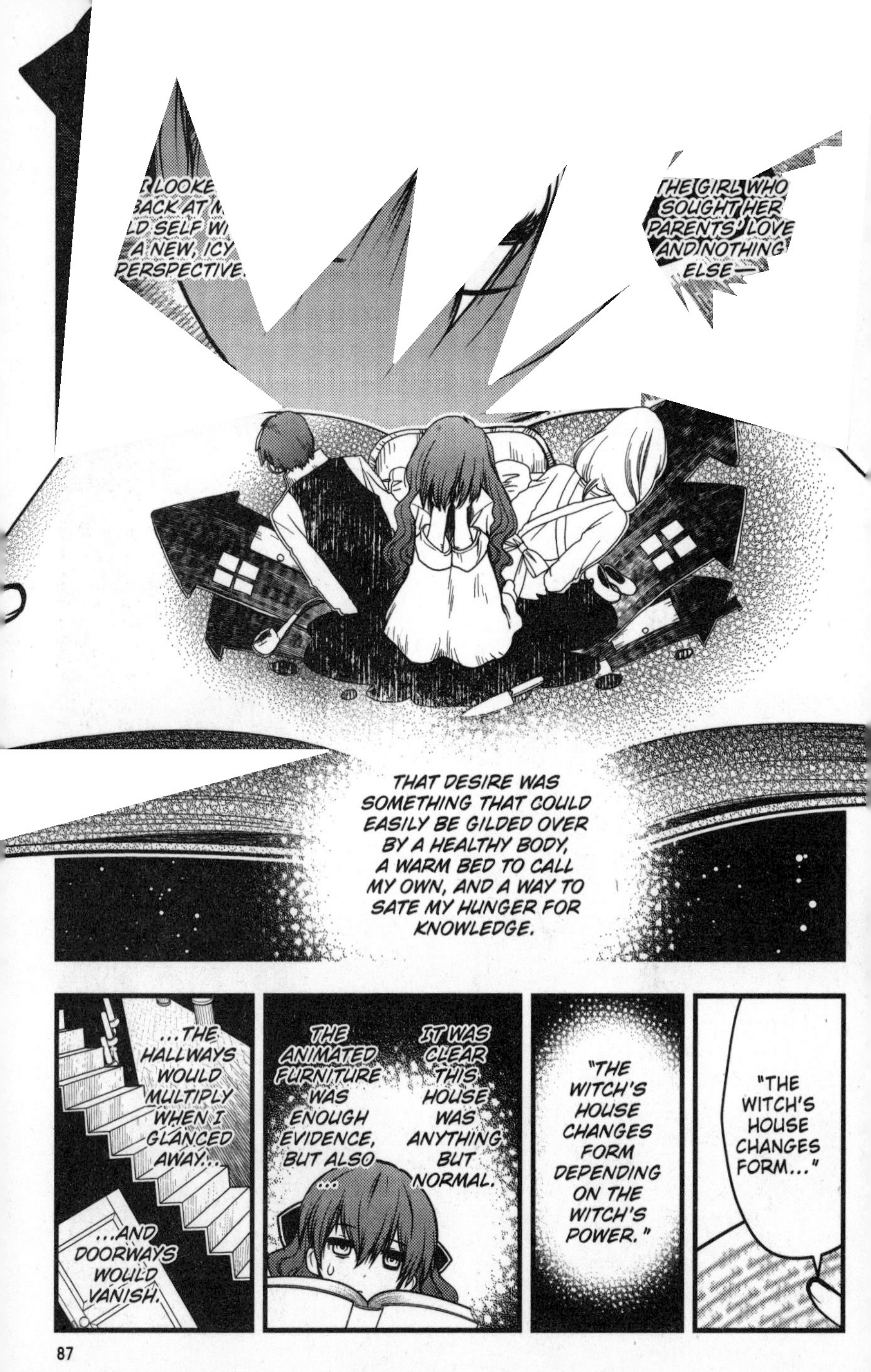
THE GIRL WHO SOUGHT HER PARENTS' LOVE AND NOTHING ELSE—
LOOKE BACK AT M LD SELF WI A NEW, ICY PERSPECTIVE.
THAT DESIRE WAS SOMETHING THAT COULD EASILY BE GILDED OVER BY A HEALTHY BODY, A WARM BED TO CALL MY OWN, AND A WAY TO SATE MY HUNGER FOR KNOWLEDGE.
"THE WITCH'S HOUSE CHANGES FORM..."
"THE WITCH'S HOUSE CHANGES FORM DEPENDING ON THE WITCH'S POWER."
IT WAS CLEAR THIS HOUSE WAS ANYTHING BUT NORMAL.
THE ANIMATED FURNITURE WAS ENOUGH EVIDENCE, BUT ALSO
...
...THE HALLWAYS WOULD MULTIPLY WHEN I GLANCED AWAY...
...AND DOORWAYS WOULD VANISH.

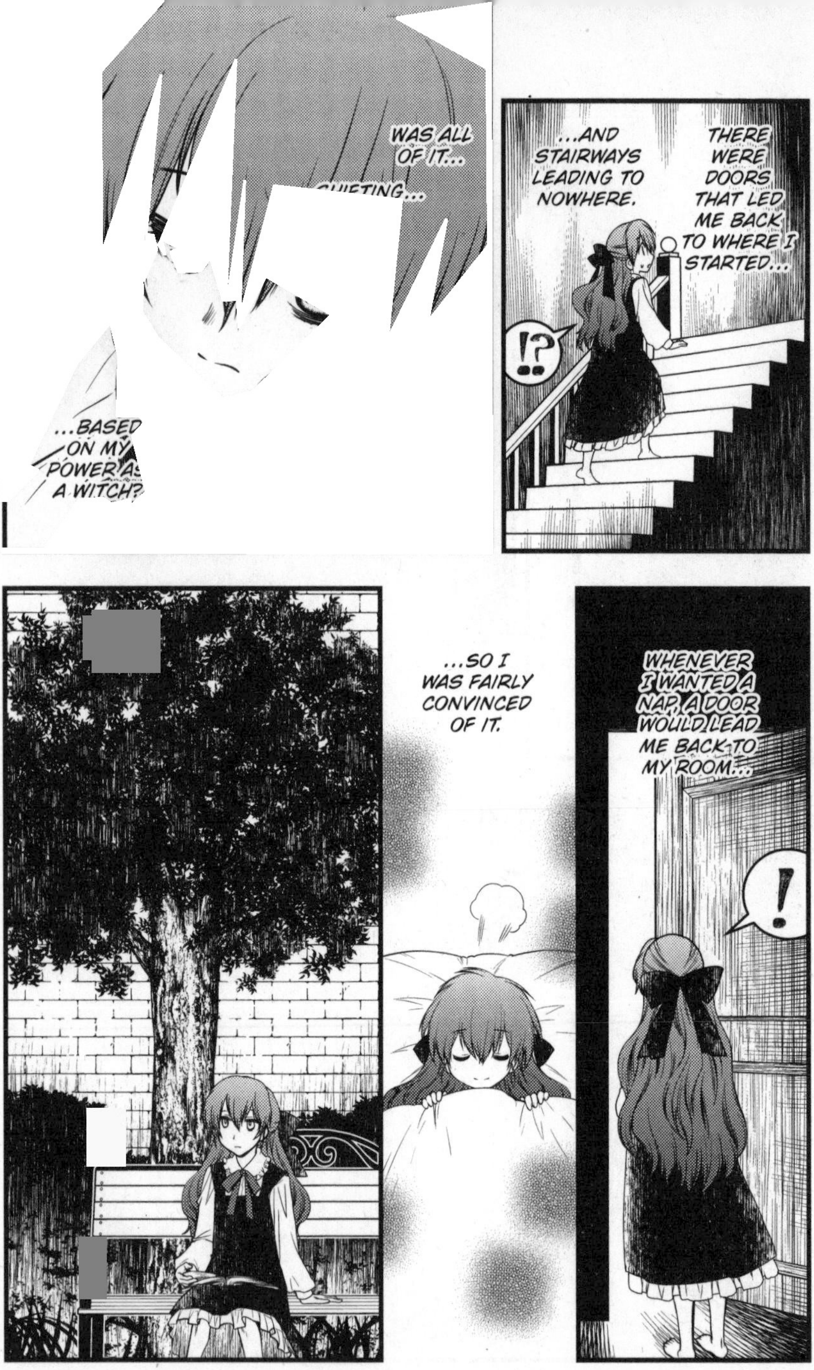
THERE WERE DOORS THAT LED ME BACK TO WHERE I STARTED...
...AND STAIRWAYS LEADING TO NOWHERE.
!?
WAS ALL OF IT...
...BASED ON MY POWER AS A WITCH?
WHENEVER I WANTED A NAP, A DOOR WOULD LEAD ME BACK TO MY ROOM...
!
...SO I WAS FAIRLY CONVINCED OF IT.

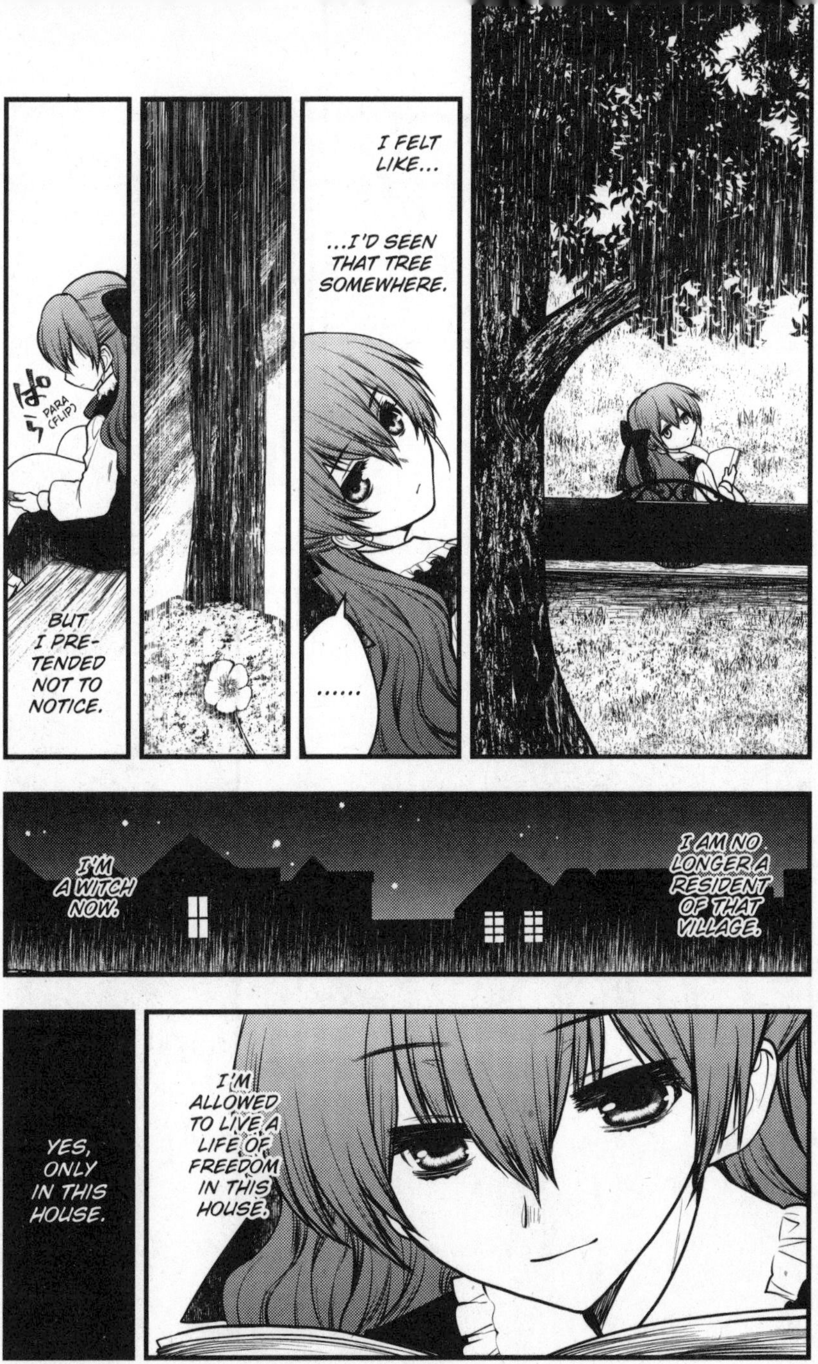
I FELT LIKE...
...I'D SEEN THAT TREE SOMEWHERE.
......
ぱら
PARA (FLIP)
BUT I PRE-TENDED NOT TO NOTICE.
I AM NO LONGER A RESIDENT OF THAT VILLAGE.
I'M A WITCH NOW.
I'M ALLOWED TO LIVE A LIFE OF FREEDOM IN THIS HOUSE.
YES, ONLY IN THIS HOUSE.

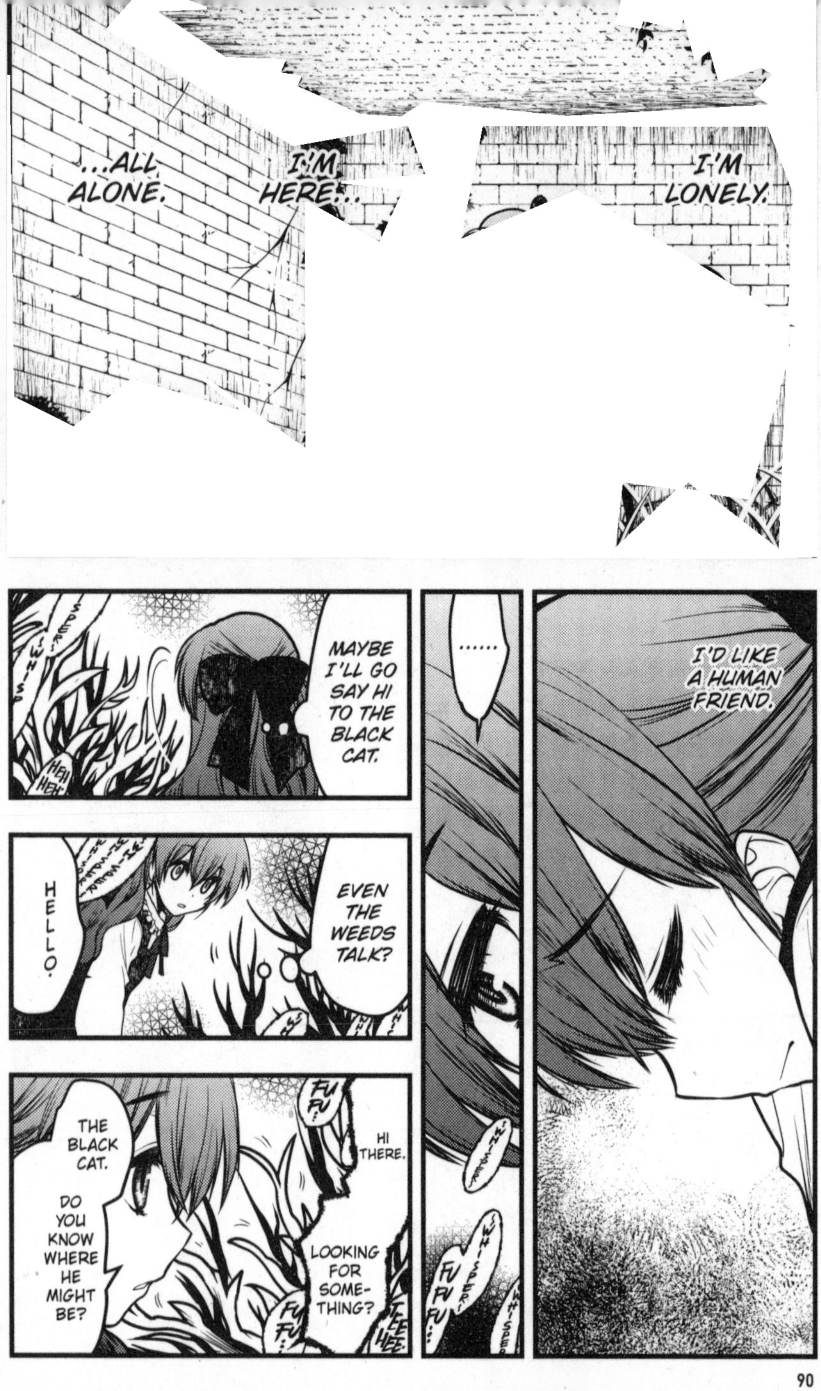
I'M LONELY.
I'M HERE...
...ALL ALONE.
I'D LIKE A HUMAN FRIEND.
......
WHISPER
FUFUFU..
WHISPER
MAYBE I'LL GO SAY HI TO THE BLACK CAT.
WHISPER
HEH HEH
EVEN THE WEEDS TALK?
HELLO.
HI THERE.
FUFU..
THE BLACK CAT.
DO YOU KNOW WHERE HE MIGHT BE?
LOOKING FOR SOME-THING?
TEE HEE.
FUFU..

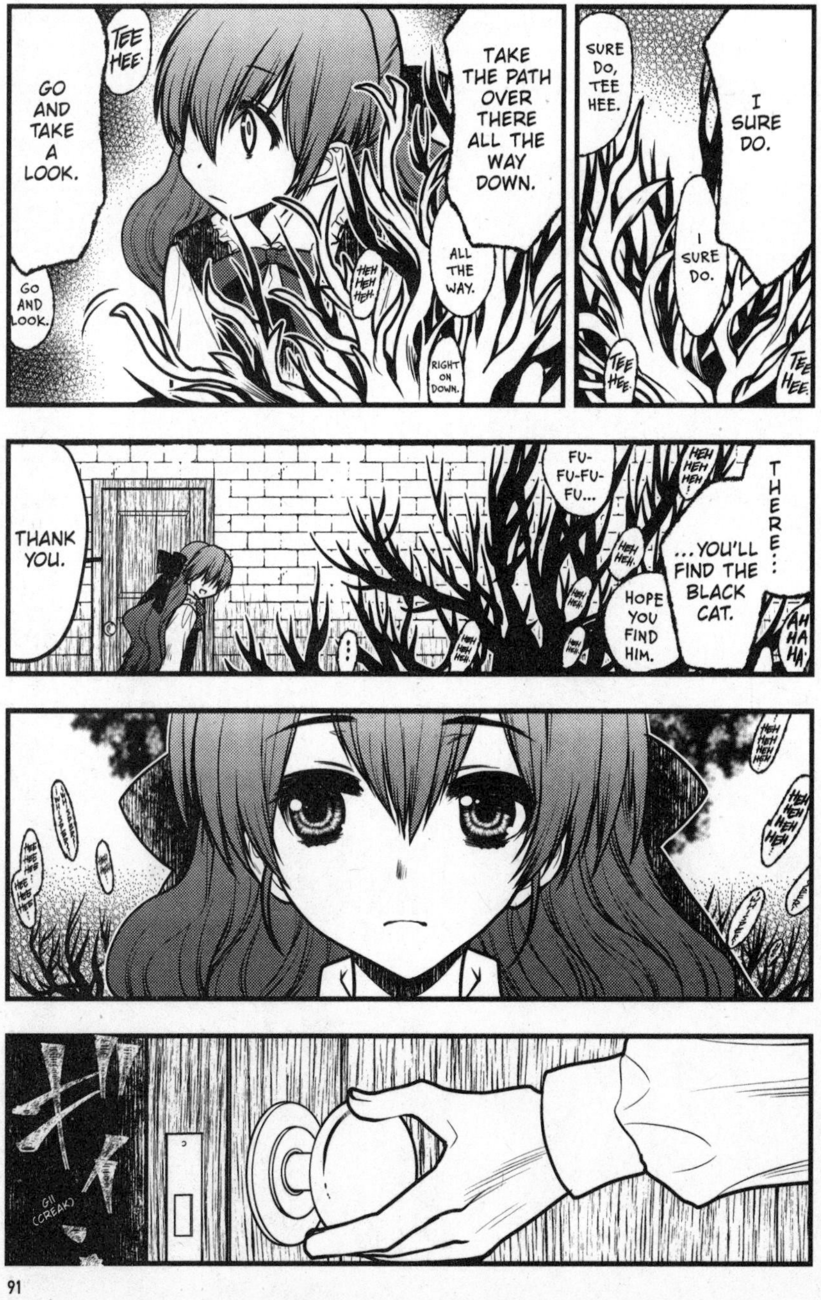
I SURE DO.
SURE DO, TEE HEE.
I SURE DO.
TEE HEE.
TEE HEE.
TAKE THE PATH OVER THERE ALL THE WAY DOWN.
ALL THE WAY.
HEH HEH HEH.
RIGHT ON DOWN.
TEE HEE.
GO AND TAKE A LOOK.
GO AND LOOK.
THERE...
...YOU'LL FIND THE BLACK CAT.
AH HA HA!
HEH HEH HEH!
FU-FU-FU-FU...
HEH HEH.
HOPE YOU FIND HIM.
HEH HEH.
HEH HEH.
HEH HEH HEH.
...
THANK YOU.
HEH HEH HEH HEH
HEH HEH HEH HEH
HEE HEE HEE
HEE HEE HEE
GII (CREAK)

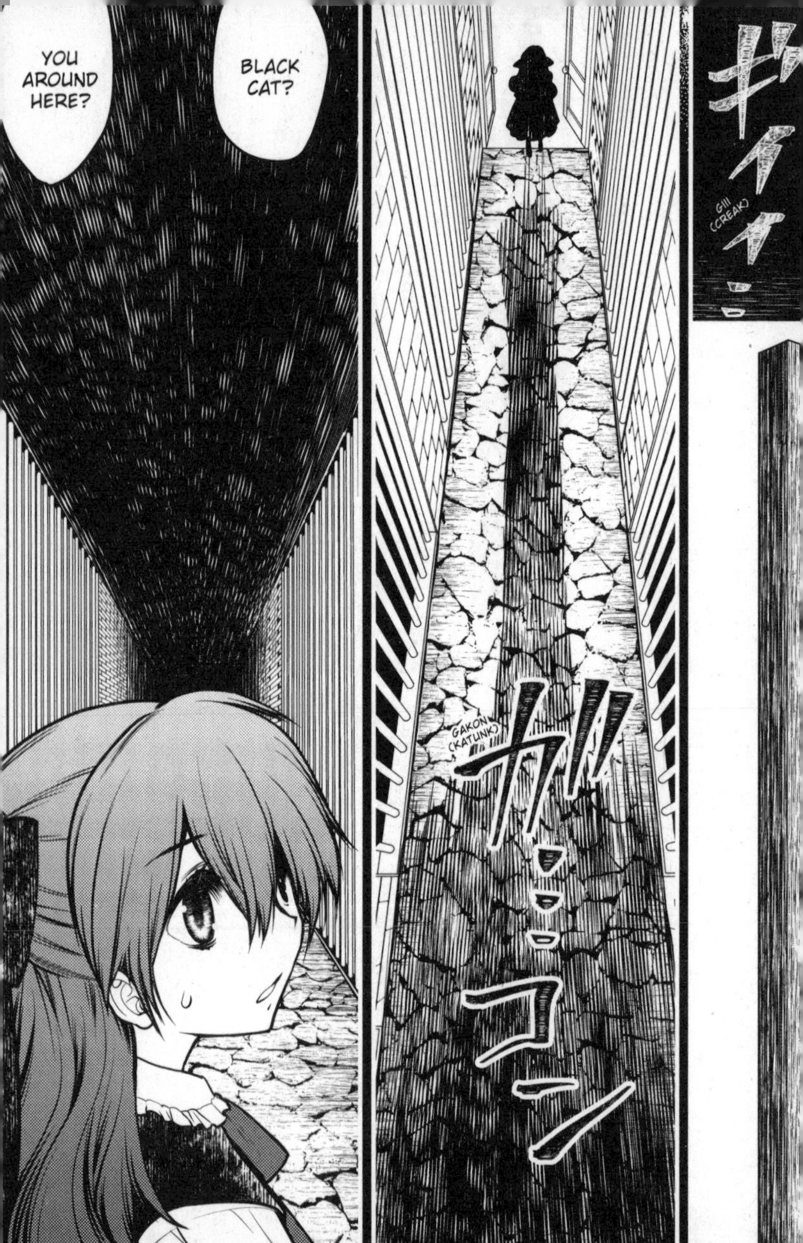
GIII (CREAK)
GAKON (KATUNK)
BLACK CAT?
YOU AROUND HERE?

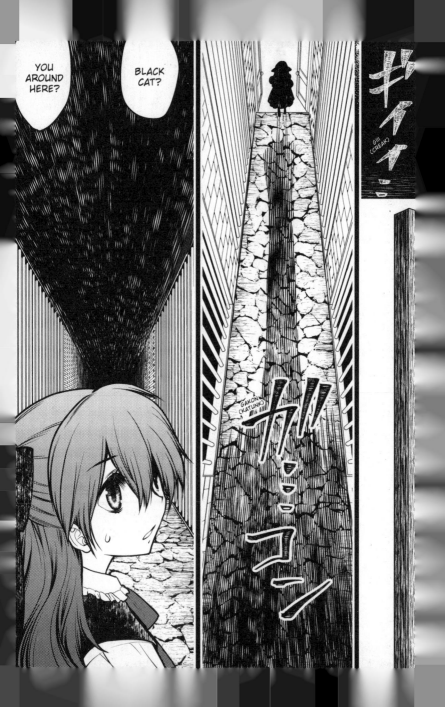

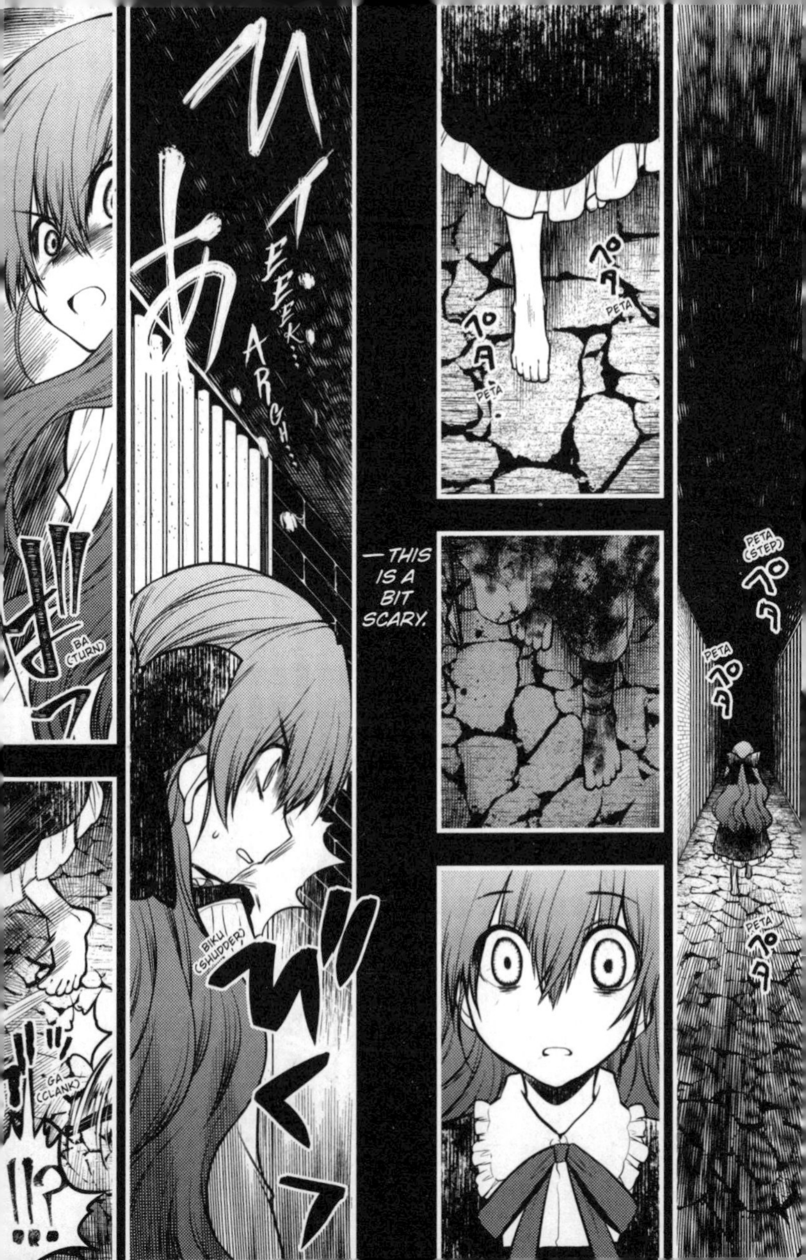
PETA (STEP)
PETA
PETA
PETA
PETA
—THIS IS A BIT SCARY.
EEEK...
ARCH...
BIKU (SHUDDER)
BA (TURN)
GA (CLANK)

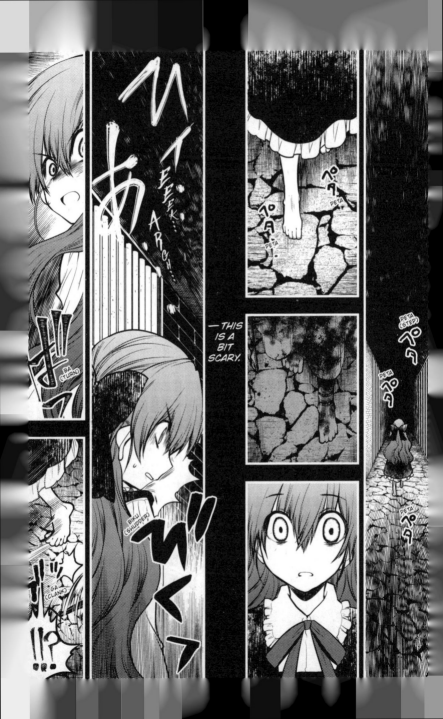

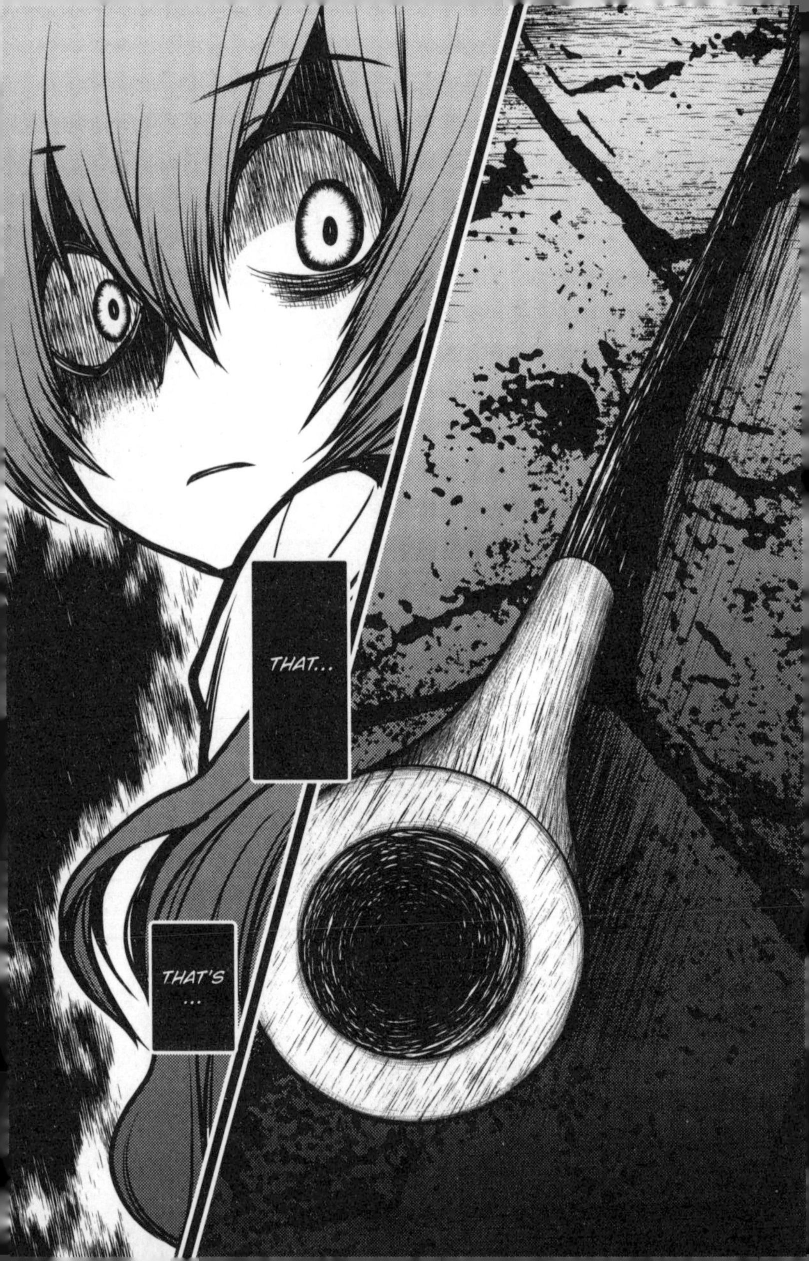
THAT...
THAT'S ...

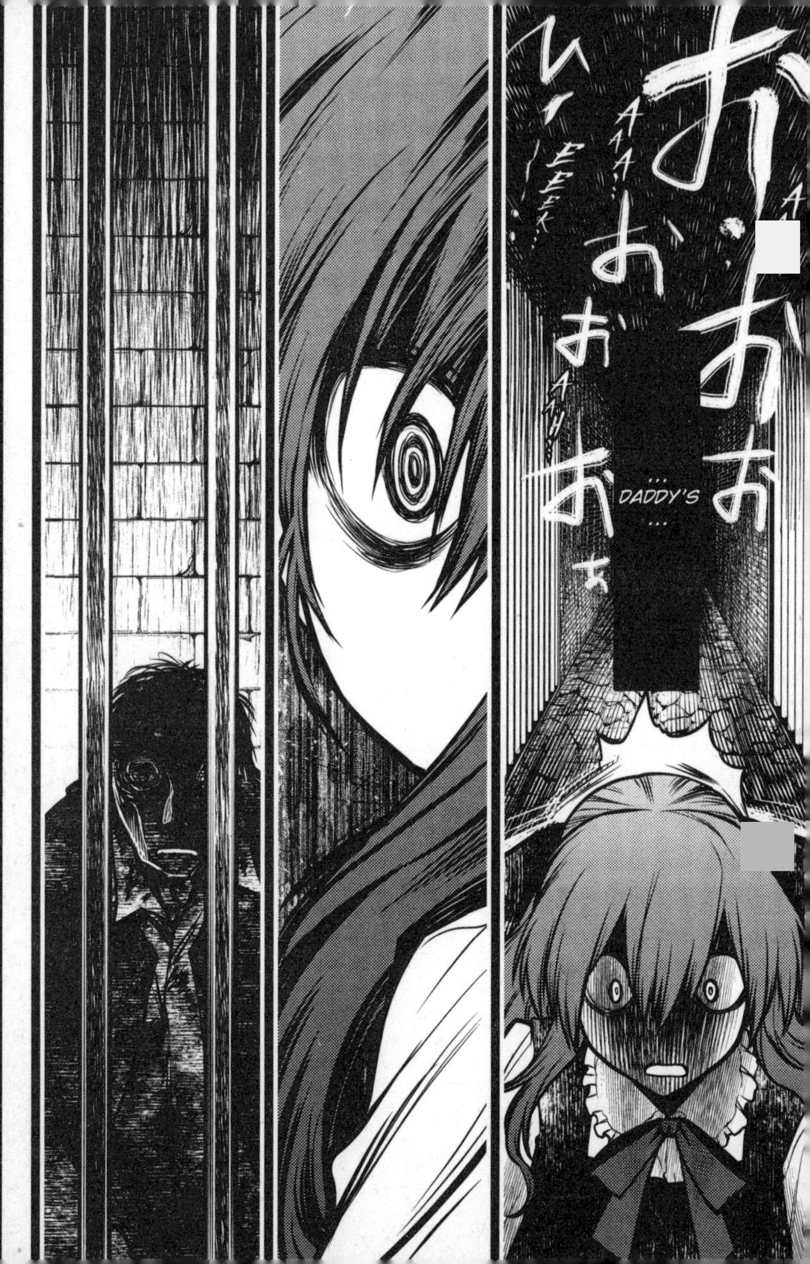
... DADDY'S ...
おおおおぉ
AAAA...
AAAH...
ひぃ
EEEEK...

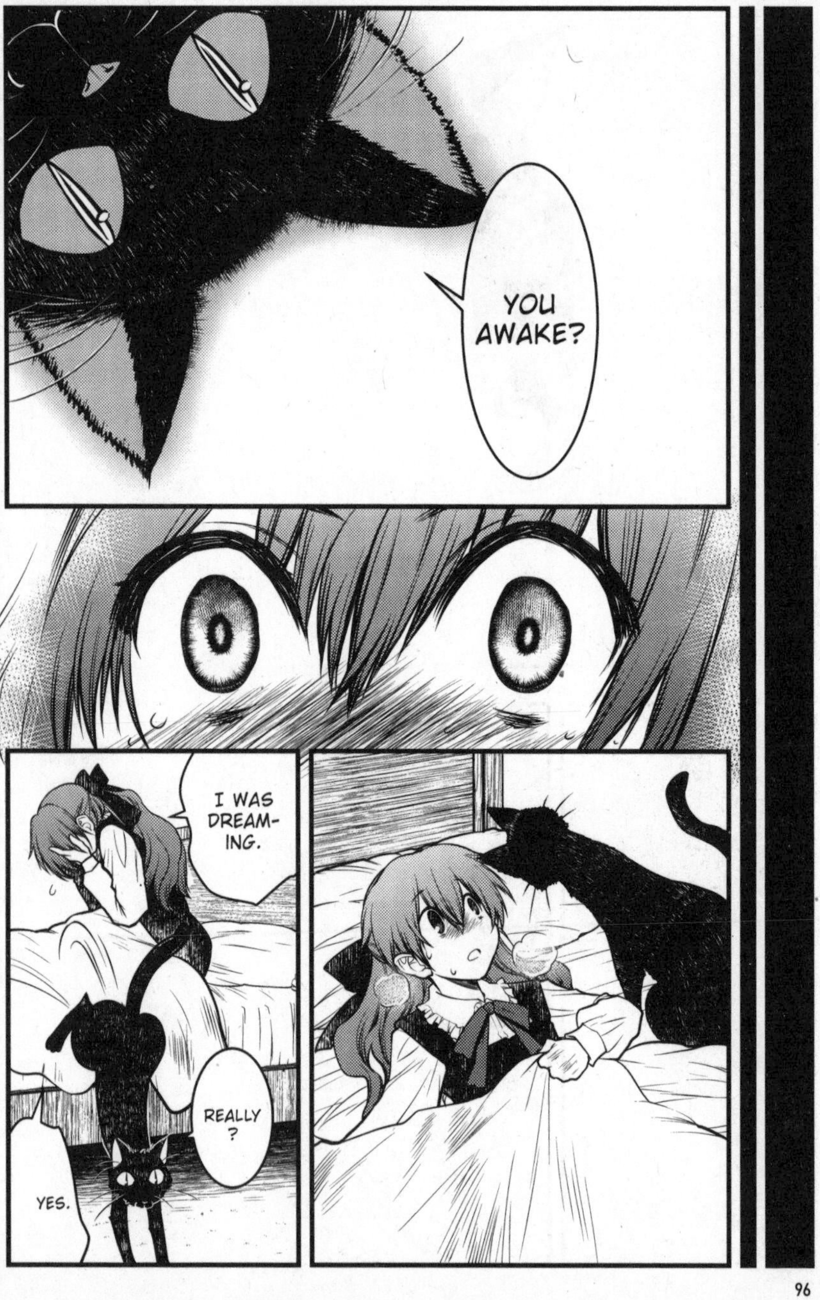
YOU AWAKE?
I WAS DREAMING.
REALLY?
YES.

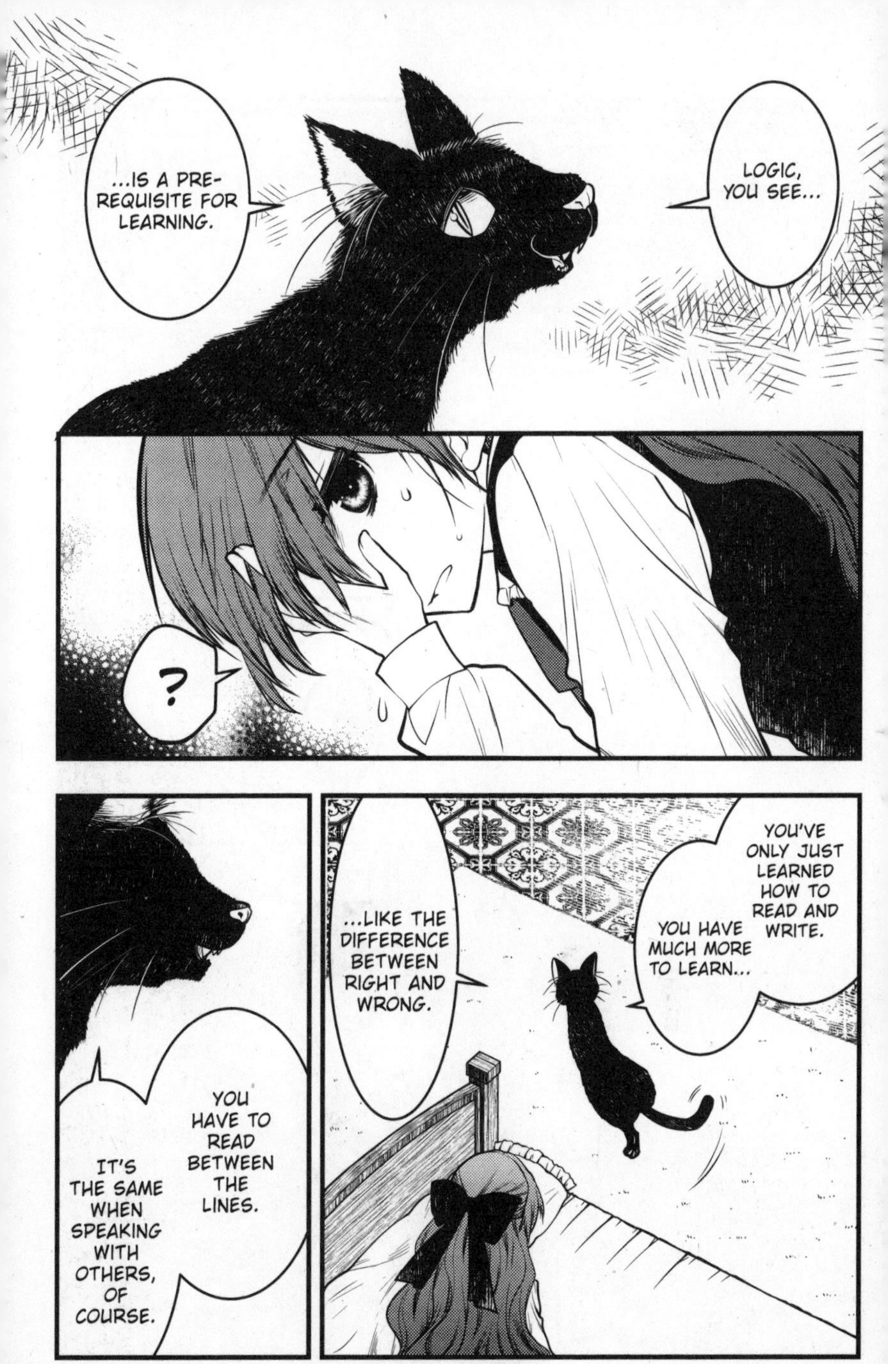
LOGIC, YOU SEE...
...IS A PRE-REQUISITE FOR LEARNING.
?
YOU'VE ONLY JUST LEARNED HOW TO READ AND WRITE.
YOU HAVE MUCH MORE TO LEARN...
...LIKE THE DIFFERENCE BETWEEN RIGHT AND WRONG.
YOU HAVE TO READ BETWEEN THE LINES.
IT'S THE SAME WHEN SPEAKING WITH OTHERS, OF COURSE.

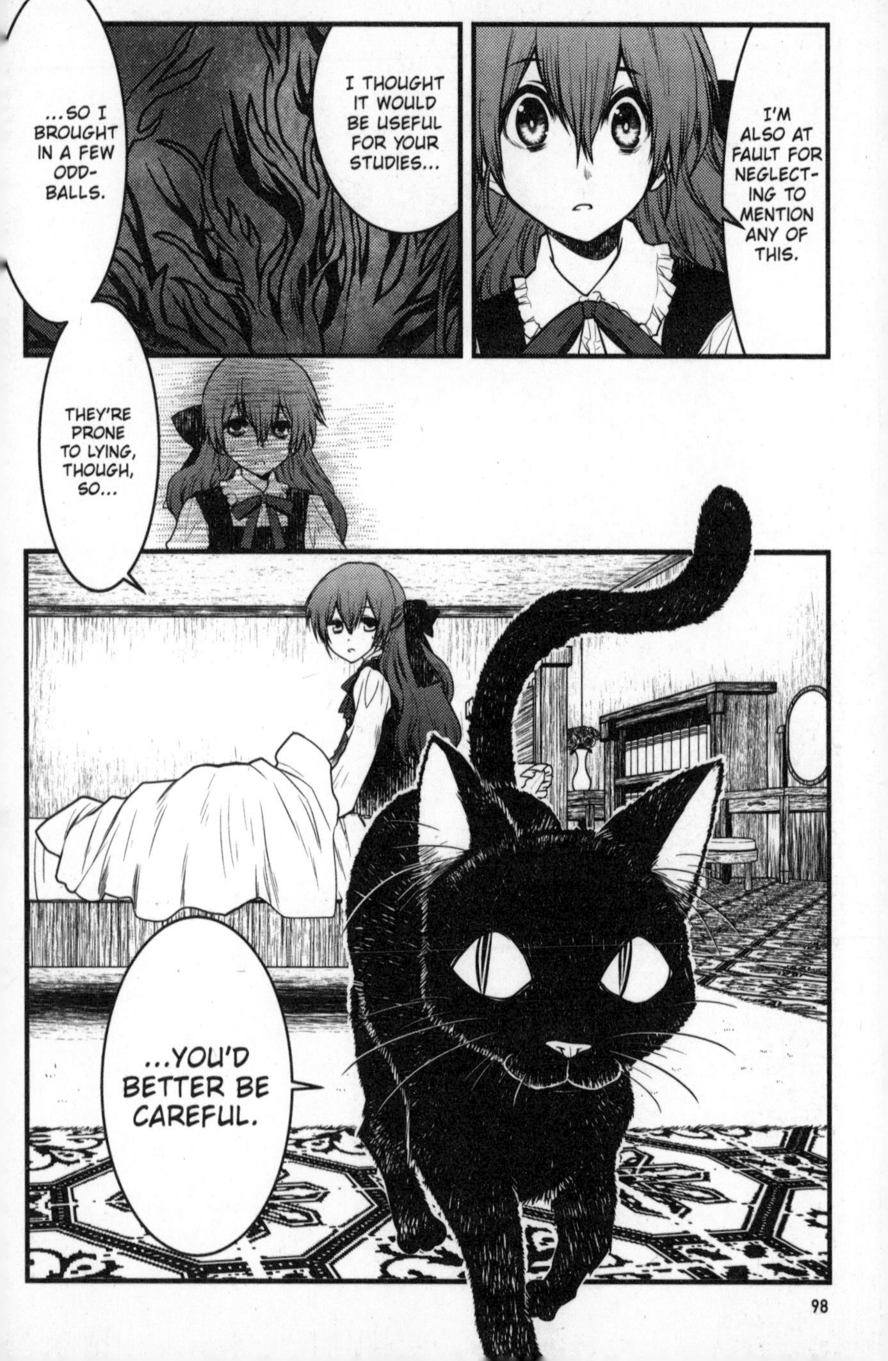
I'M ALSO AT FAULT FOR NEGLECTING TO MENTION ANY OF THIS.
I THOUGHT IT WOULD BE USEFUL FOR YOUR STUDIES...
...SO I BROUGHT IN A FEW ODD-BALLS.
THEY'RE PRONE TO LYING, THOUGH, SO...
...YOU'D BETTER BE CAREFUL.

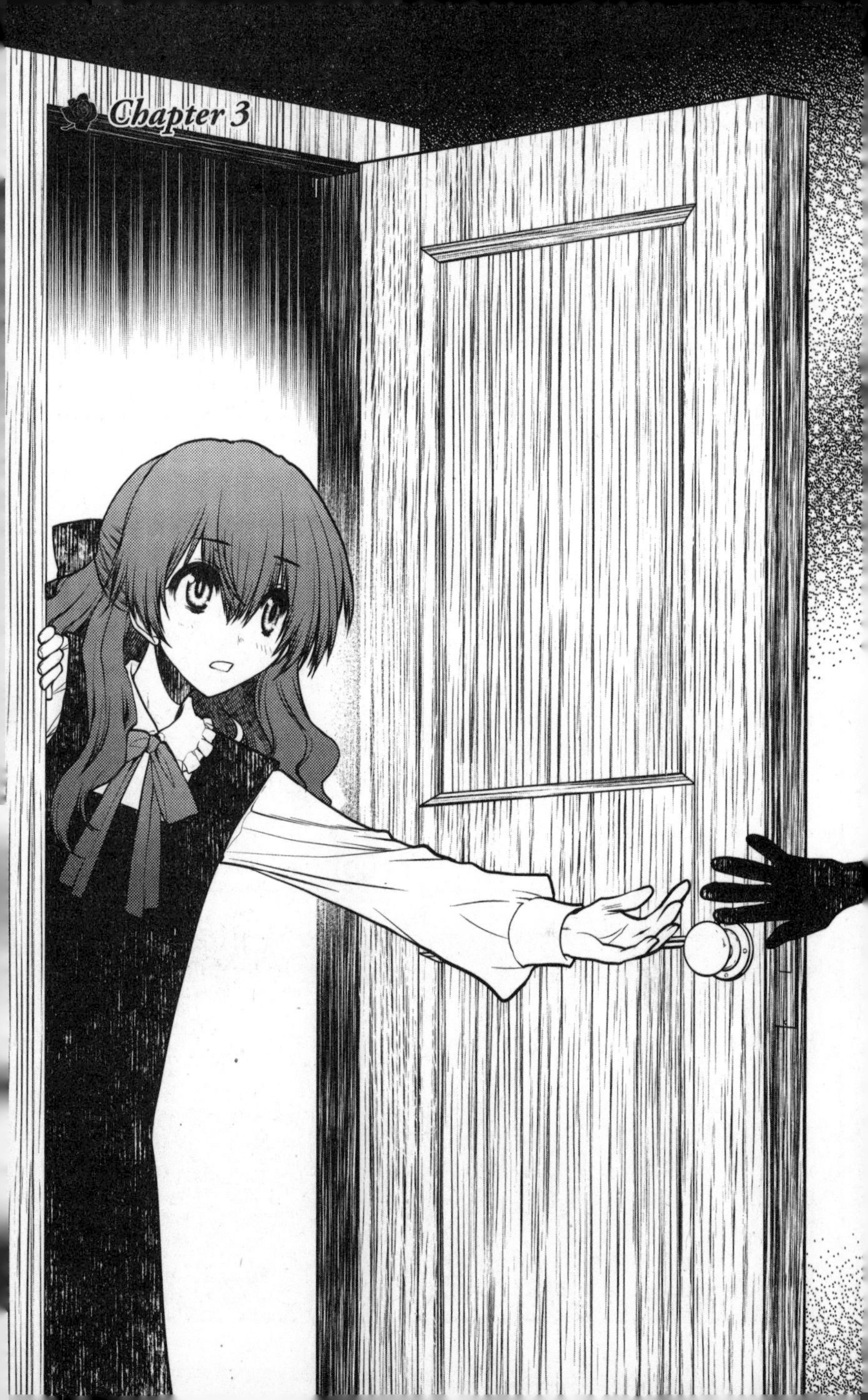
Chapter 3

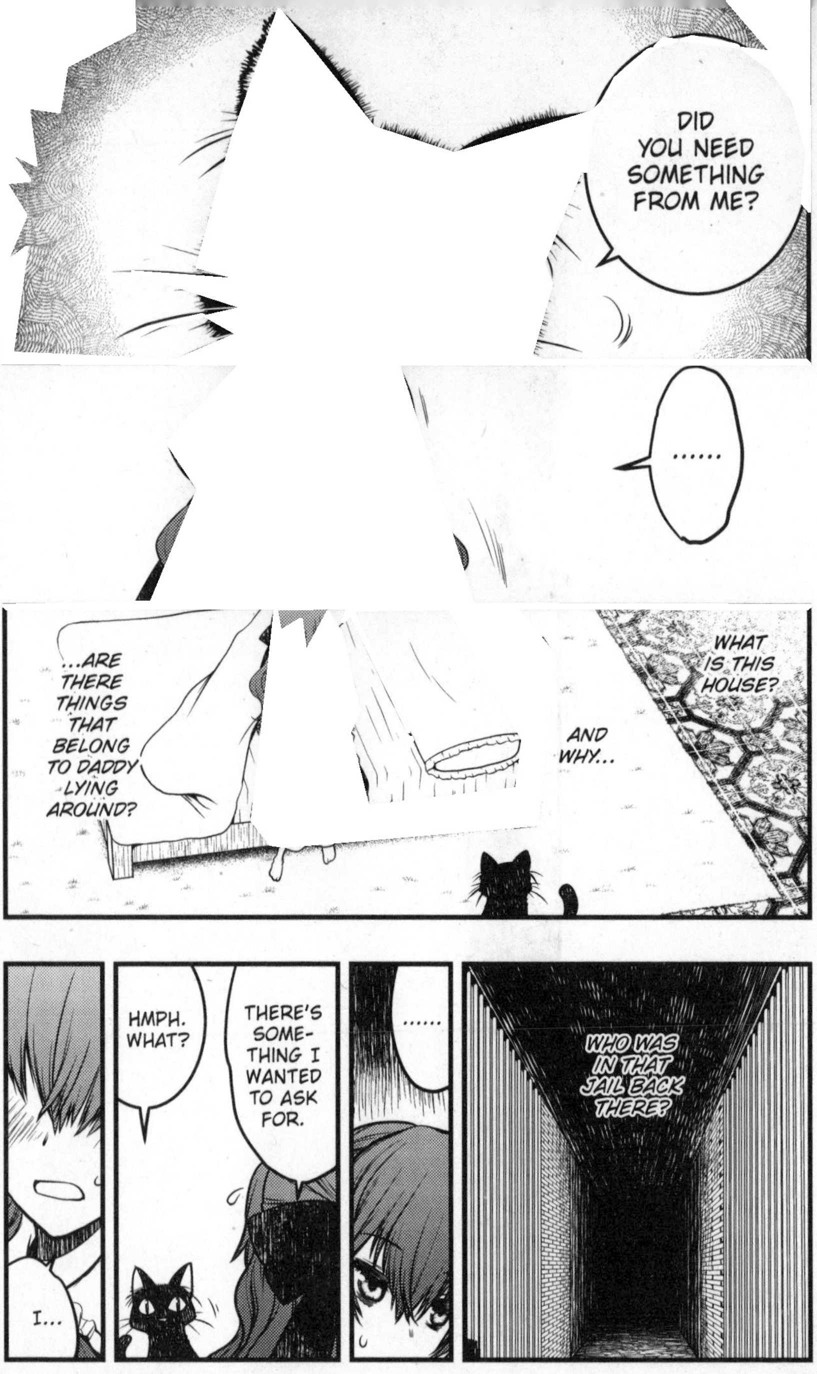
DID YOU NEED SOMETHING FROM ME?
......
WHAT IS THIS HOUSE?
AND WHY...
...ARE THERE THINGS THAT BELONG TO DADDY LYING AROUND?
WHO WAS IN THAT JAIL BACK THERE?
......
THERE'S SOME-THING I WANTED TO ASK FOR.
HMPH. WHAT?
I...

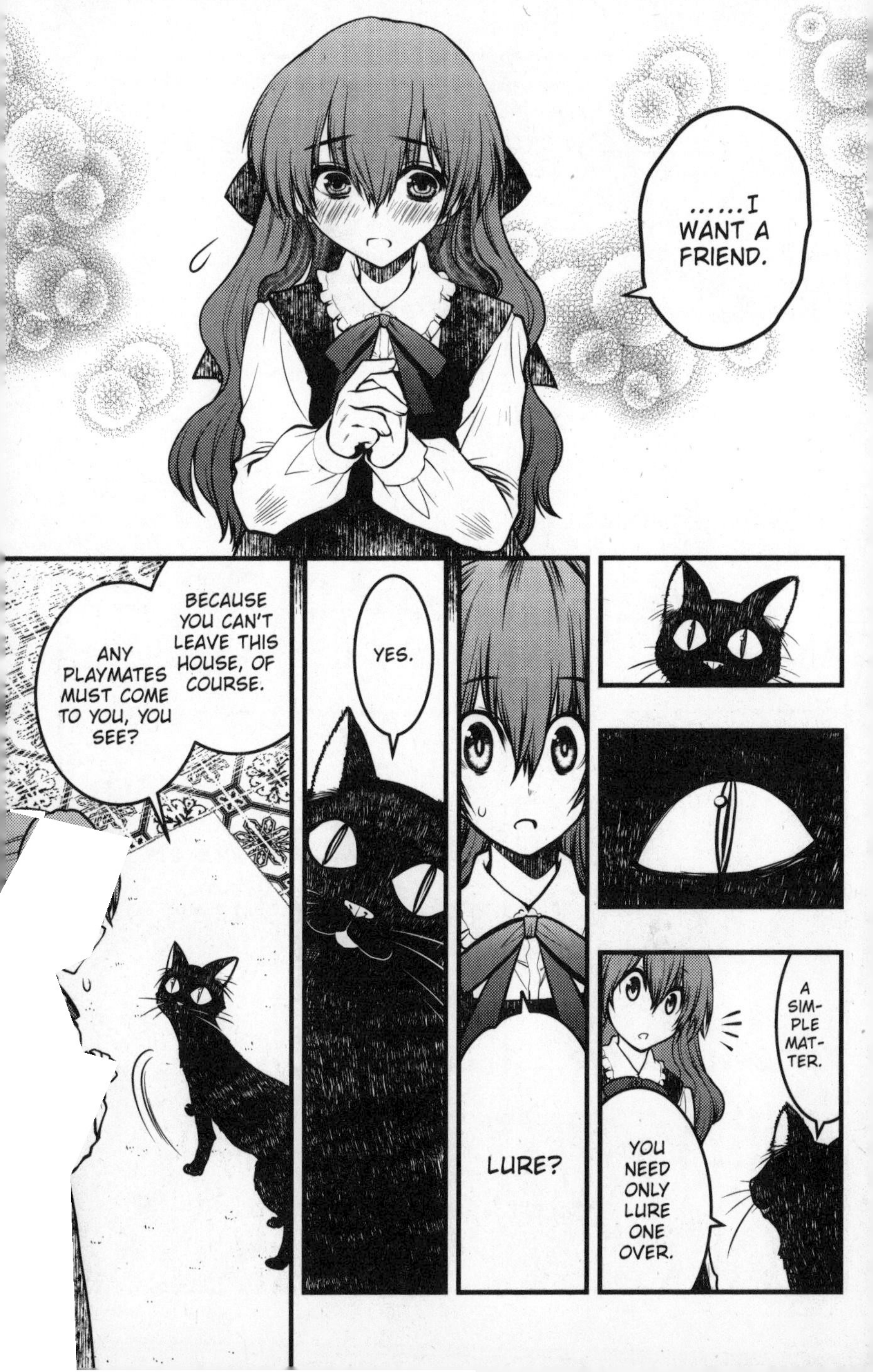
......I WANT A FRIEND.
A SIM-PLE MAT-TER.
YOU NEED ONLY LURE ONE OVER.
LURE?
YES.
BECAUSE YOU CAN'T LEAVE THIS HOUSE, OF COURSE.
ANY PLAYMATES MUST COME TO YOU, YOU SEE?

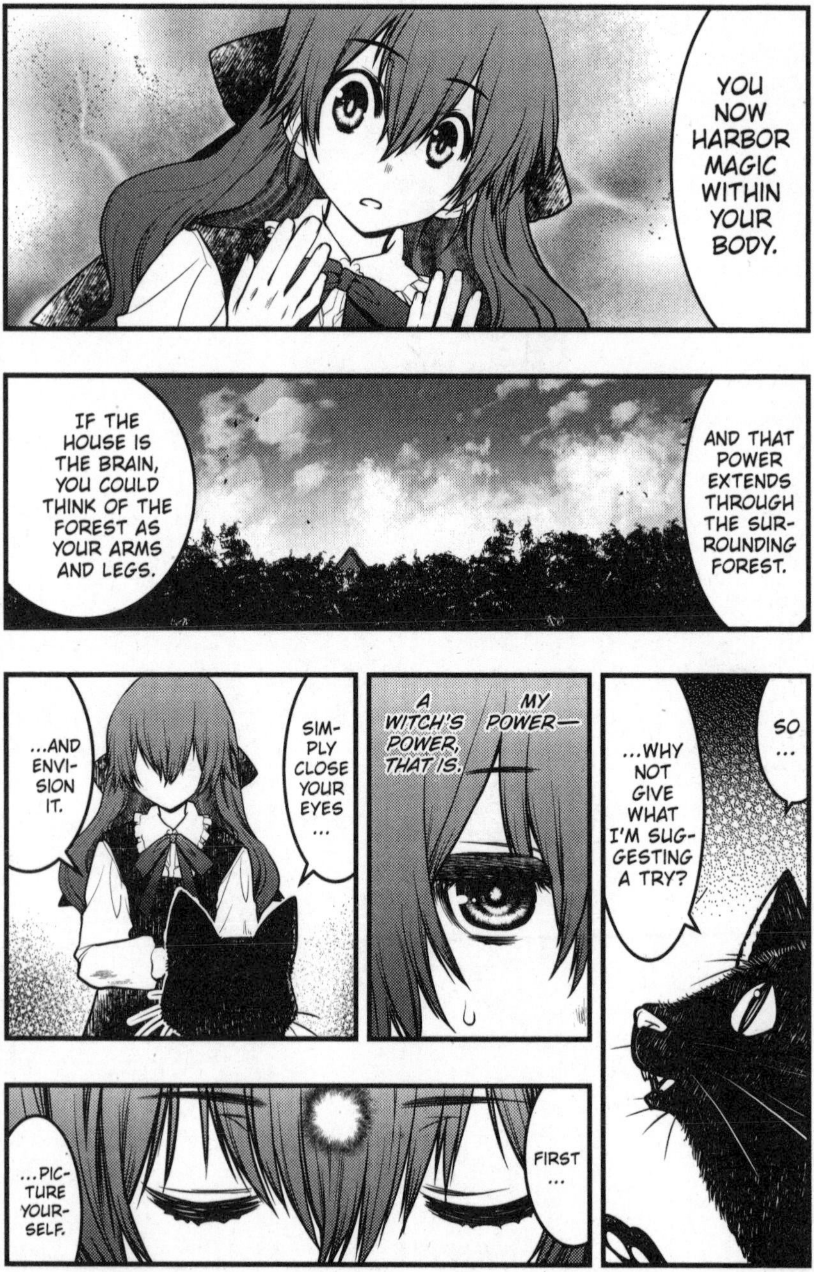
YOU NOW HARBOR MAGIC WITHIN YOUR BODY.
AND THAT POWER EXTENDS THROUGH THE SURROUNDING FOREST.
IF THE HOUSE IS THE BRAIN, YOU COULD THINK OF THE FOREST AS YOUR ARMS AND LEGS.
SO ...
...WHY NOT GIVE WHAT I'M SUGGESTING A TRY?
MY POWER—
A WITCH'S POWER, THAT IS.
SIMPLY CLOSE YOUR EYES ...
...AND ENVISION IT.
FIRST ...
...PICTURE YOURSELF.

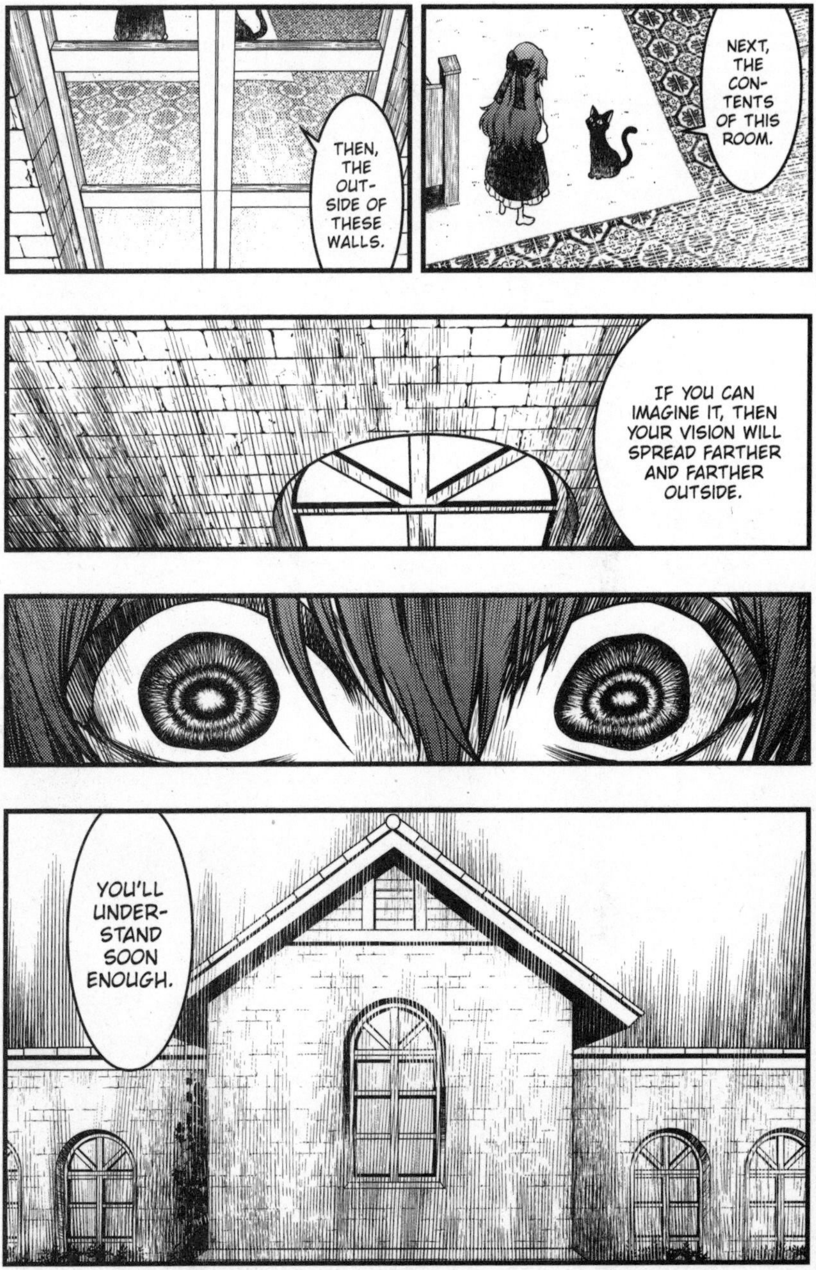
NEXT, THE CON-TENTS OF THIS ROOM.
THEN, THE OUT-SIDE OF THESE WALLS.
IF YOU CAN IMAGINE IT, THEN YOUR VISION WILL SPREAD FARTHER AND FARTHER OUTSIDE.
YOU'LL UNDER-STAND SOON ENOUGH.

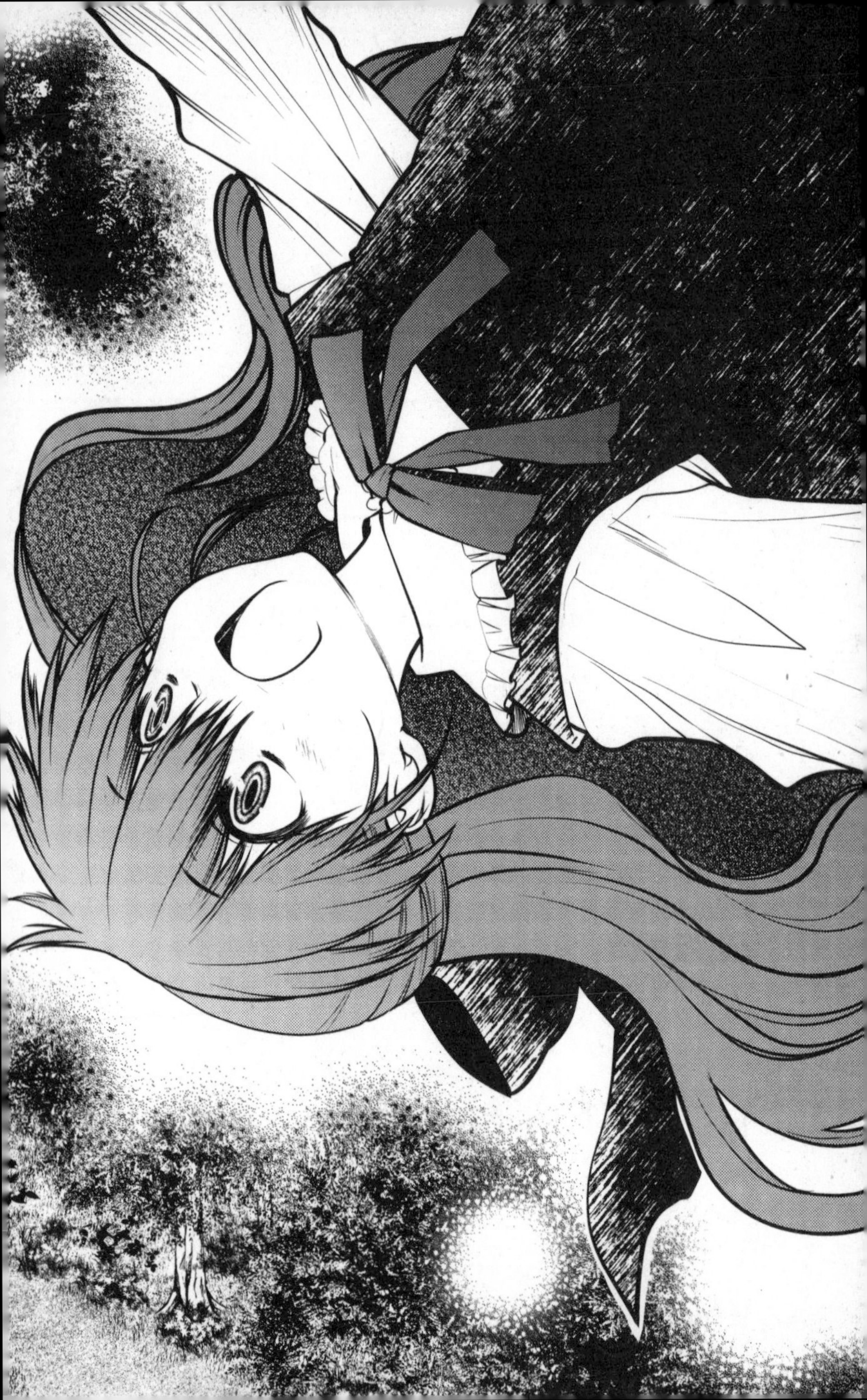

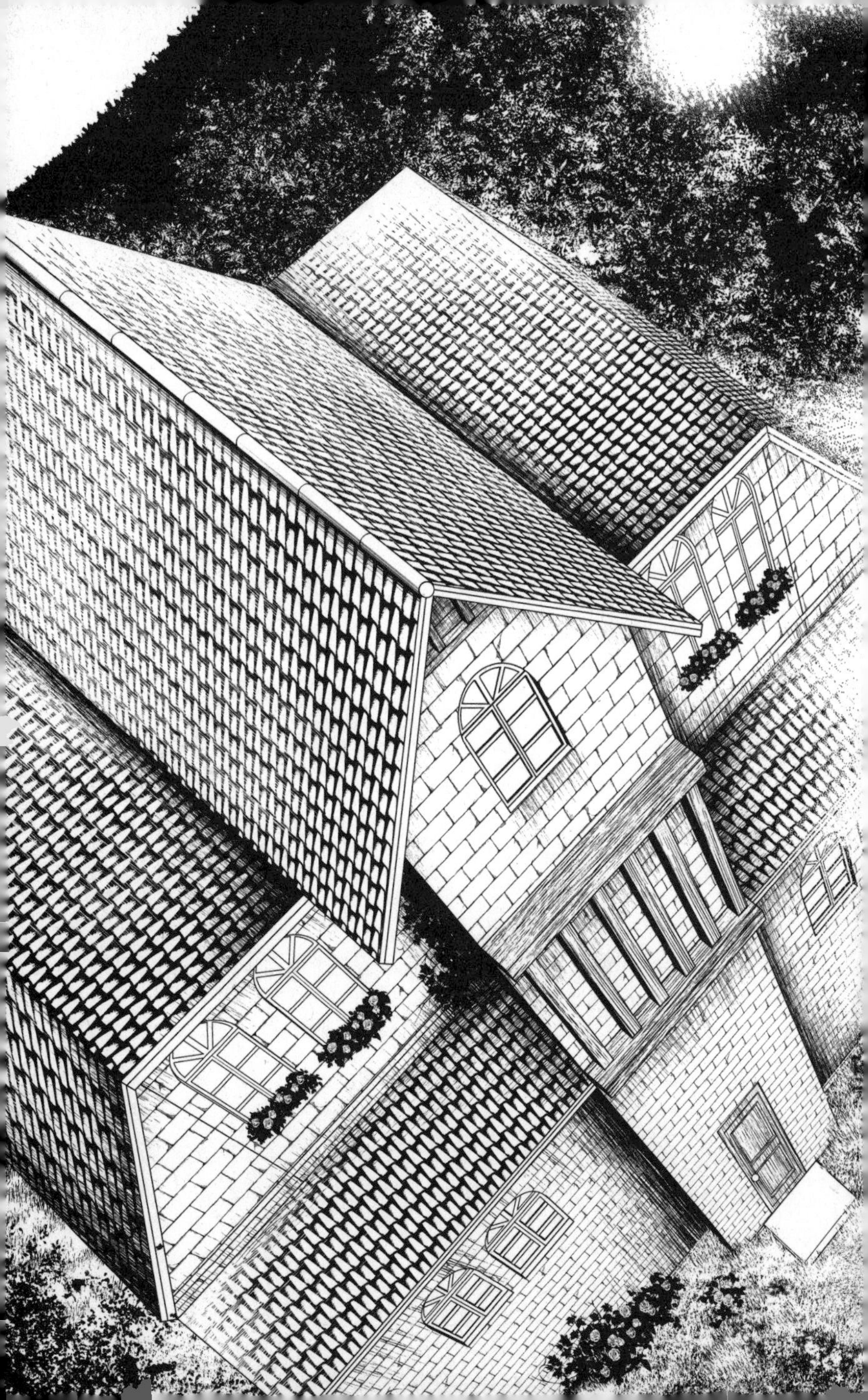

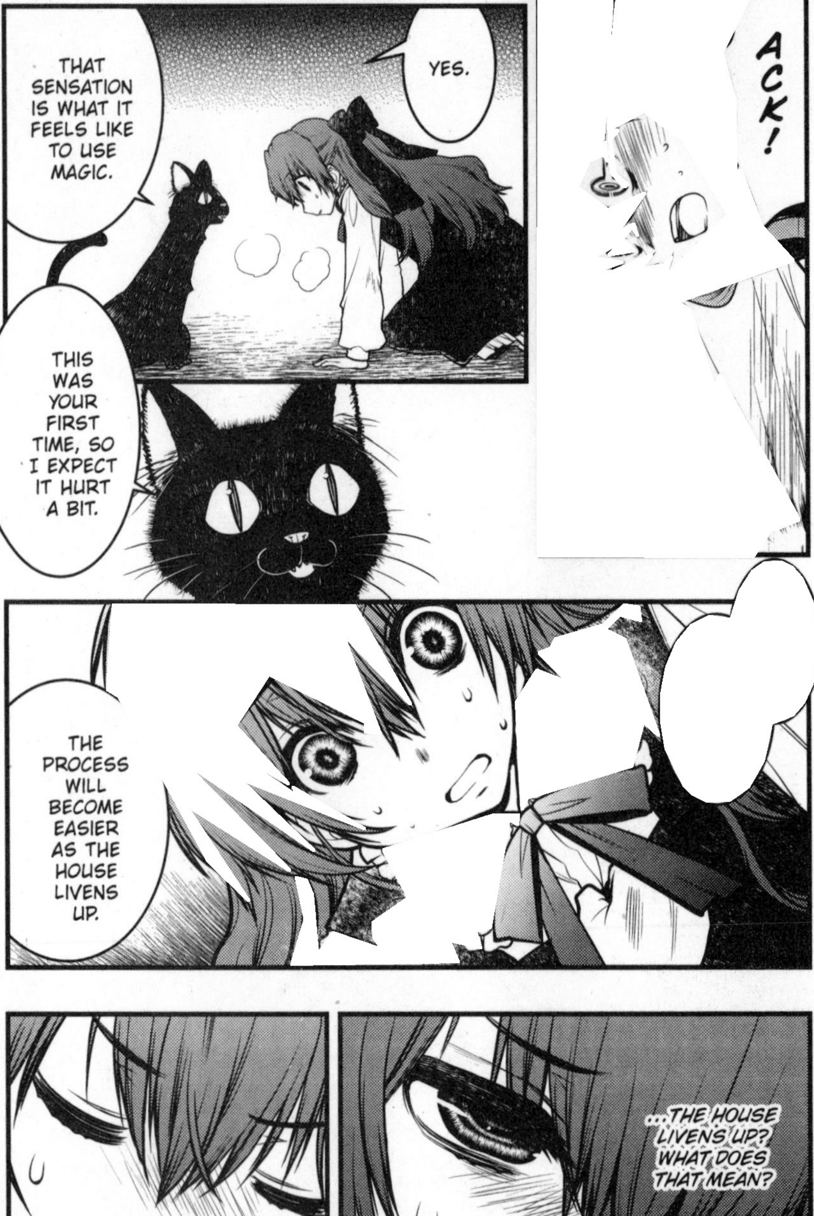
ACK!
YES.
THAT SENSATION IS WHAT IT FEELS LIKE TO USE MAGIC.
THIS WAS YOUR FIRST TIME, SO I EXPECT IT HURT A BIT.
THE PROCESS WILL BECOME EASIER AS THE HOUSE LIVENS UP.
...THE HOUSE LIVENS UP? WHAT DOES THAT MEAN?

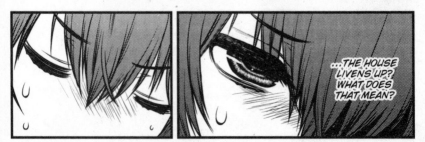

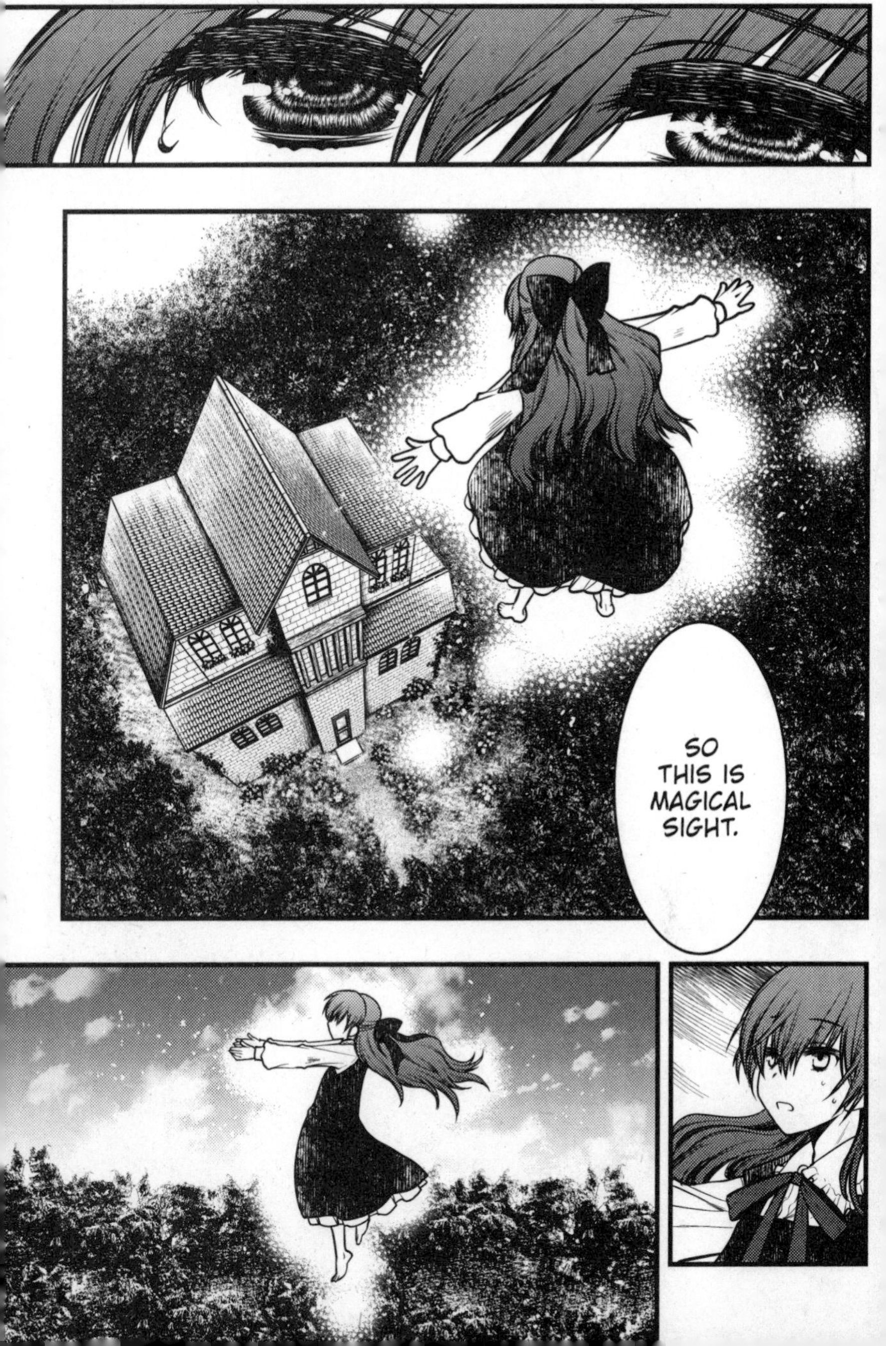
SO THIS IS MAGICAL SIGHT.

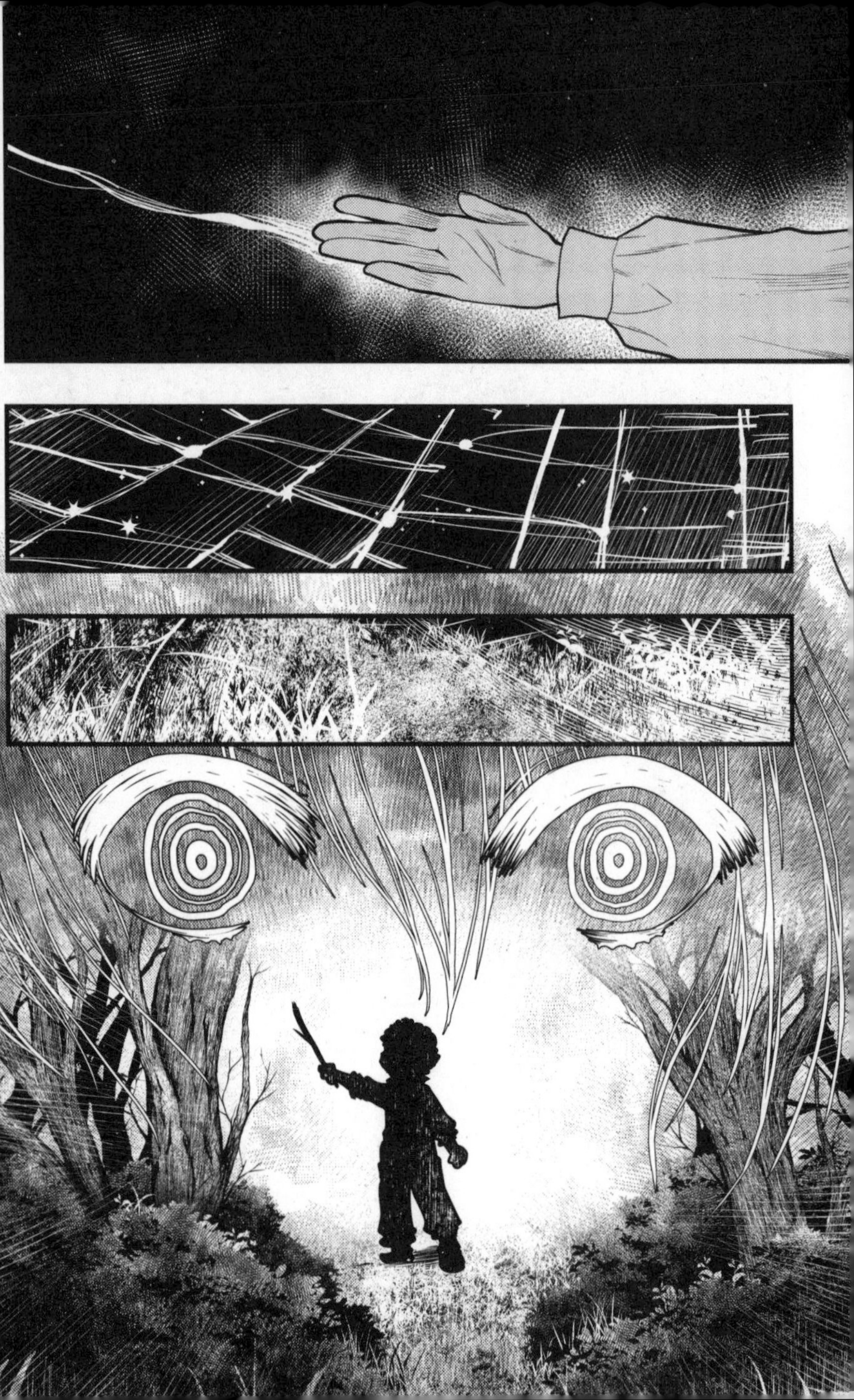

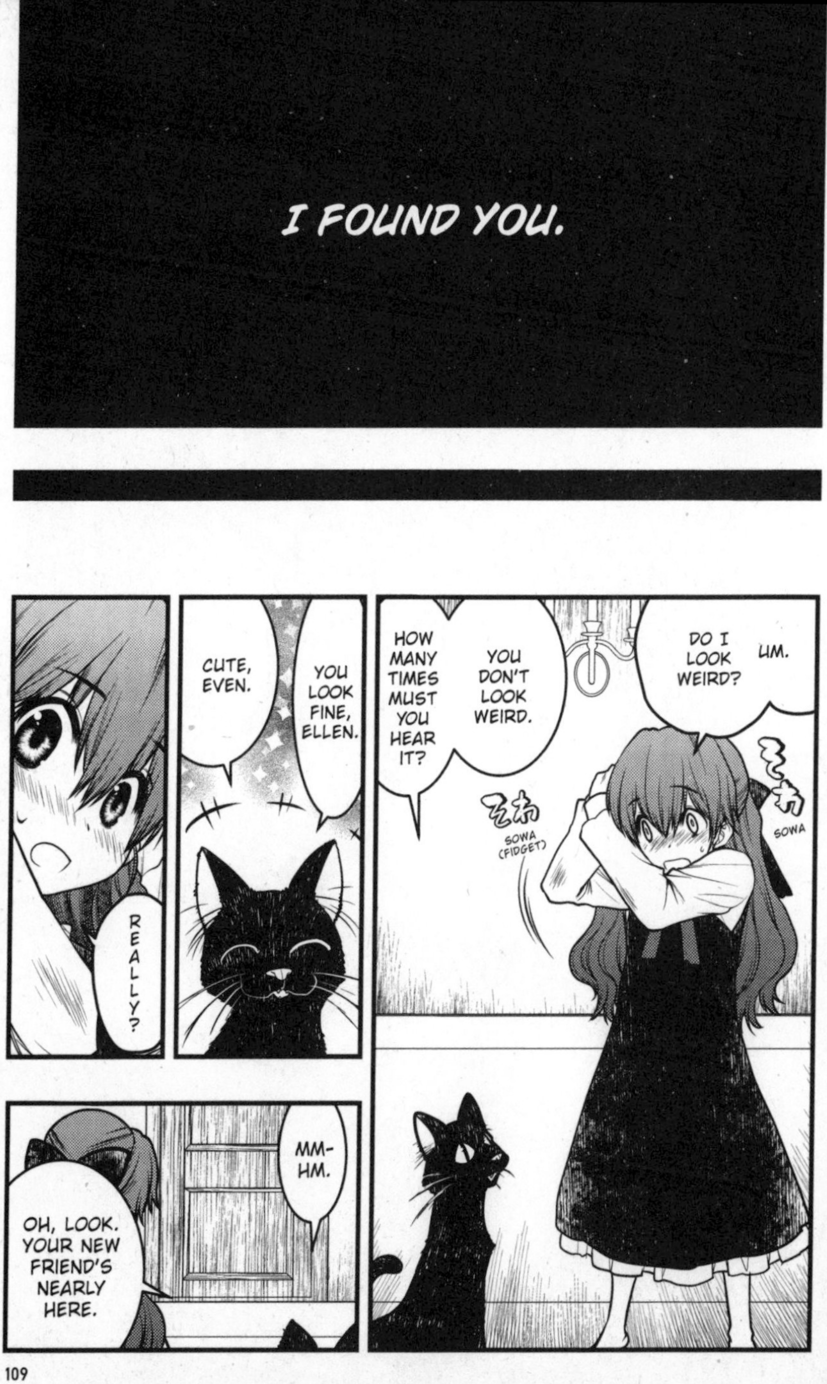

I FOUND YOU.
UM.
DO I LOOK WEIRD?
そわ
SOWA
そわ
SOWA (FIDGET)
YOU DON'T LOOK WEIRD.
HOW MANY TIMES MUST YOU HEAR IT?
YOU LOOK FINE, ELLEN.
CUTE, EVEN.
REALLY?
MM-HM.
OH, LOOK. YOUR NEW FRIEND'S NEARLY HERE.

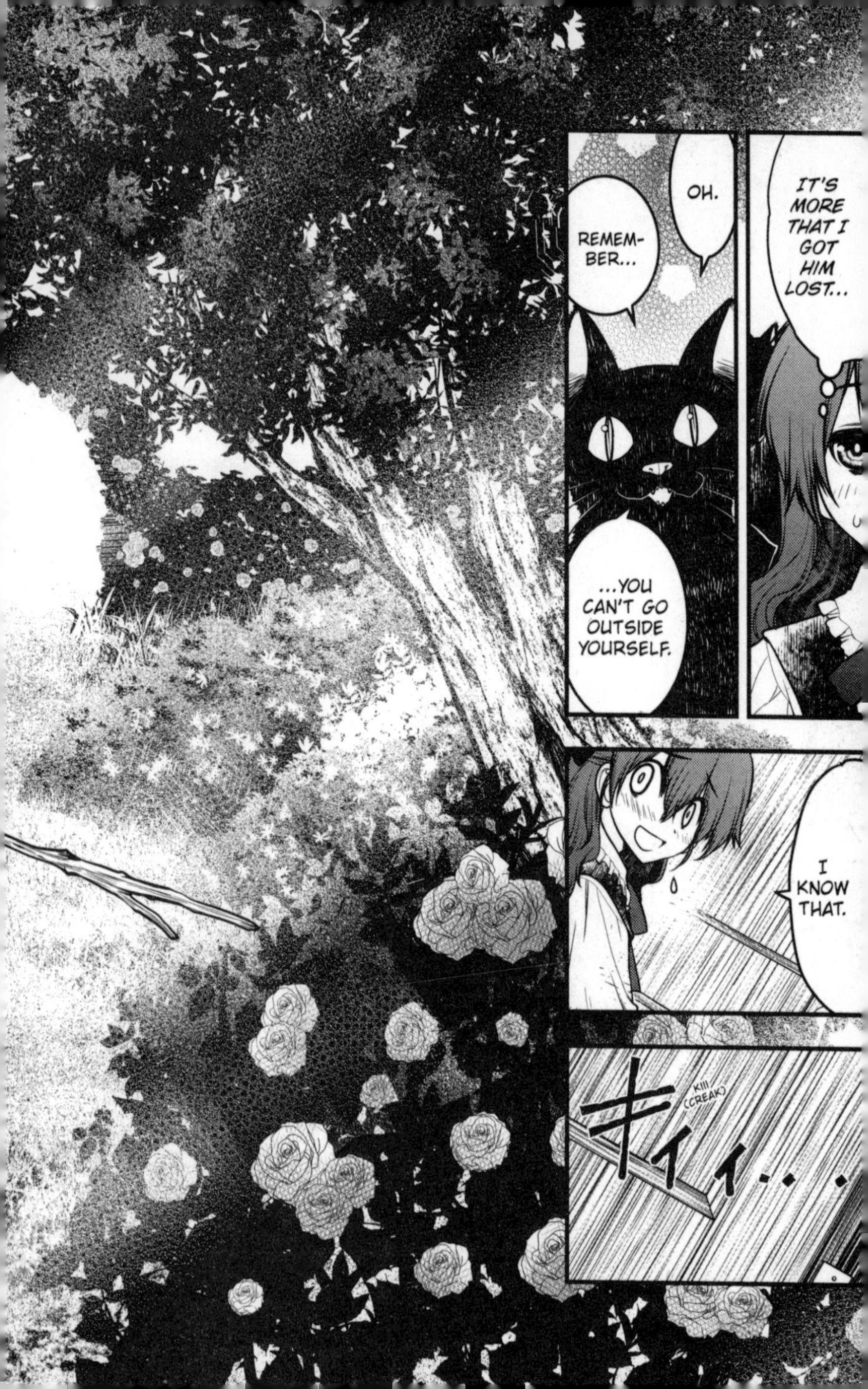
IT'S MORE THAT I GOT HIM LOST...
OH.
REMEMBER...
...YOU CAN'T GO OUTSIDE YOURSELF.
I KNOW THAT.
KIII (CREAK)

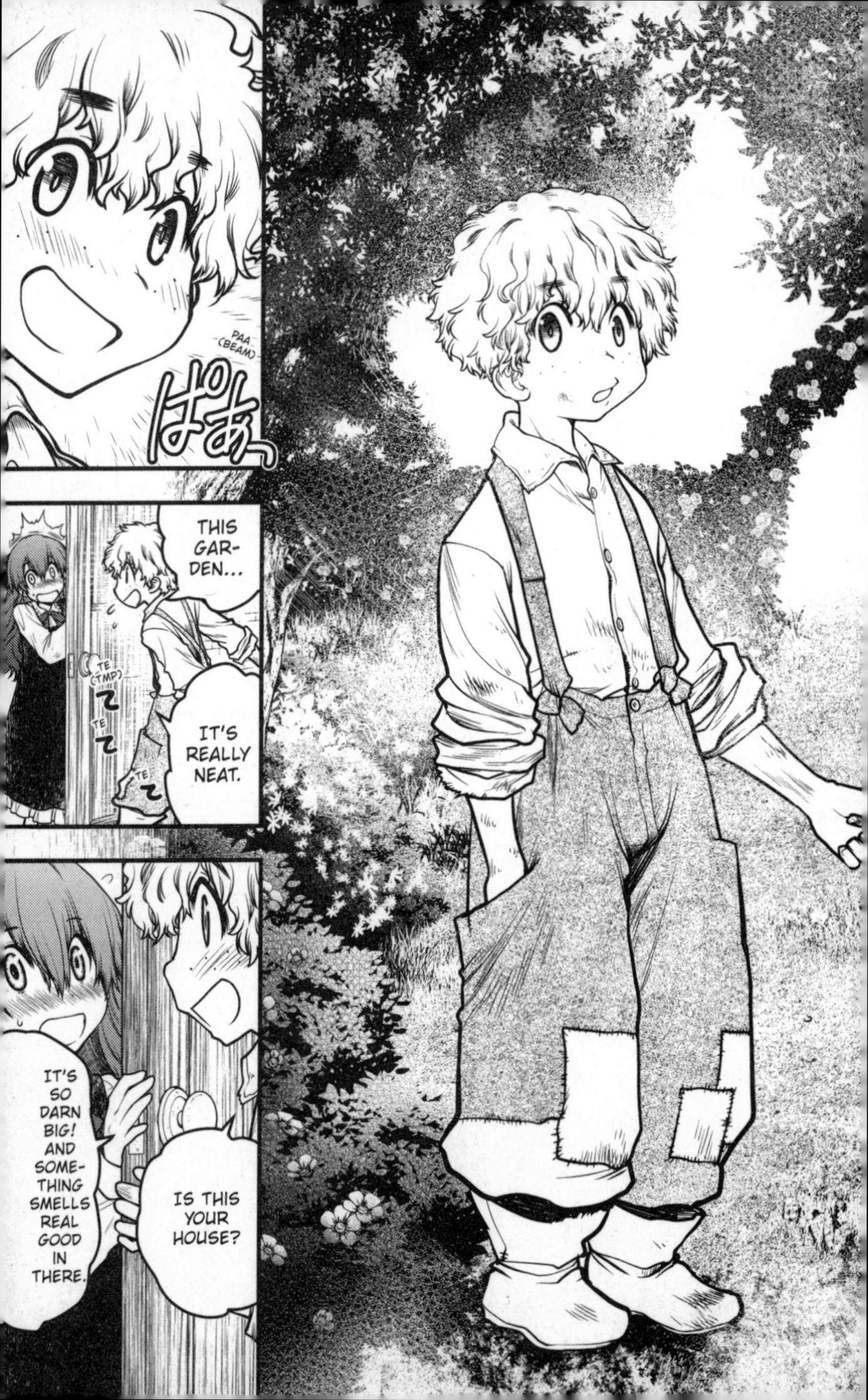
PAA (BEAM)
ぱあっ
THIS GARDEN...
IT'S REALLY NEAT.
TE (TMP) て
TE て
TE て
IS THIS YOUR HOUSE?
IT'S SO DARN BIG! AND SOMETHING SMELLS REAL GOOD IN THERE.

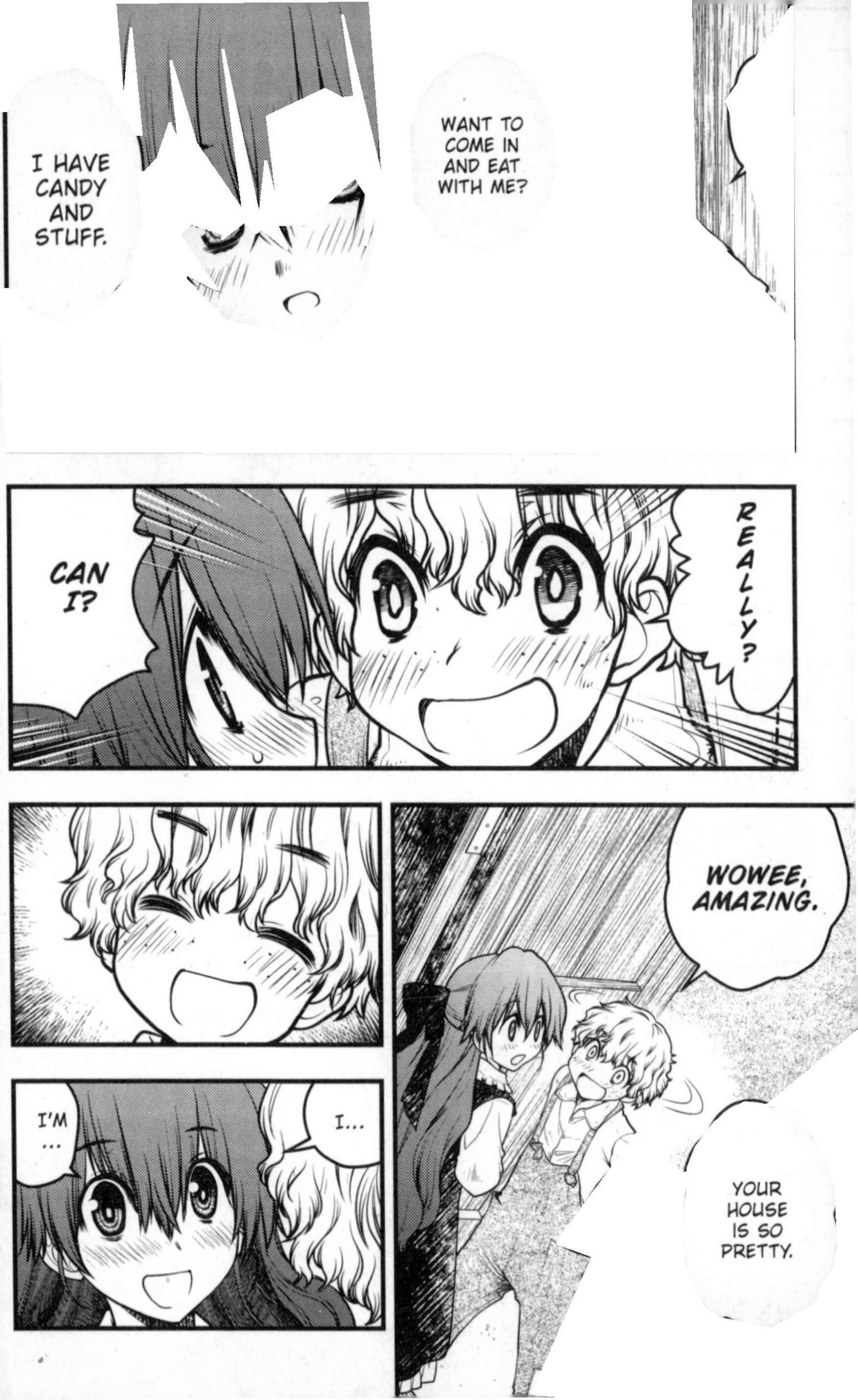
WANT TO COME IN AND EAT WITH ME?
I HAVE CANDY AND STUFF.
REALLY?
CAN I?
WOWEE, AMAZING.
YOUR HOUSE IS SO PRETTY.
I...
I'M ...

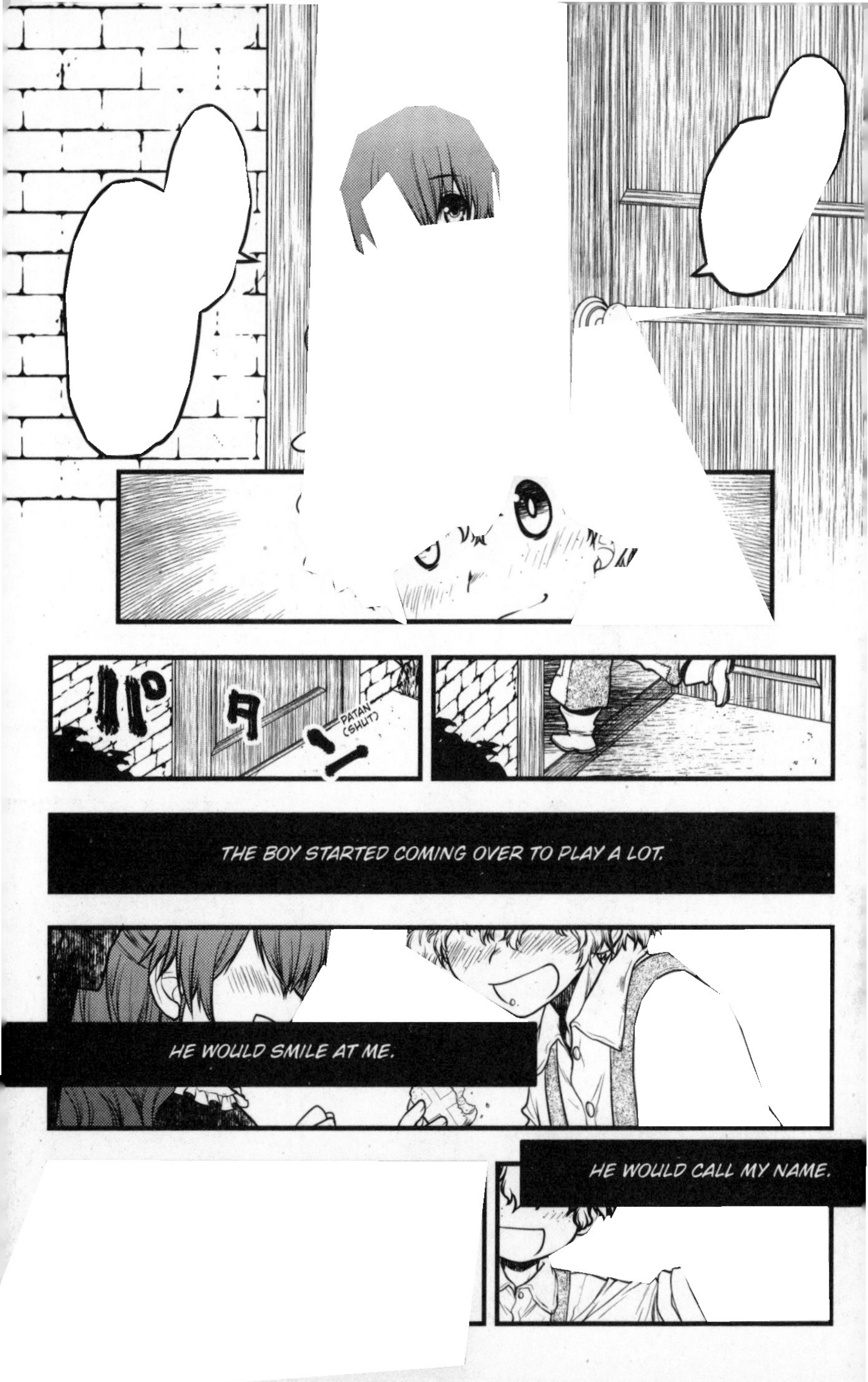
PATAN
(SHUT)
THE BOY STARTED COMING OVER TO PLAY A LOT.
HE WOULD SMILE AT ME.
HE WOULD CALL MY NAME.

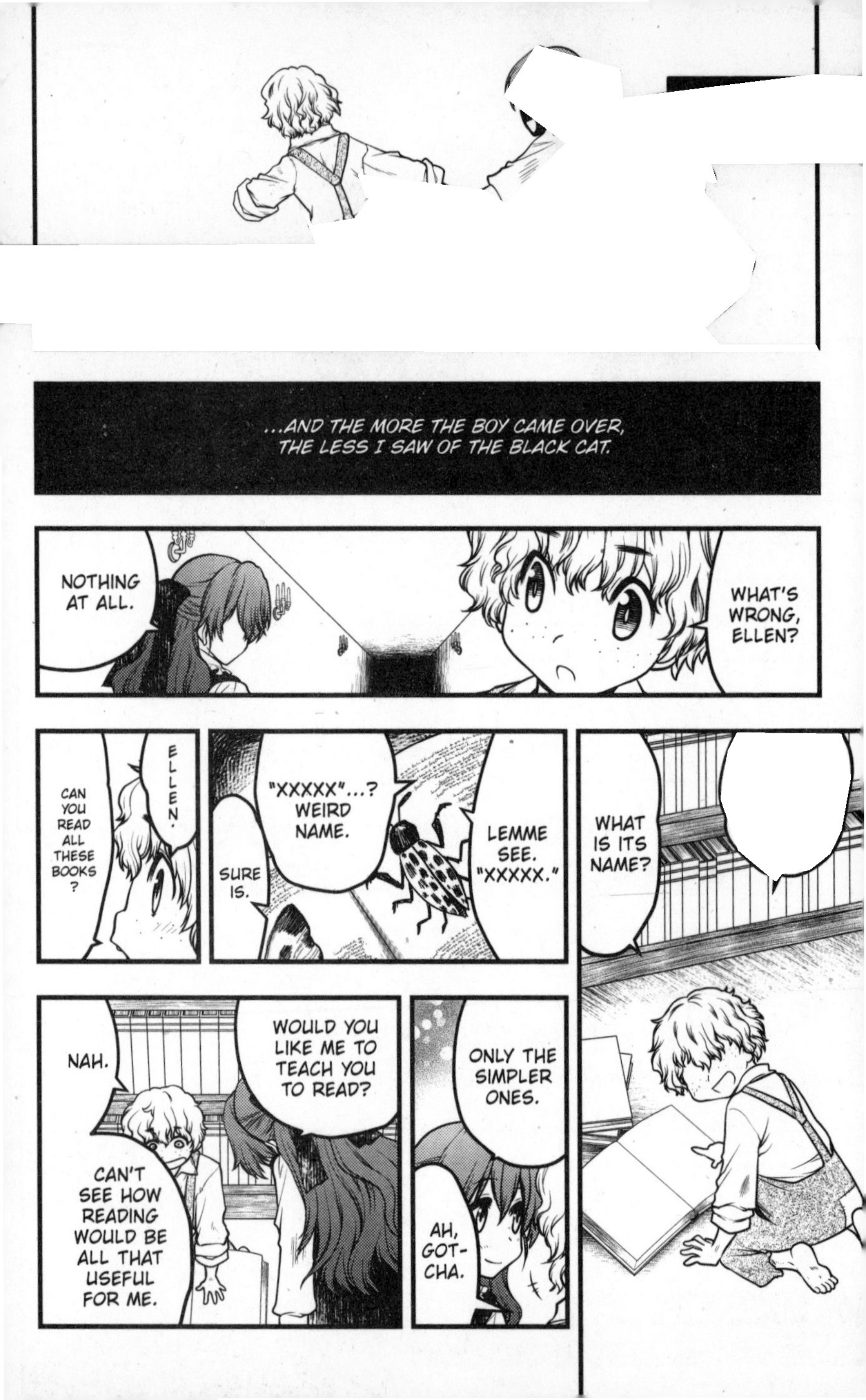
...AND THE MORE THE BOY CAME OVER, THE LESS I SAW OF THE BLACK CAT.
WHAT'S WRONG, ELLEN?
NOTHING AT ALL.
WHAT IS ITS NAME?
LEMME SEE. "XXXXX."
"XXXXX"...? WEIRD NAME.
SURE IS.
ELLEN.
CAN YOU READ ALL THESE BOOKS?
ONLY THE SIMPLER ONES.
AH, GOTCHA.
WOULD YOU LIKE ME TO TEACH YOU TO READ?
NAH.
CAN'T SEE HOW READING WOULD BE ALL THAT USEFUL FOR ME.

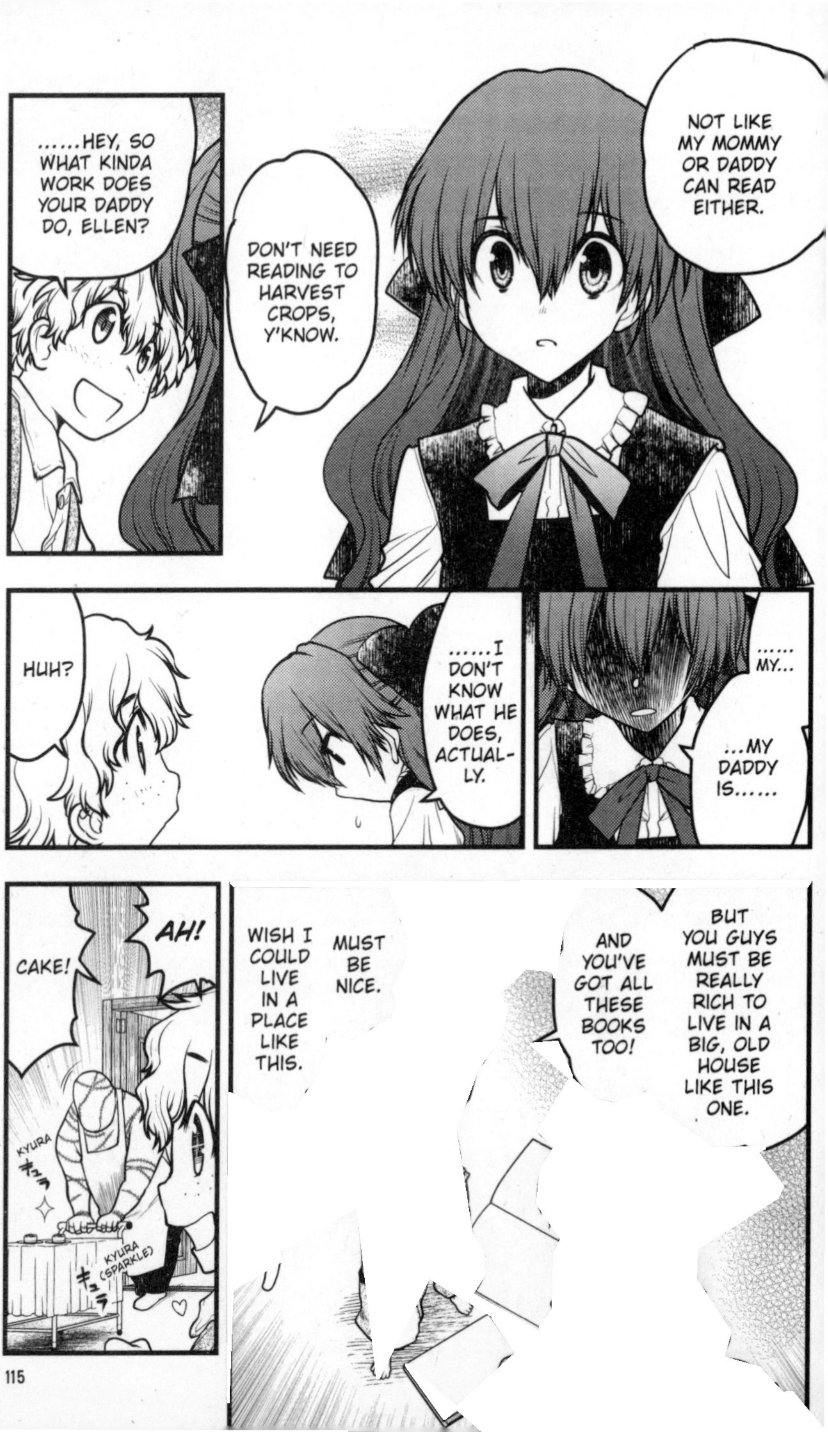
NOT LIKE MY MOMMY OR DADDY CAN READ EITHER.
DON'T NEED READING TO HARVEST CROPS, Y'KNOW.
......HEY, SO WHAT KINDA WORK DOES YOUR DADDY DO, ELLEN?
...... MY...
...MY DADDY IS......
......I DON'T KNOW WHAT HE DOES, ACTUAL-LY.
HUH?
BUT YOU GUYS MUST BE REALLY RICH TO LIVE IN A BIG, OLD HOUSE LIKE THIS ONE.
AND YOU'VE GOT ALL THESE BOOKS TOO!
MUST BE NICE.
WISH I COULD LIVE IN A PLACE LIKE THIS.
AH!
CAKE!
KYURA
キュラ
KYURA (SPARKLE)
キュラ

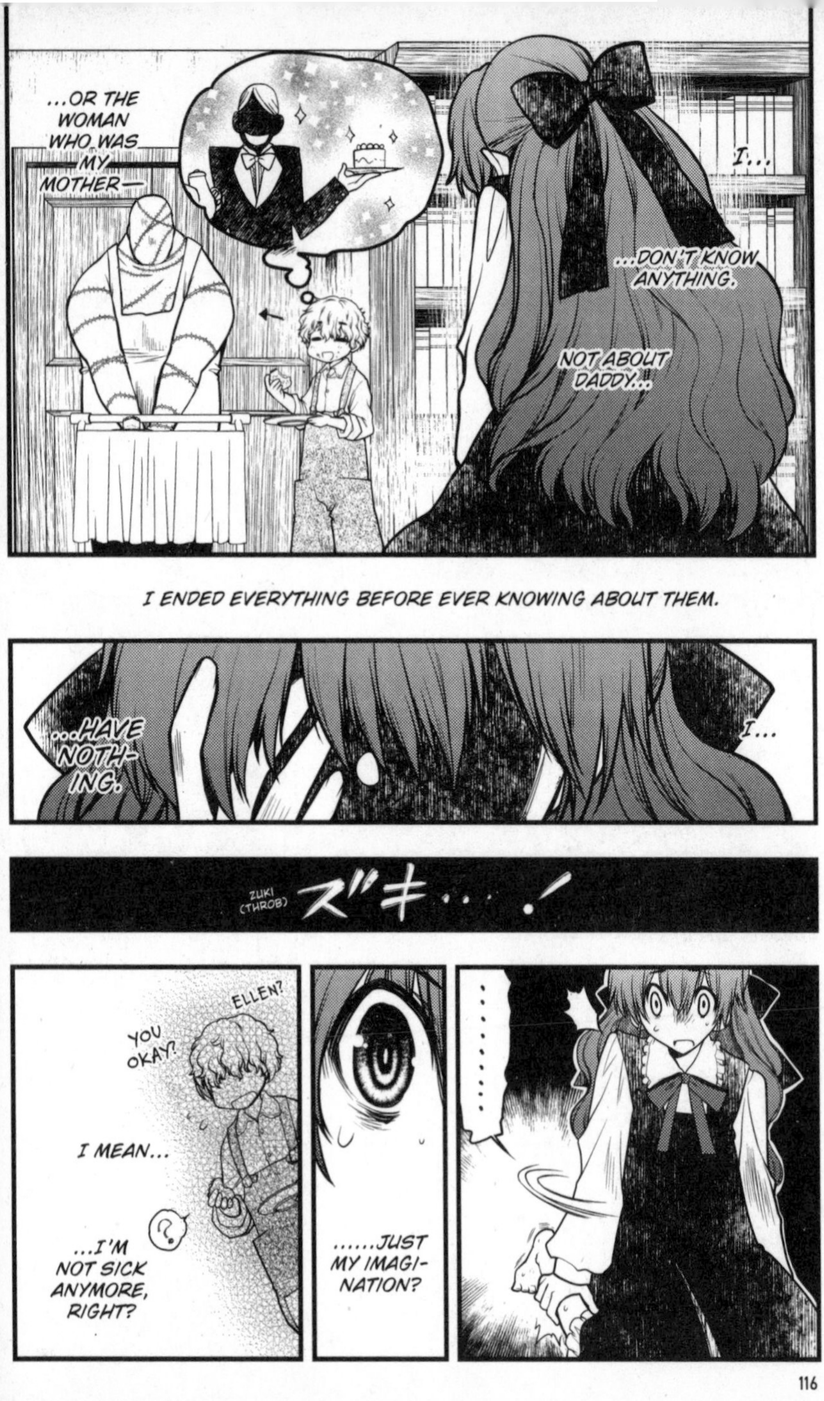
I...
...DON'T KNOW ANYTHING.
NOT ABOUT DADDY...
...OR THE WOMAN WHO WAS MY MOTHER—
I ENDED EVERYTHING BEFORE EVER KNOWING ABOUT THEM.
I...
...HAVE NOTHING.
ZUKI (THROB)
ズキ…!
......
......JUST MY IMAGINATION?
ELLEN?
YOU OKAY?
I MEAN...
...I'M NOT SICK ANYMORE, RIGHT?

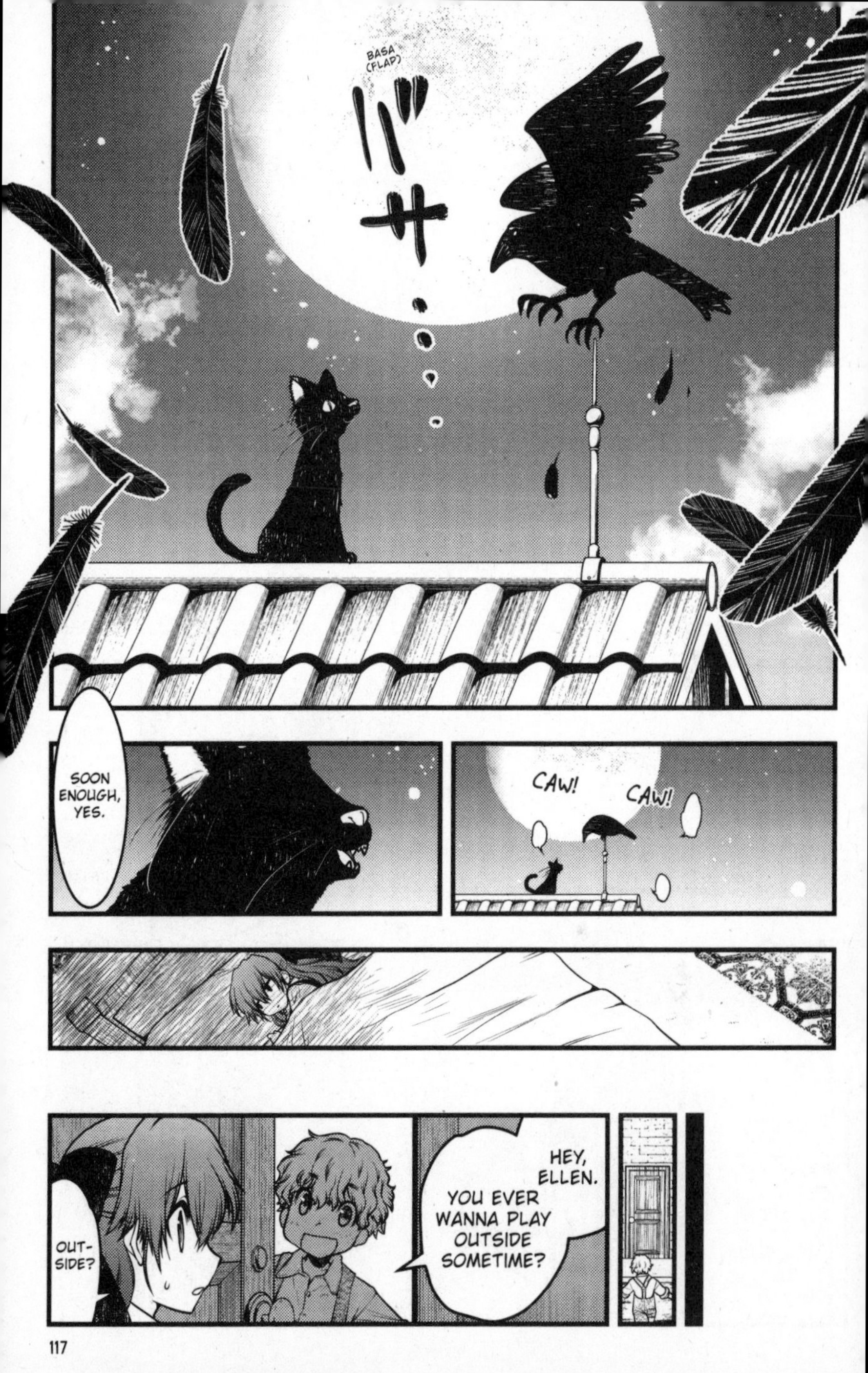
BASA (FLAP)
バサッ
CAW!
CAW!
SOON ENOUGH, YES.
HEY, ELLEN.
YOU EVER WANNA PLAY OUTSIDE SOMETIME?
OUT-SIDE?

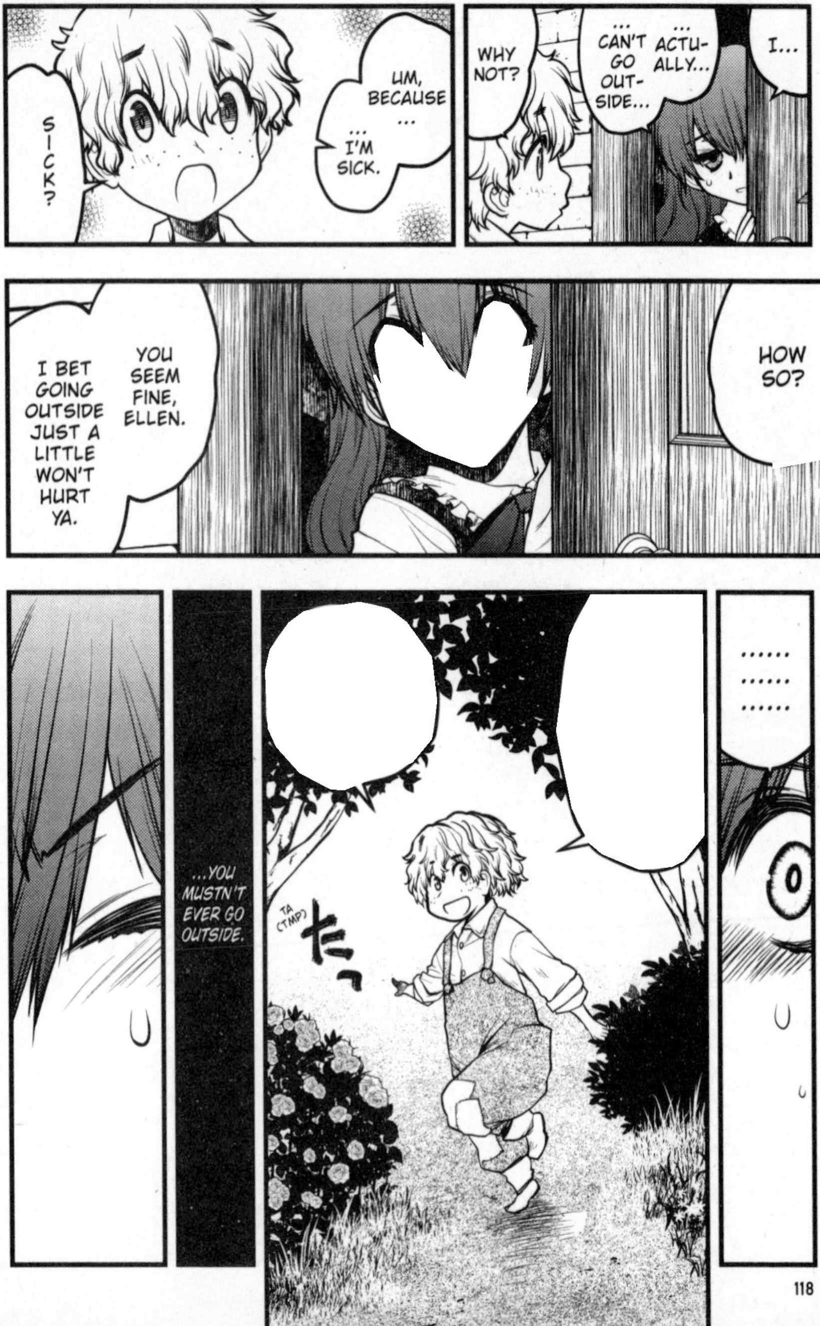
I...
...ACTUALLY...
...CAN'T GO OUTSIDE...
WHY NOT?
UM, BECAUSE... ...I'M SICK.
SICK?
HOW SO?
YOU SEEM FINE, ELLEN.
I BET GOING OUTSIDE JUST A LITTLE WON'T HURT YA.
....
TA (TMP)
...YOU MUSTN'T EVER GO OUTSIDE.

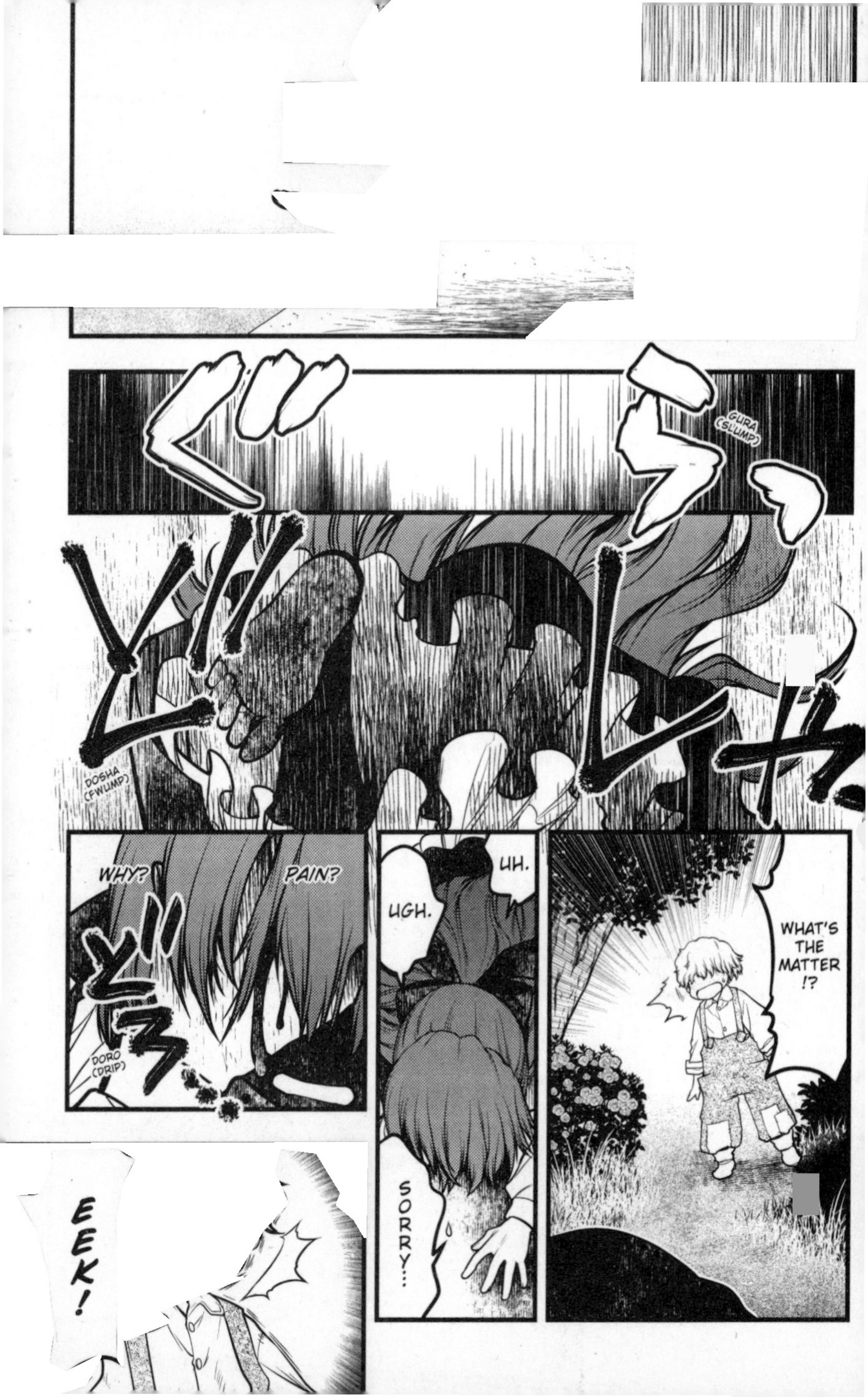

GURA (SLUMP)
DOSHA (FWUMP)
WHAT'S THE MATTER !?
UH.
UGH.
SORRY...
PAIN?
WHY?
DORO (DRIP)
EEK!

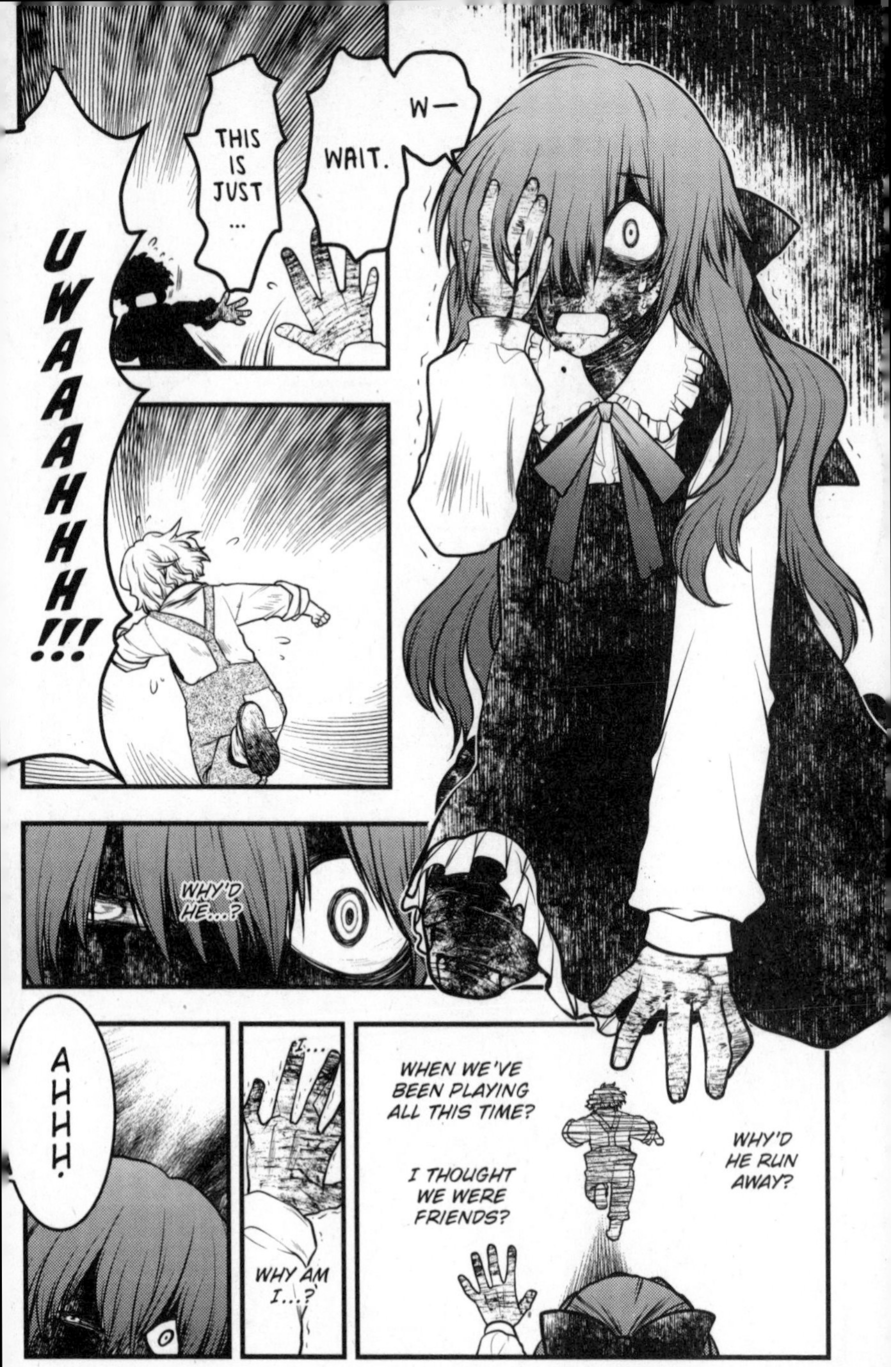
W—
WAIT.
THIS IS JUST ...
UWAAAAHHHH!!!
WHY'D HE...?
WHY'D HE RUN AWAY?
WHEN WE'VE BEEN PLAYING ALL THIS TIME?
I THOUGHT WE WERE FRIENDS?
I...
WHY AM I...?
AHHH.

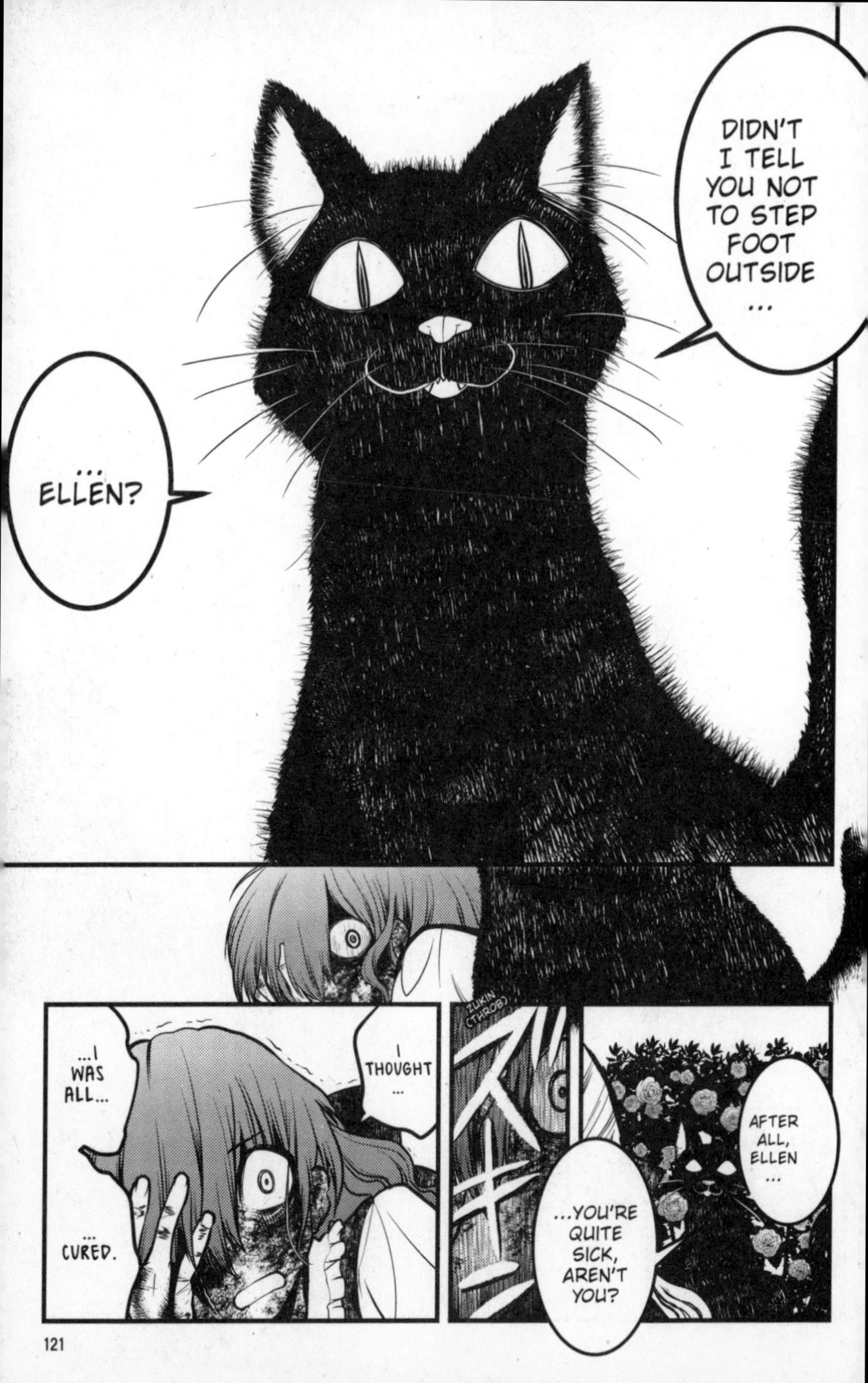
DIDN'T I TELL YOU NOT TO STEP FOOT OUTSIDE ...
... ELLEN?
AFTER ALL, ELLEN ...
...YOU'RE QUITE SICK, AREN'T YOU?
ZUKIN (THROB)
I THOUGHT ...
...I WAS ALL...
... CURED.

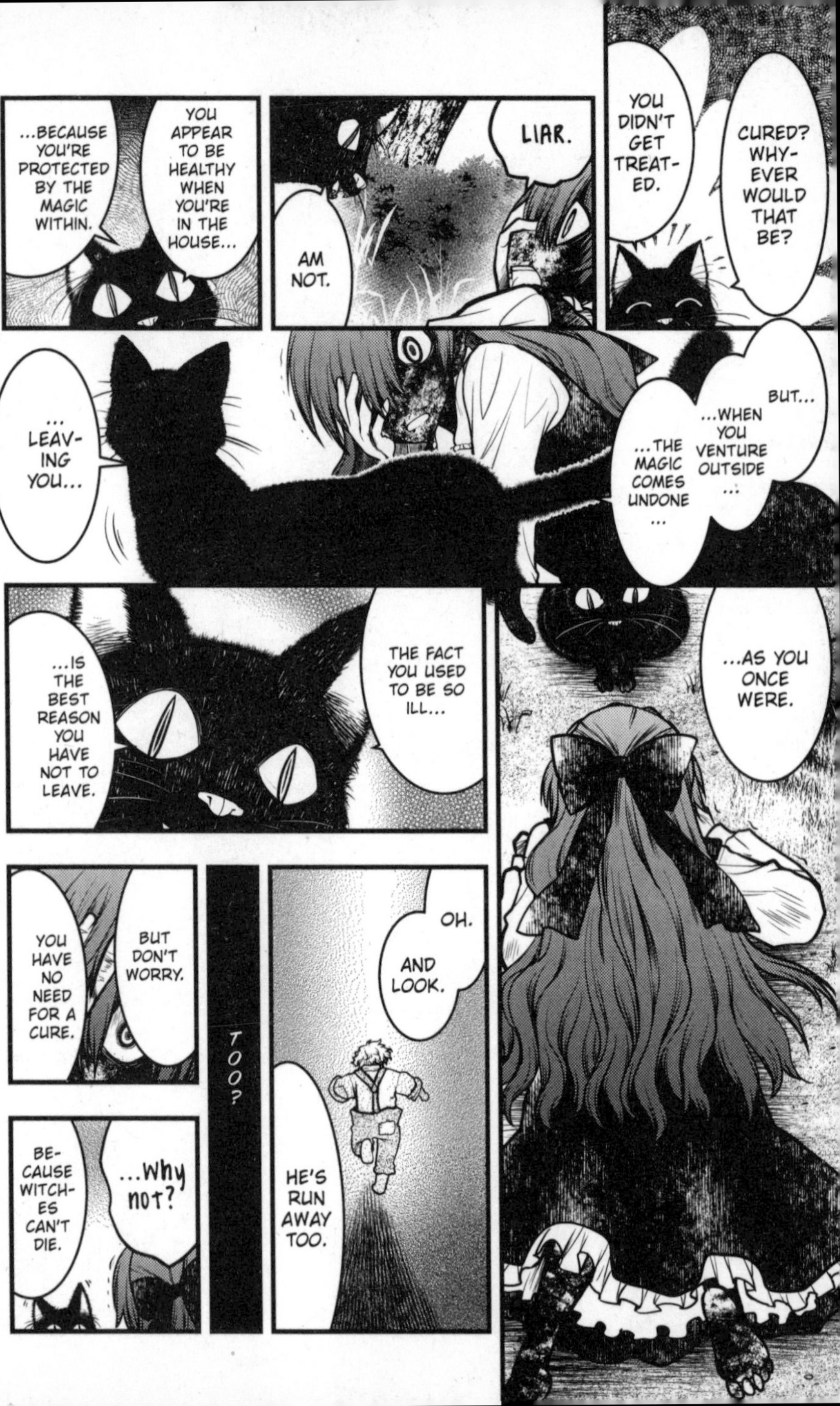
CURED? WHY-EVER WOULD THAT BE?
YOU DIDN'T GET TREAT-ED.
LIAR.
AM NOT.
YOU APPEAR TO BE HEALTHY WHEN YOU'RE IN THE HOUSE...
...BECAUSE YOU'RE PROTECTED BY THE MAGIC WITHIN.
BUT...
...WHEN YOU VENTURE OUTSIDE...
...THE MAGIC COMES UNDONE...
...LEAV-ING YOU...
...AS YOU ONCE WERE.
THE FACT YOU USED TO BE SO ILL...
...IS THE BEST REASON YOU HAVE NOT TO LEAVE.
OH.
AND LOOK.
HE'S RUN AWAY TOO.
TOO?
BUT DON'T WORRY.
YOU HAVE NO NEED FOR A CURE.
...why not?
BE-CAUSE WITCH-ES CAN'T DIE.

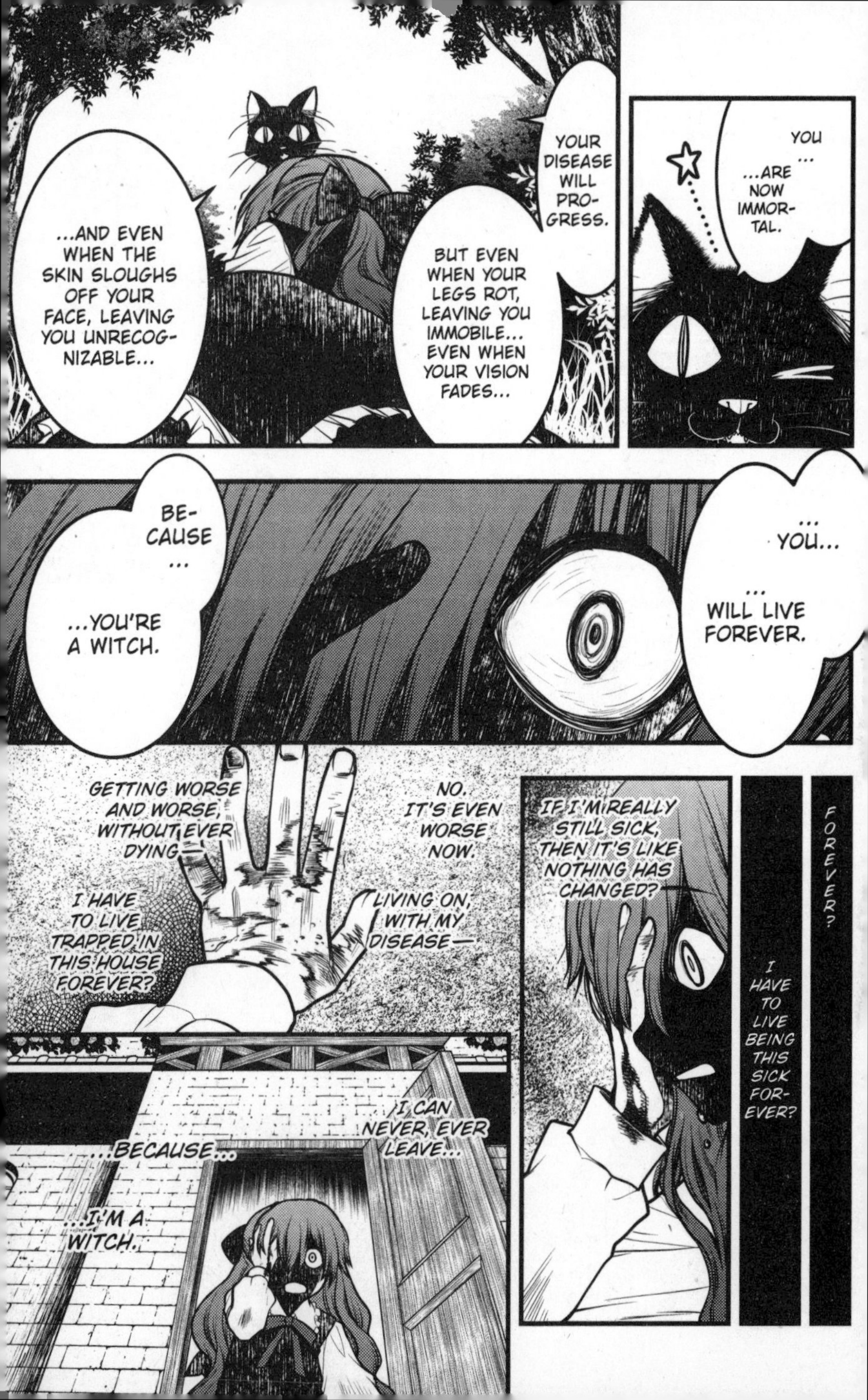
YOU ... ...ARE NOW IMMORTAL.
YOUR DISEASE WILL PROGRESS.
BUT EVEN WHEN YOUR LEGS ROT, LEAVING YOU IMMOBILE... EVEN WHEN YOUR VISION FADES...
...AND EVEN WHEN THE SKIN SLOUGHS OFF YOUR FACE, LEAVING YOU UNRECOGNIZABLE...
... YOU...
... WILL LIVE FOREVER.
BECAUSE...
...YOU'RE A WITCH.
FOREVER?
I HAVE TO LIVE BEING THIS SICK FOREVER?
IF I'M REALLY STILL SICK, THEN IT'S LIKE NOTHING HAS CHANGED?
NO. IT'S EVEN WORSE NOW.
LIVING ON, WITH MY DISEASE—
GETTING WORSE AND WORSE, WITHOUT EVER DYING—
I HAVE TO LIVE TRAPPED IN THIS HOUSE FOREVER?
I CAN NEVER, EVER LEAVE...
...BECAUSE...
...I'M A WITCH.

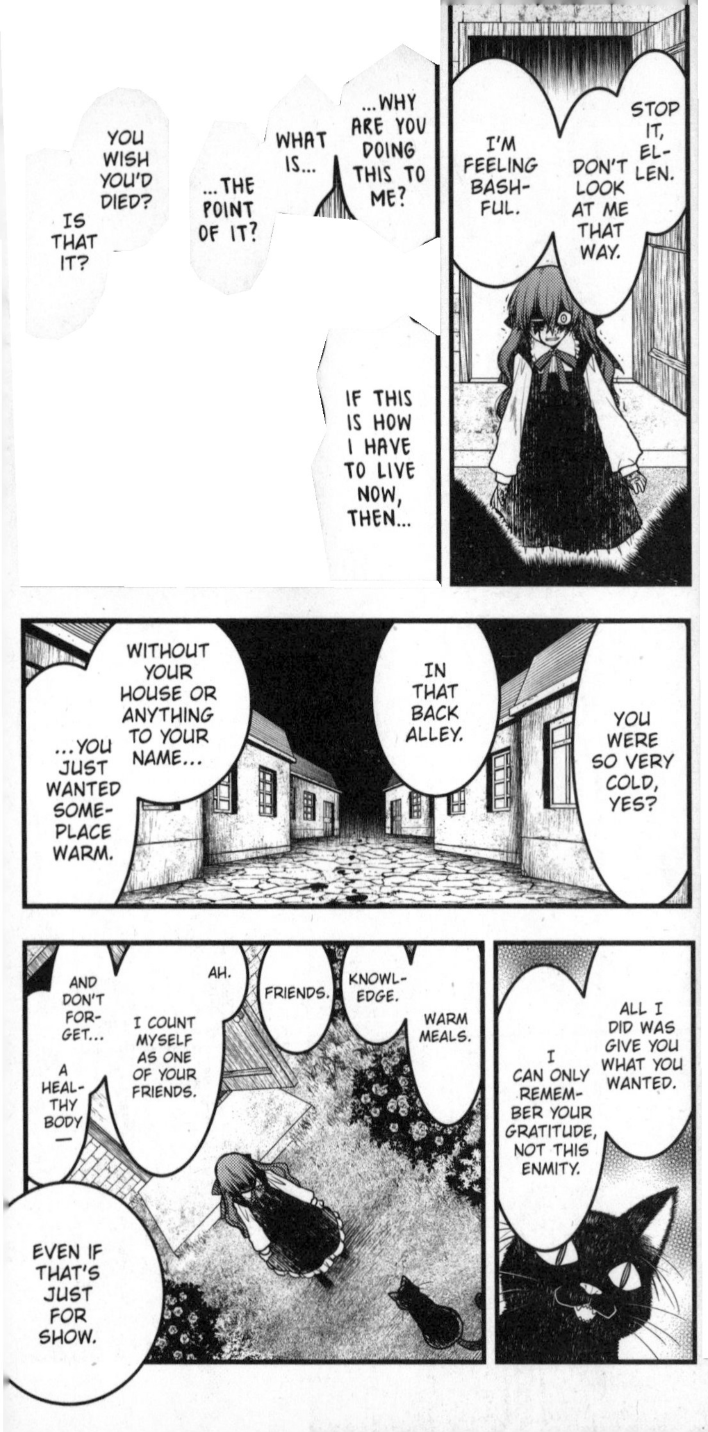
STOP IT, EL-LEN.
DON'T LOOK AT ME THAT WAY.
I'M FEELING BASH-FUL.
...WHY ARE YOU DOING THIS TO ME?
WHAT IS...
...THE POINT OF IT?
YOU WISH YOU'D DIED?
IS THAT IT?
IF THIS IS HOW I HAVE TO LIVE NOW, THEN...
YOU WERE SO VERY COLD, YES?
IN THAT BACK ALLEY.
WITHOUT YOUR HOUSE OR ANYTHING TO YOUR NAME...
...YOU JUST WANTED SOME-PLACE WARM.
ALL I DID WAS GIVE YOU WHAT YOU WANTED.
I CAN ONLY REMEM-BER YOUR GRATITUDE, NOT THIS ENMITY.
KNOWL-EDGE.
WARM MEALS.
FRIENDS.
AH.
I COUNT MYSELF AS ONE OF YOUR FRIENDS.
AND DON'T FOR-GET...
A HEAL-THY BODY—
EVEN IF THAT'S JUST FOR SHOW.

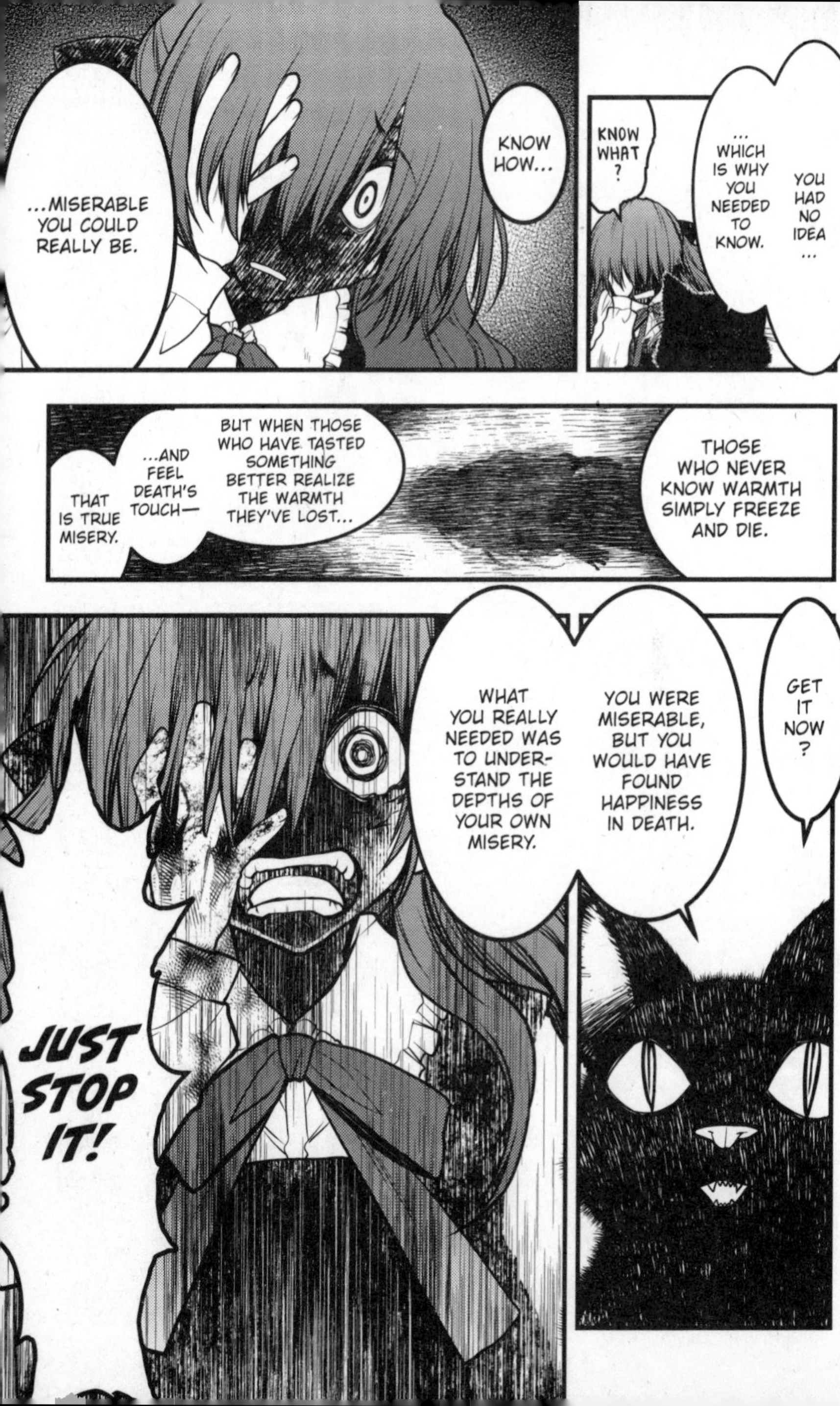
YOU HAD NO IDEA...
...WHICH IS WHY YOU NEEDED TO KNOW.
KNOW WHAT?
KNOW HOW...
...MISERABLE YOU COULD REALLY BE.
THOSE WHO NEVER KNOW WARMTH SIMPLY FREEZE AND DIE.
BUT WHEN THOSE WHO HAVE TASTED SOMETHING BETTER REALIZE THE WARMTH THEY'VE LOST...
...AND FEEL DEATH'S TOUCH—
THAT IS TRUE MISERY.
GET IT NOW?
YOU WERE MISERABLE, BUT YOU WOULD HAVE FOUND HAPPINESS IN DEATH.
WHAT YOU REALLY NEEDED WAS TO UNDER-STAND THE DEPTHS OF YOUR OWN MISERY.
JUST STOP IT!

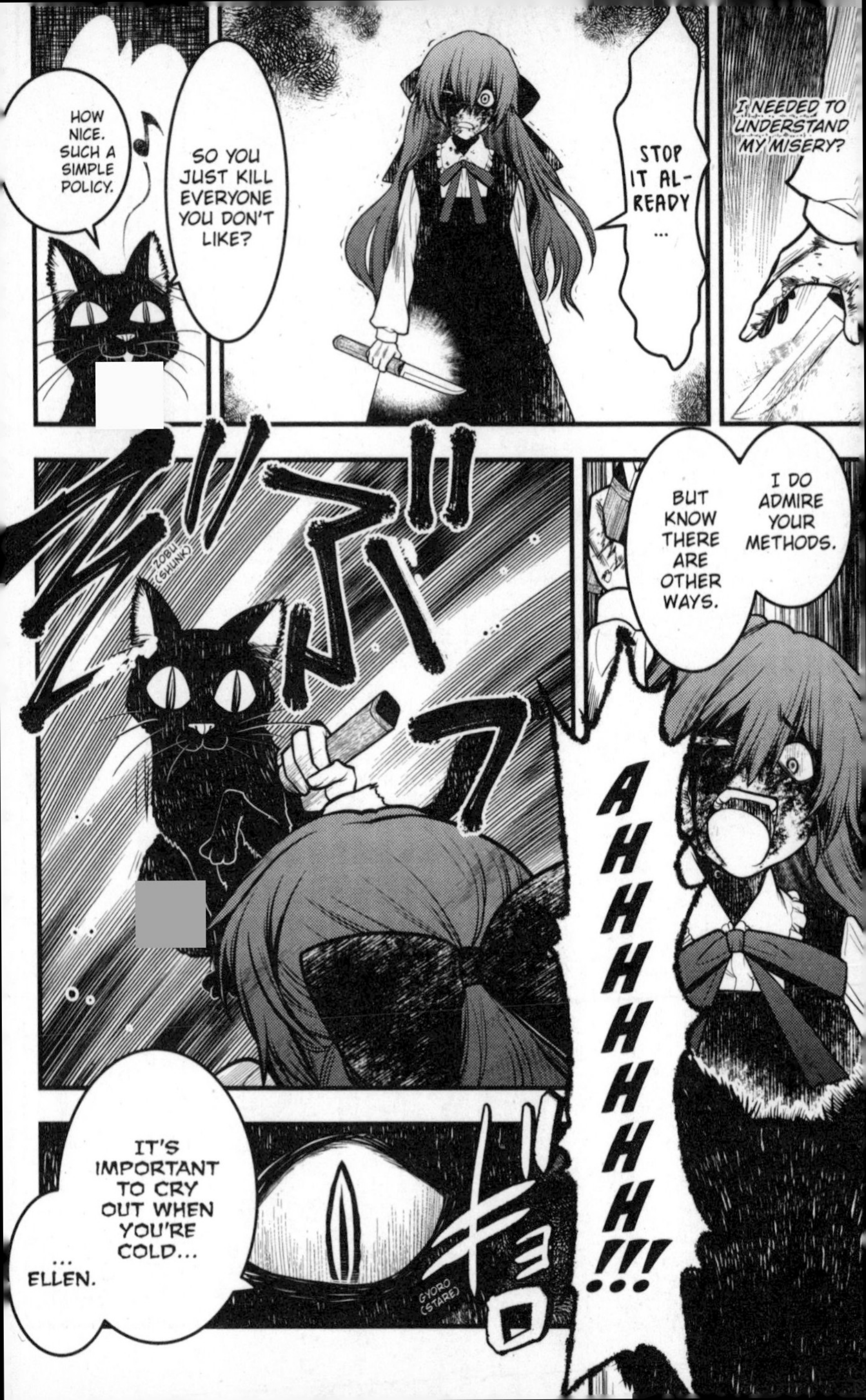
I NEEDED TO UNDERSTAND MY MISERY?
STOP IT AL- READY ...
SO YOU JUST KILL EVERYONE YOU DON'T LIKE?
HOW NICE. SUCH A SIMPLE POLICY.
I DO ADMIRE YOUR METHODS.
BUT KNOW THERE ARE OTHER WAYS.
AHHHHHHHHH!!!
ZOBU (SHUNK)
IT'S IMPORTANT TO CRY OUT WHEN YOU'RE COLD... ... ELLEN.
GYORO (STARE)

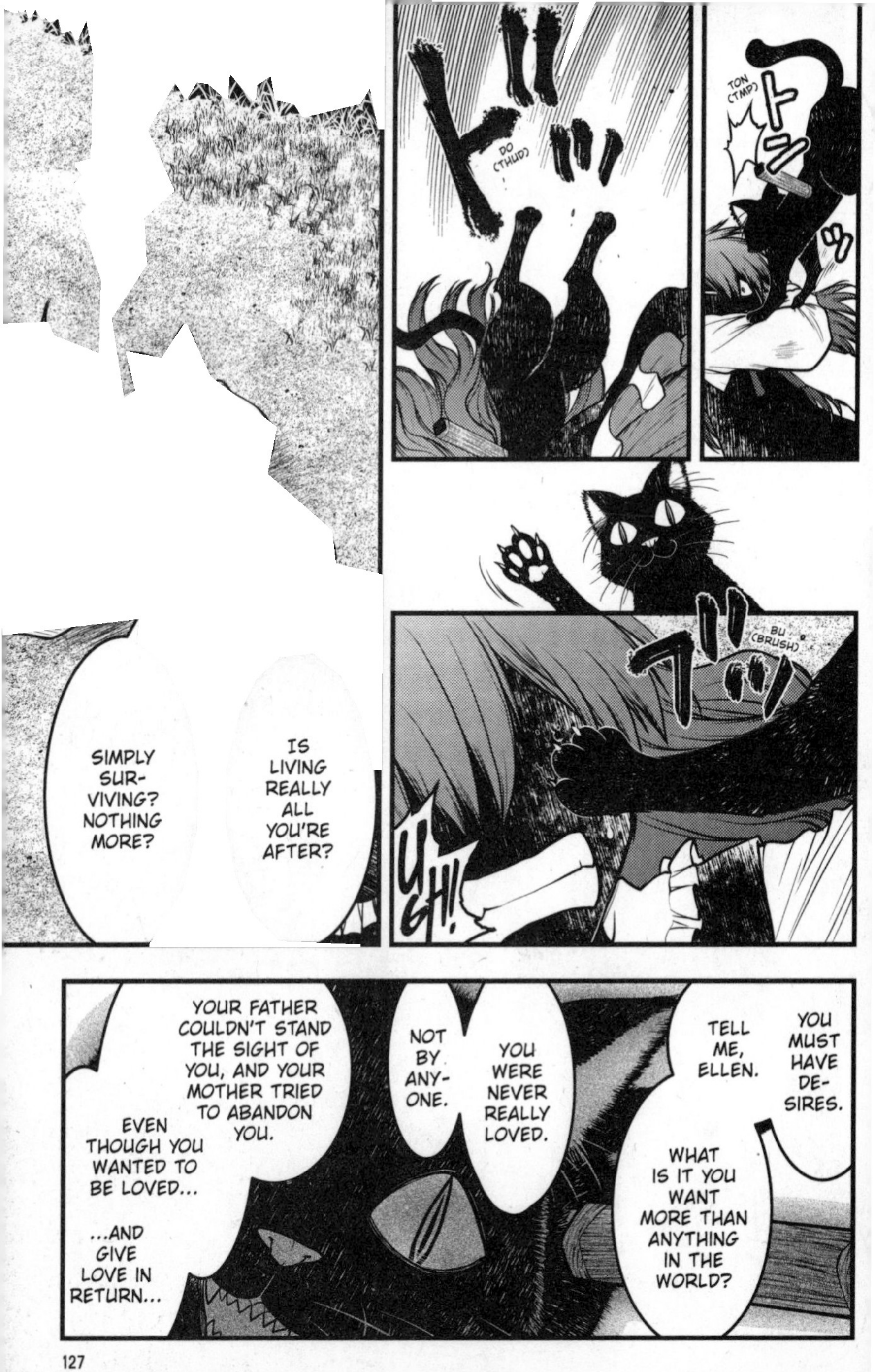
TON (TMP)
DO (THUD)
BU (BRUSH)
UGH!
IS LIVING REALLY ALL YOU'RE AFTER?
SIMPLY SURVIVING? NOTHING MORE?
YOU MUST HAVE DESIRES.
TELL ME, ELLEN.
WHAT IS IT YOU WANT MORE THAN ANYTHING IN THE WORLD?
YOU WERE NEVER REALLY LOVED.
NOT BY ANYONE.
YOUR FATHER COULDN'T STAND THE SIGHT OF YOU, AND YOUR MOTHER TRIED TO ABANDON YOU.
EVEN THOUGH YOU WANTED TO BE LOVED...
...AND GIVE LOVE IN RETURN...

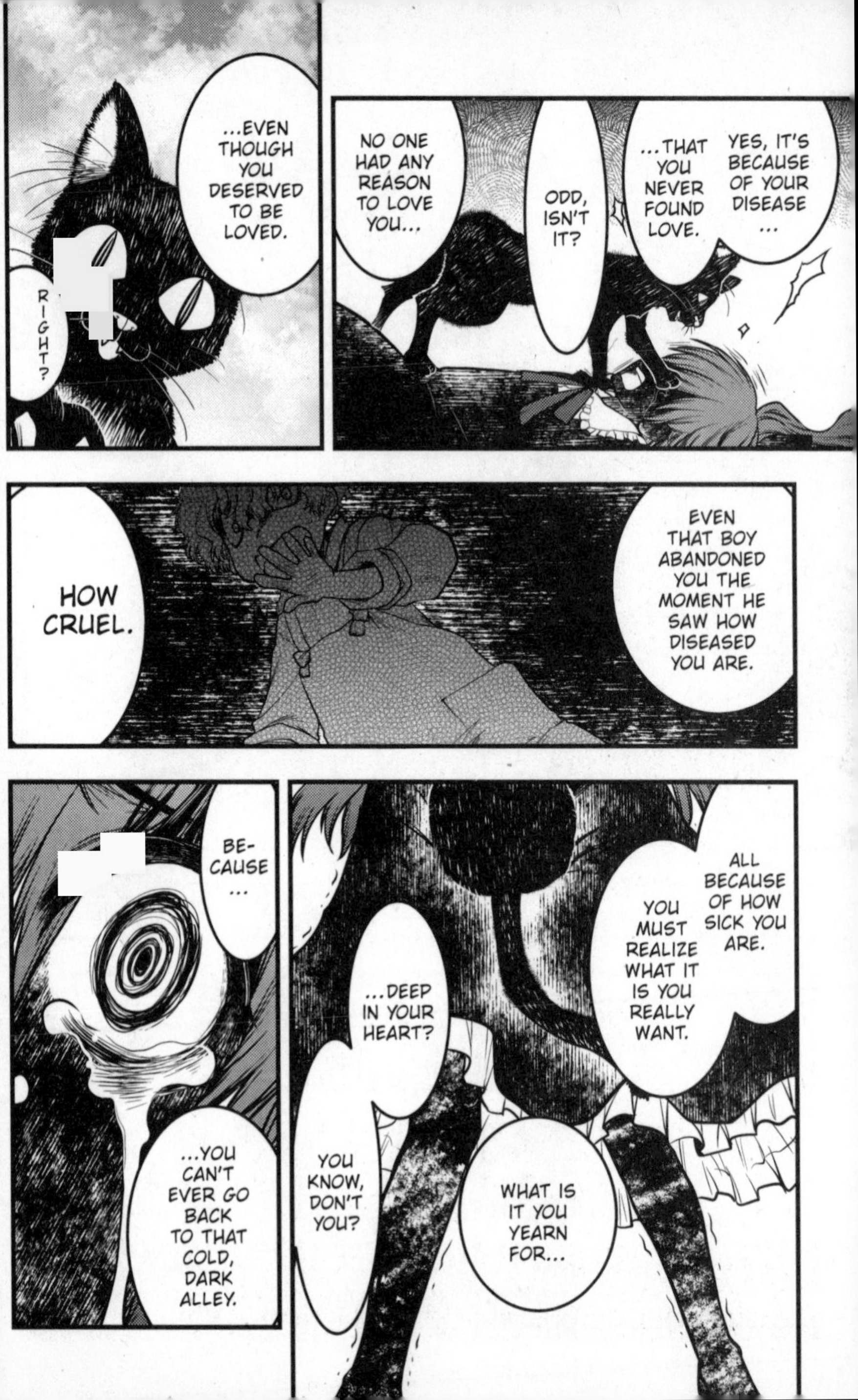
YES, IT'S BECAUSE OF YOUR DISEASE ...
...THAT YOU NEVER FOUND LOVE.
ODD, ISN'T IT?
NO ONE HAD ANY REASON TO LOVE YOU...
...EVEN THOUGH YOU DESERVED TO BE LOVED.
RIGHT?
EVEN THAT BOY ABANDONED YOU THE MOMENT HE SAW HOW DISEASED YOU ARE.
HOW CRUEL.
ALL BECAUSE OF HOW SICK YOU ARE.
YOU MUST REALIZE WHAT IT IS YOU REALLY WANT.
...DEEP IN YOUR HEART?
WHAT IS IT YOU YEARN FOR...
YOU KNOW, DON'T YOU?
BE-CAUSE ...
...YOU CAN'T EVER GO BACK TO THAT COLD, DARK ALLEY.

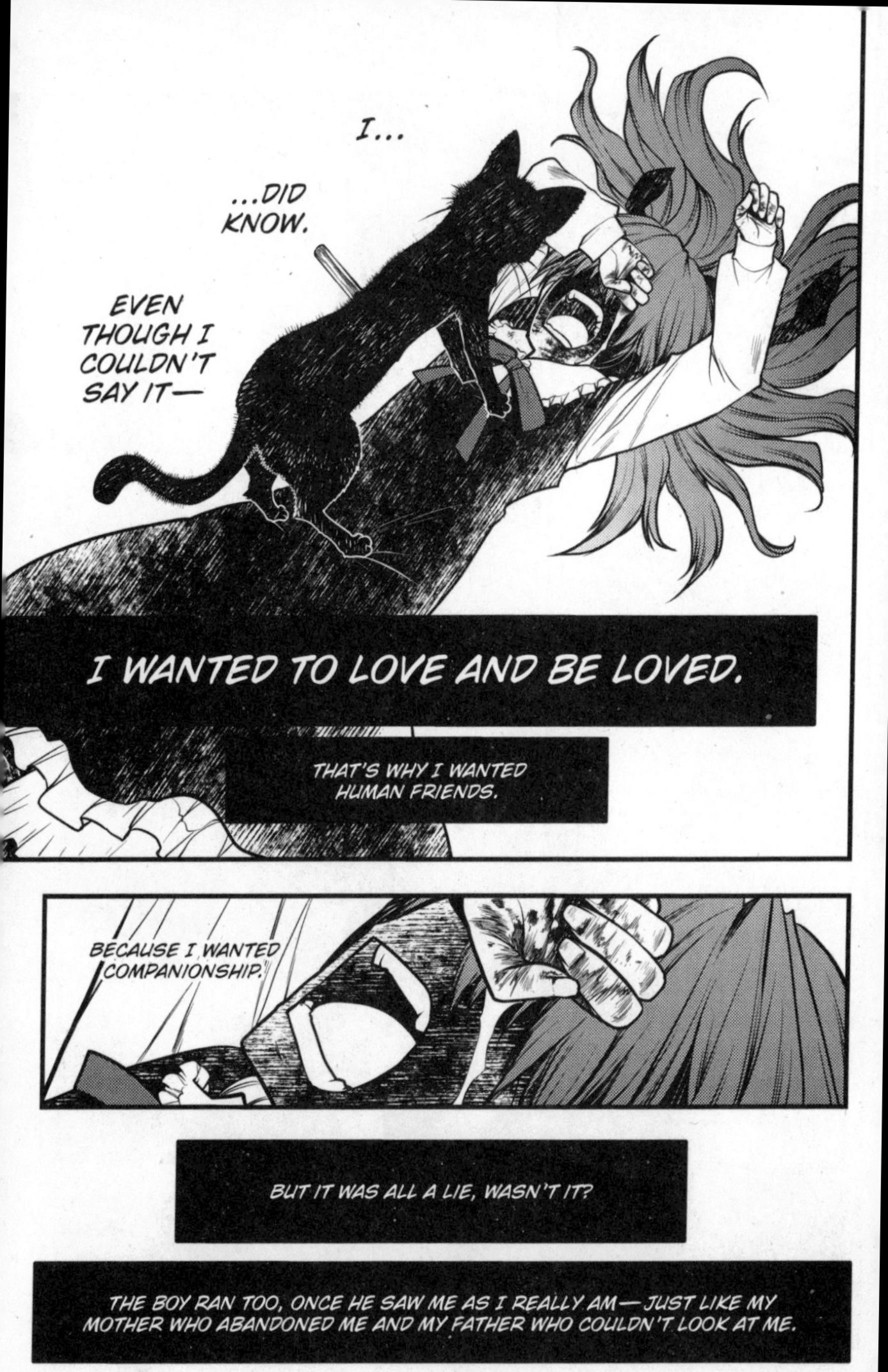
I...
...DID KNOW.
EVEN THOUGH I COULDN'T SAY IT—
I WANTED TO LOVE AND BE LOVED.
THAT'S WHY I WANTED HUMAN FRIENDS.
BECAUSE I WANTED COMPANIONSHIP.
BUT IT WAS ALL A LIE, WASN'T IT?
THE BOY RAN TOO, ONCE HE SAW ME AS I REALLY AM—JUST LIKE MY MOTHER WHO ABANDONED ME AND MY FATHER WHO COULDN'T LOOK AT ME.

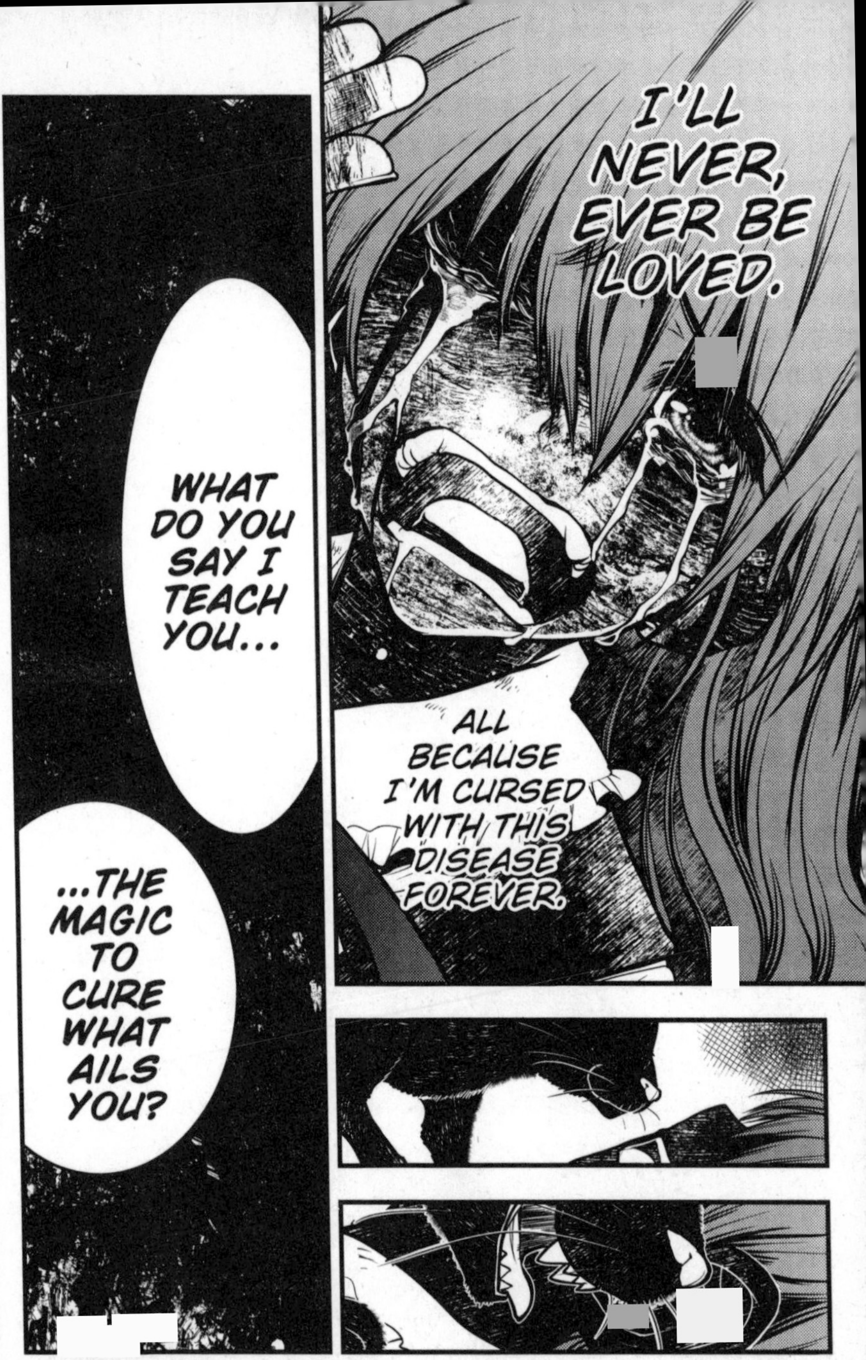
I'LL NEVER, EVER BE LOVED.
ALL BECAUSE I'M CURSED WITH THIS DISEASE FOREVER.
WHAT DO YOU SAY I TEACH YOU...
...THE MAGIC TO CURE WHAT AILS YOU?

THE WITCH'S HOUSE

The Diary of Ellen

THE WITCH'S HOUSE
The Diary of Ellen

Chapter 4

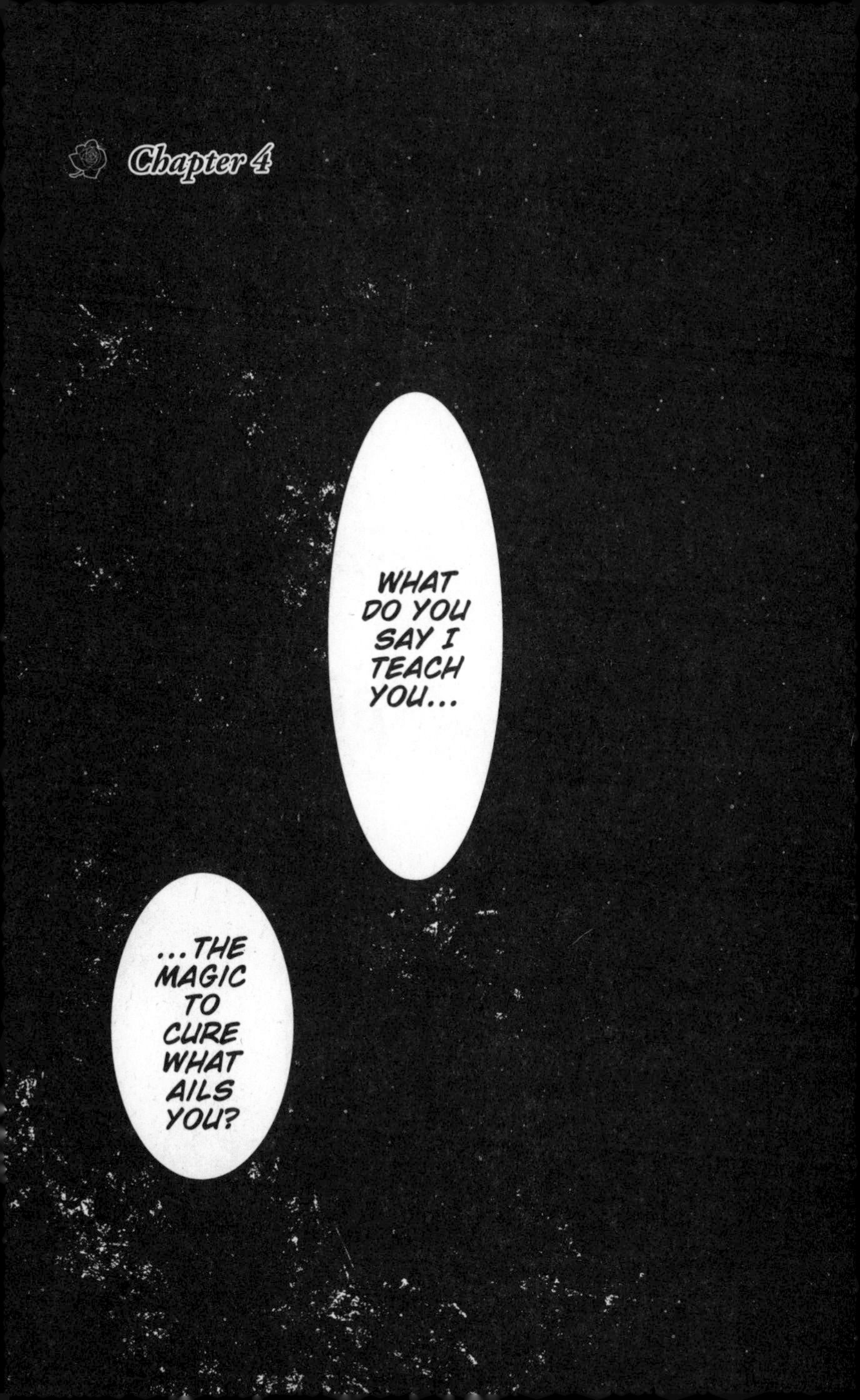
WHAT DO YOU SAY I TEACH YOU...
...THE MAGIC TO CURE WHAT AILS YOU?

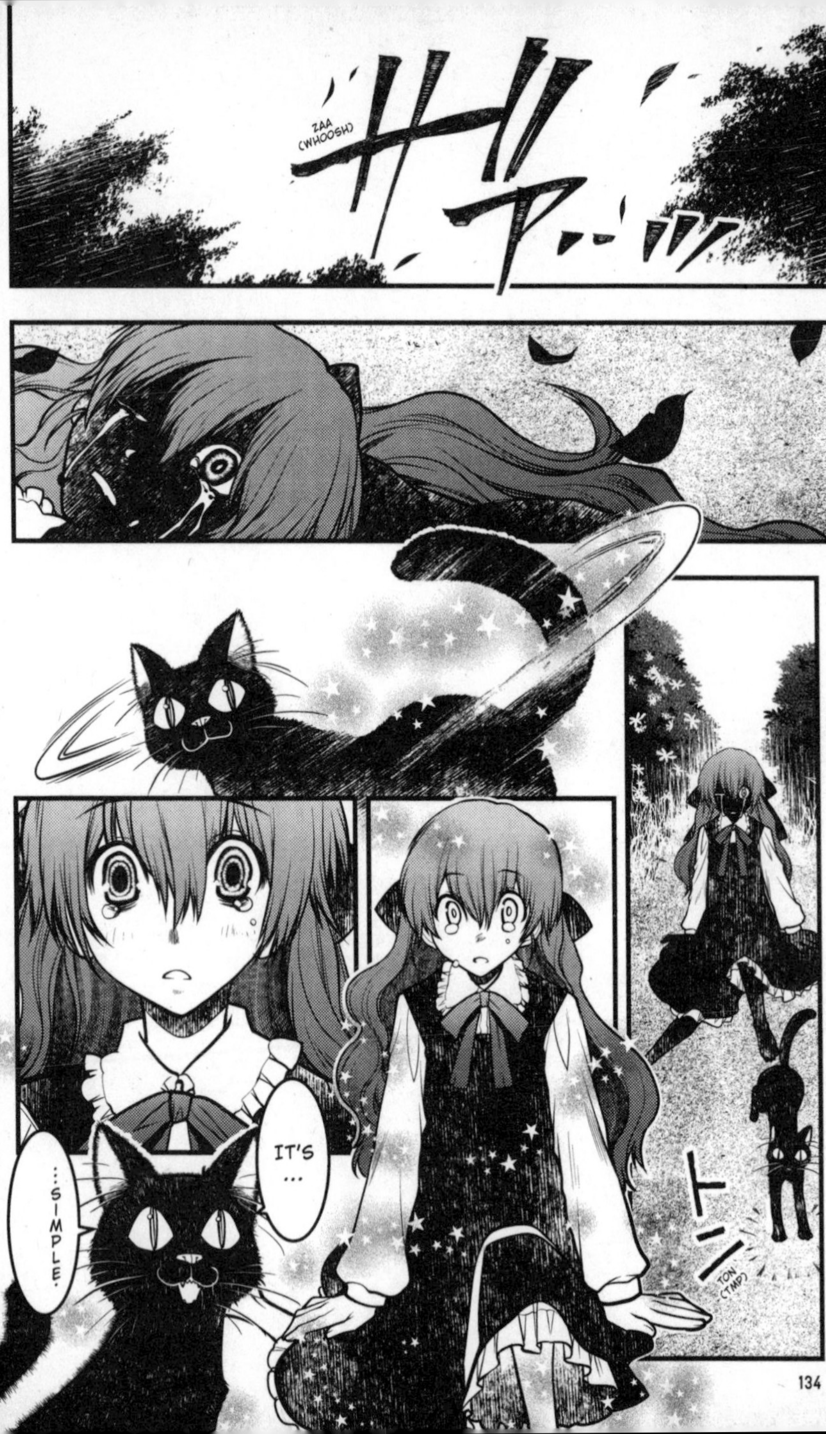
ZAA (WHOOSH)
TON (TMP)
IT'S ...
...SIMPLE.

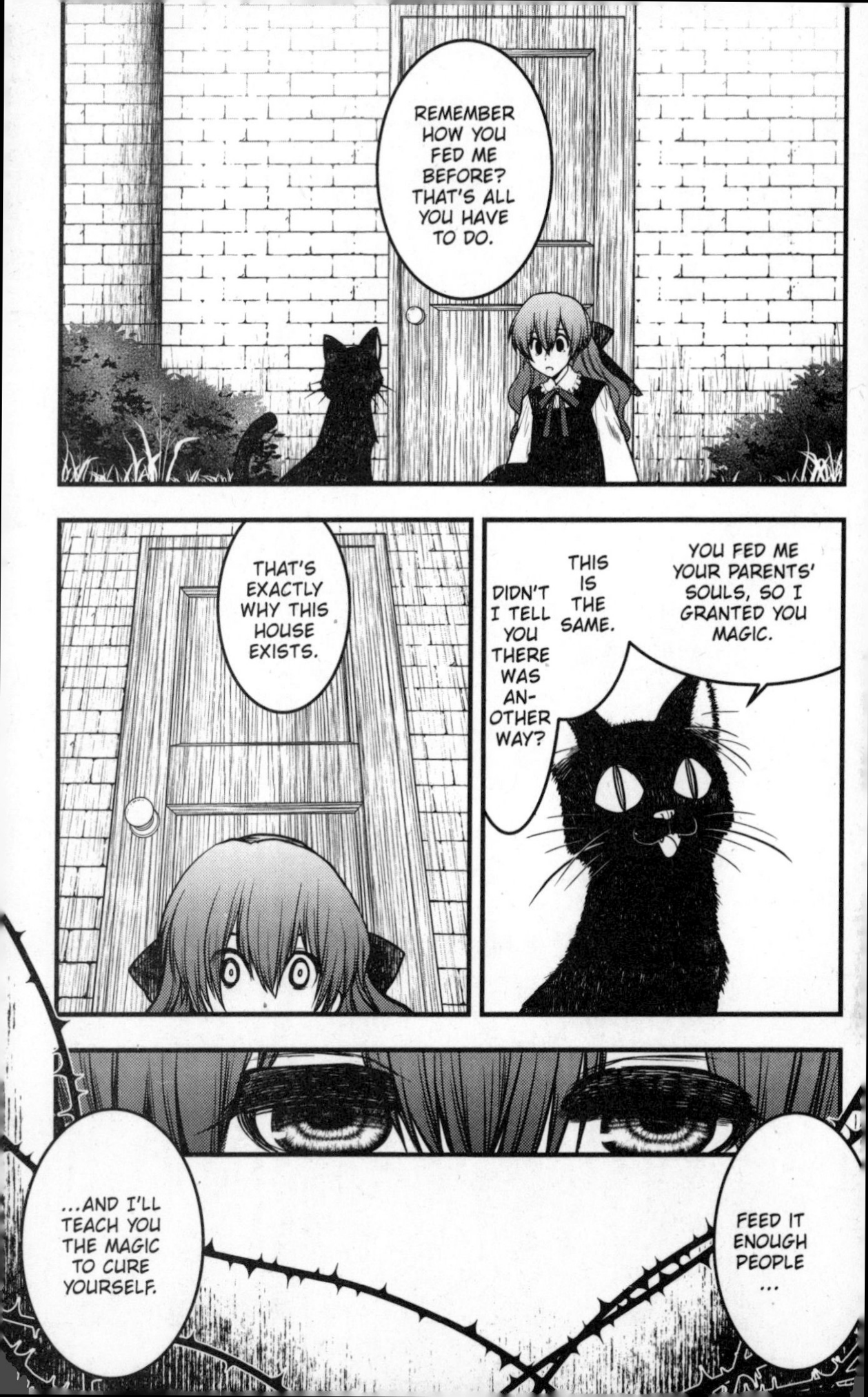
REMEMBER HOW YOU FED ME BEFORE? THAT'S ALL YOU HAVE TO DO.
YOU FED ME YOUR PARENTS' SOULS, SO I GRANTED YOU MAGIC.
THIS IS THE SAME.
DIDN'T I TELL YOU THERE WAS AN-OTHER WAY?
THAT'S EXACTLY WHY THIS HOUSE EXISTS.
FEED IT ENOUGH PEOPLE ...
...AND I'LL TEACH YOU THE MAGIC TO CURE YOURSELF.

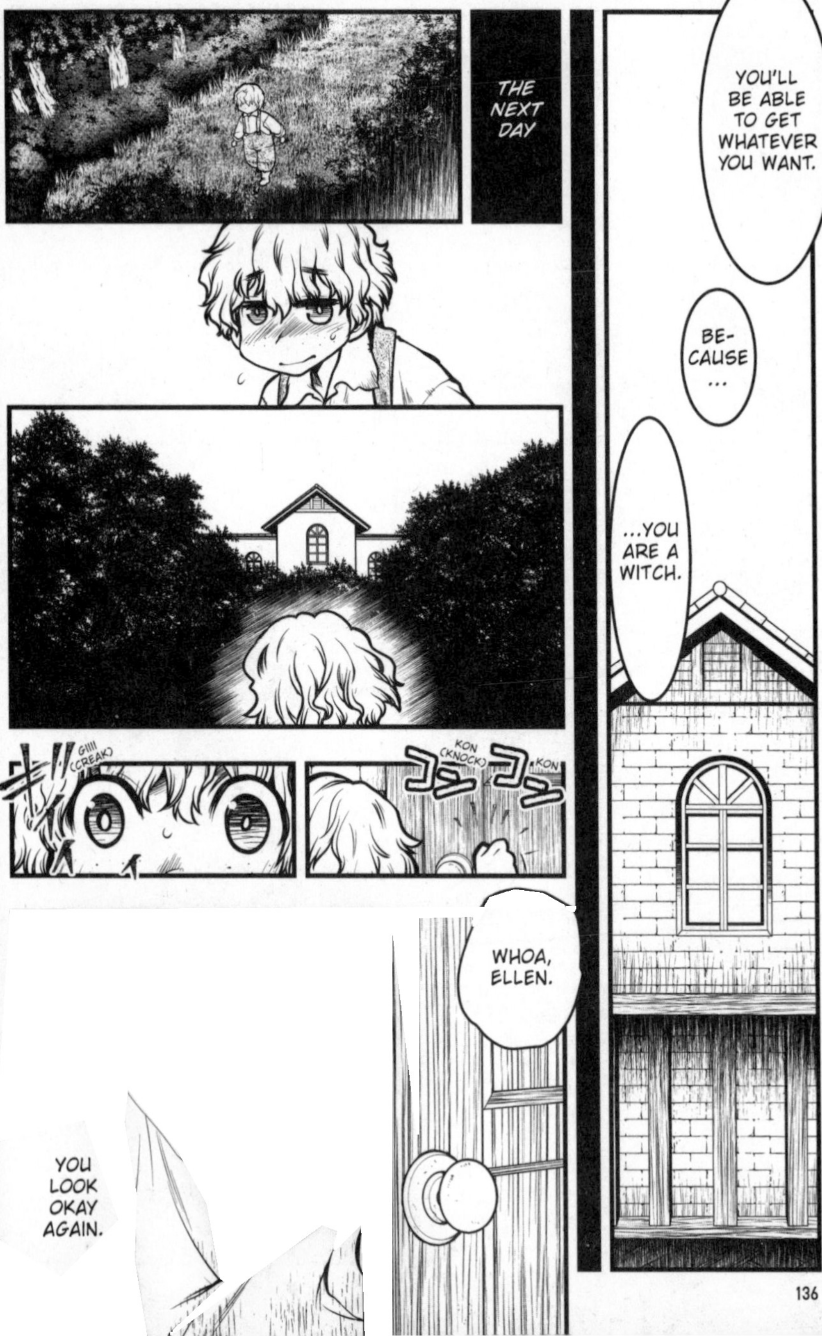
YOU'LL BE ABLE TO GET WHATEVER YOU WANT.
BE-CAUSE ...
...YOU ARE A WITCH.
THE NEXT DAY
KON (KNOCK) KON
GIIII (CREAK)
WHOA, ELLEN.
YOU LOOK OKAY AGAIN.

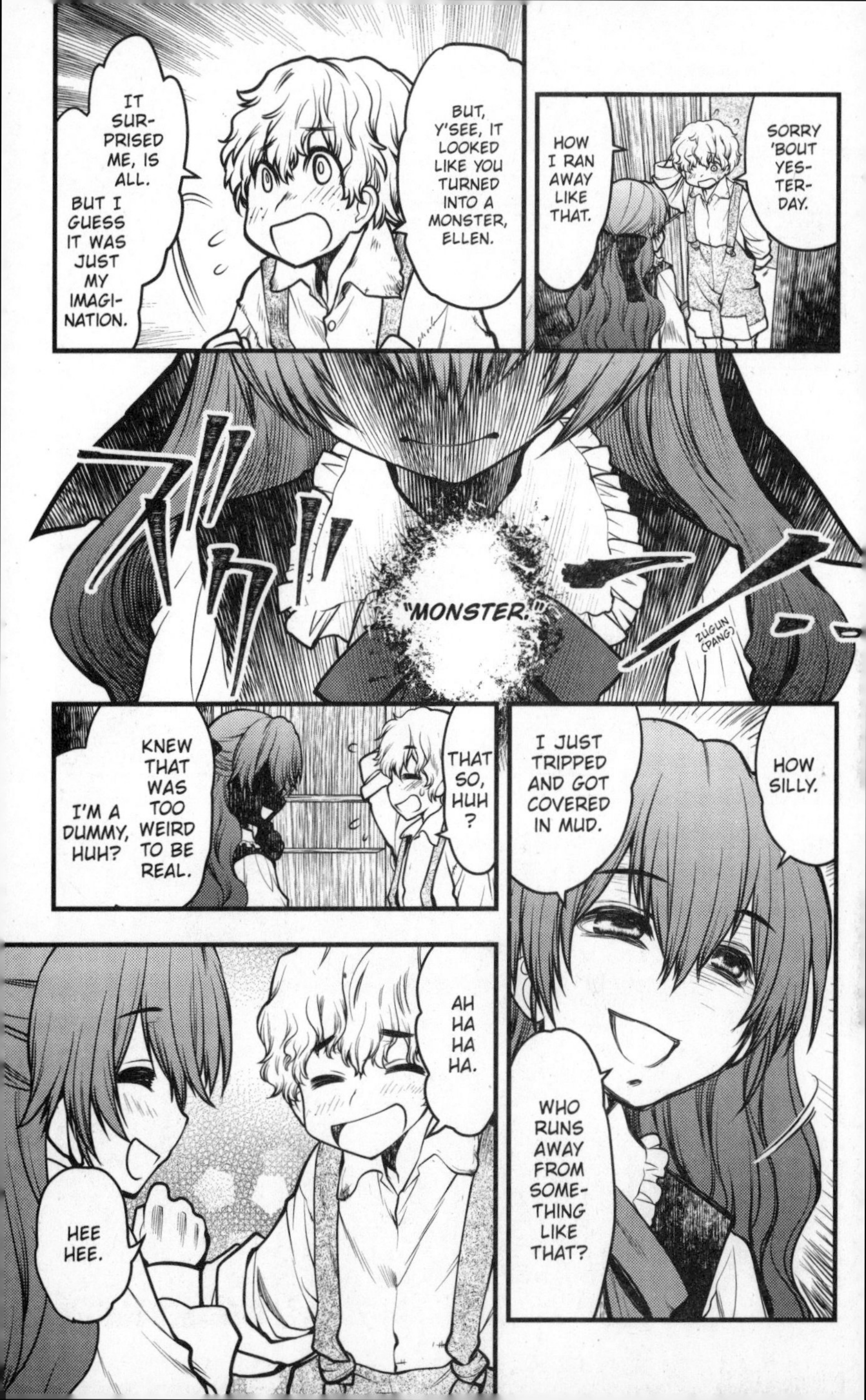
SORRY 'BOUT YESTERDAY.
HOW I RAN AWAY LIKE THAT.
BUT, Y'SEE, IT LOOKED LIKE YOU TURNED INTO A MONSTER, ELLEN.
IT SURPRISED ME, IS ALL.
BUT I GUESS IT WAS JUST MY IMAGINATION.
"MONSTER."
ZUGUN (PANG)
HOW SILLY.
I JUST TRIPPED AND GOT COVERED IN MUD.
WHO RUNS AWAY FROM SOMETHING LIKE THAT?
THAT SO, HUH?
KNEW THAT WAS TOO WEIRD TO BE REAL.
I'M A DUMMY, HUH?
AH HA HA HA.
HEE HEE.

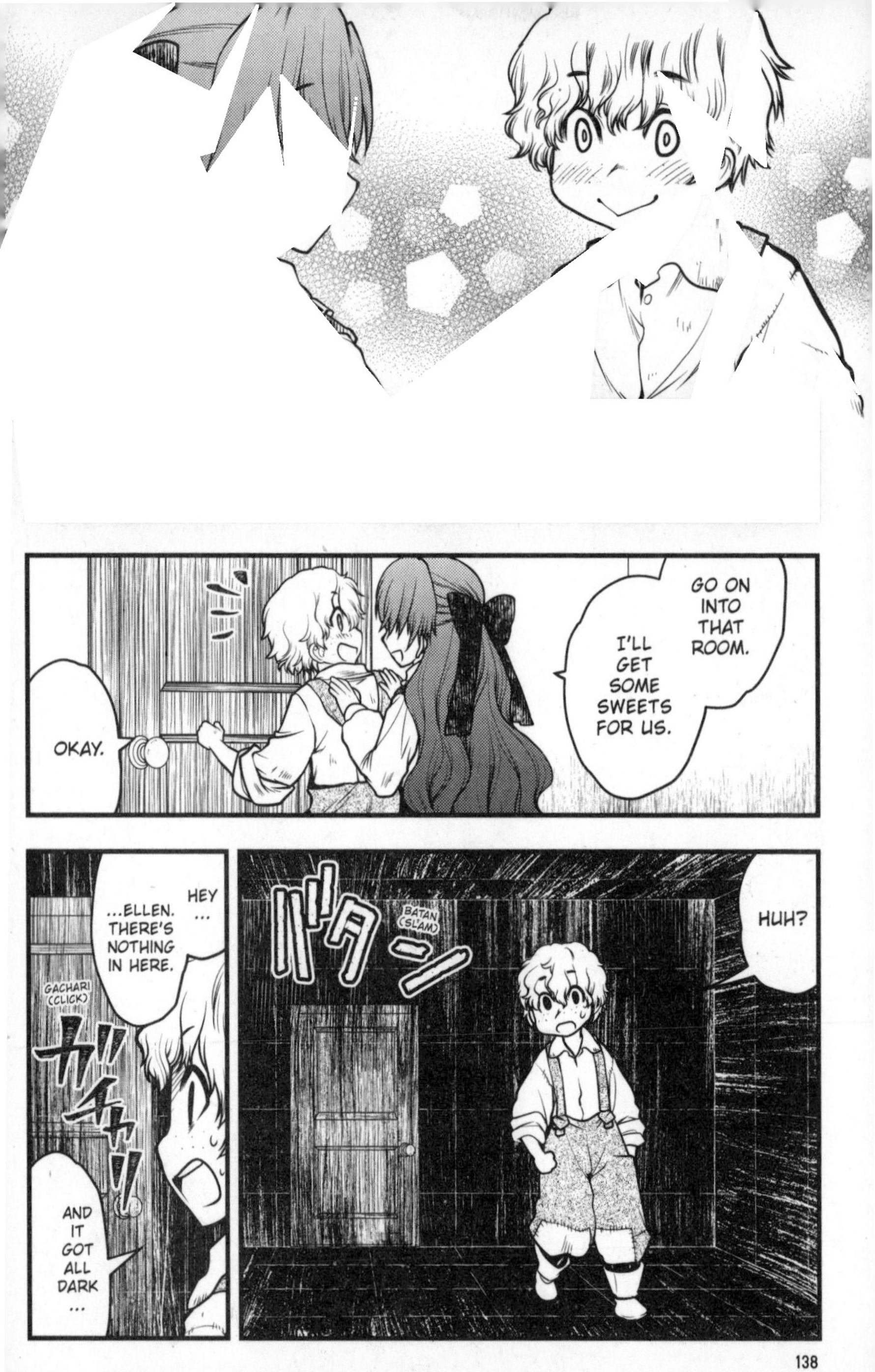
GO ON INTO THAT ROOM.
I'LL GET SOME SWEETS FOR US.
OKAY.
HUH?
BATAN (SLAM)
HEY ...
...ELLEN. THERE'S NOTHING IN HERE.
GACHARI (CLICK)
AND IT GOT ALL DARK ...

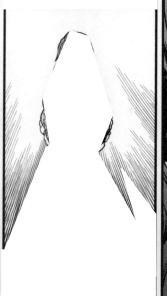

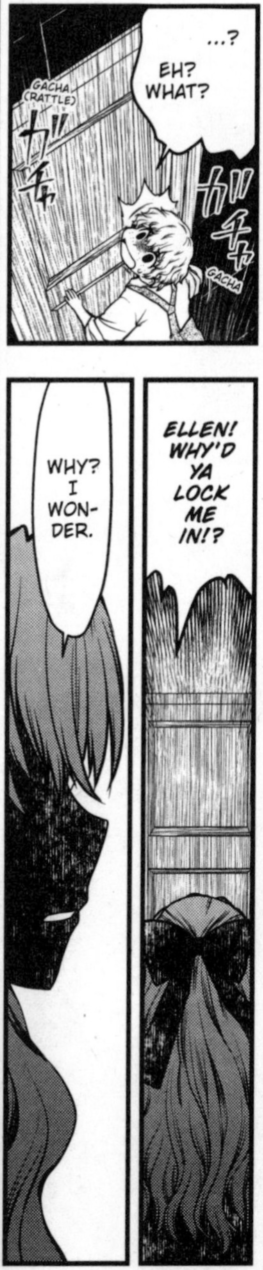
...?
EH? WHAT?
GACHA (RATTLE)
GACHA
ELLEN! WHY'D YA LOCK ME IN!?
WHY? I WONDER.

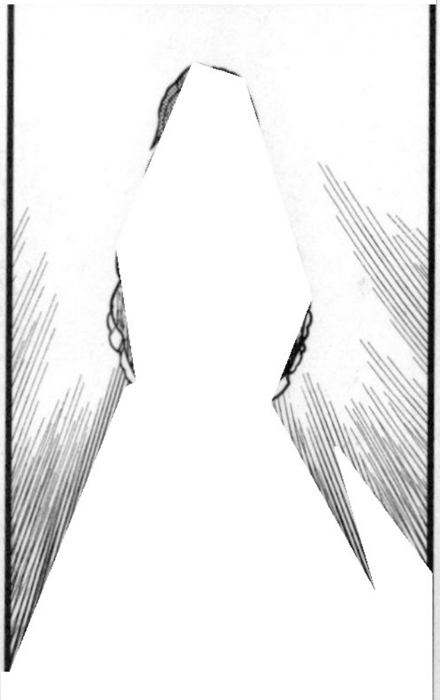

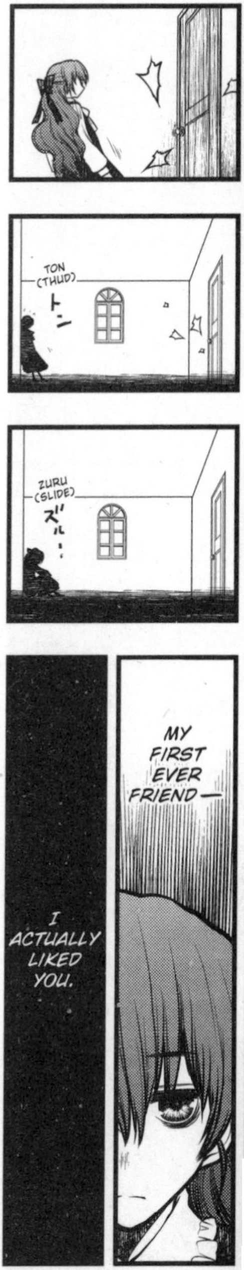
TON (THUD)
ZURU (SLIDE)
MY FIRST EVER FRIEND—
I ACTUALLY LIKED YOU.

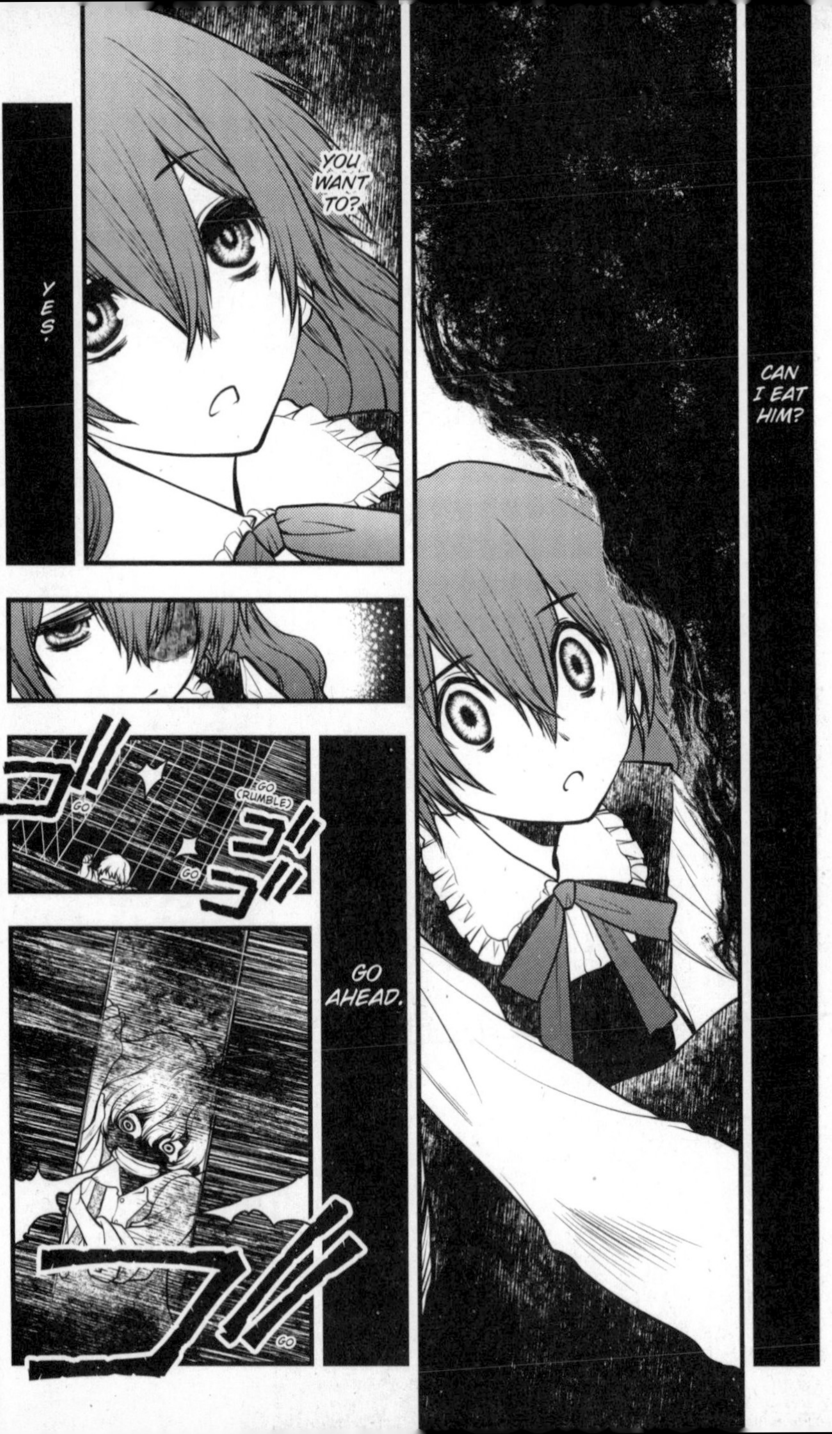
CAN I EAT HIM?
YOU WANT TO?
YES.
GO (RUMBLE)
GO
GO
GO AHEAD.
GO

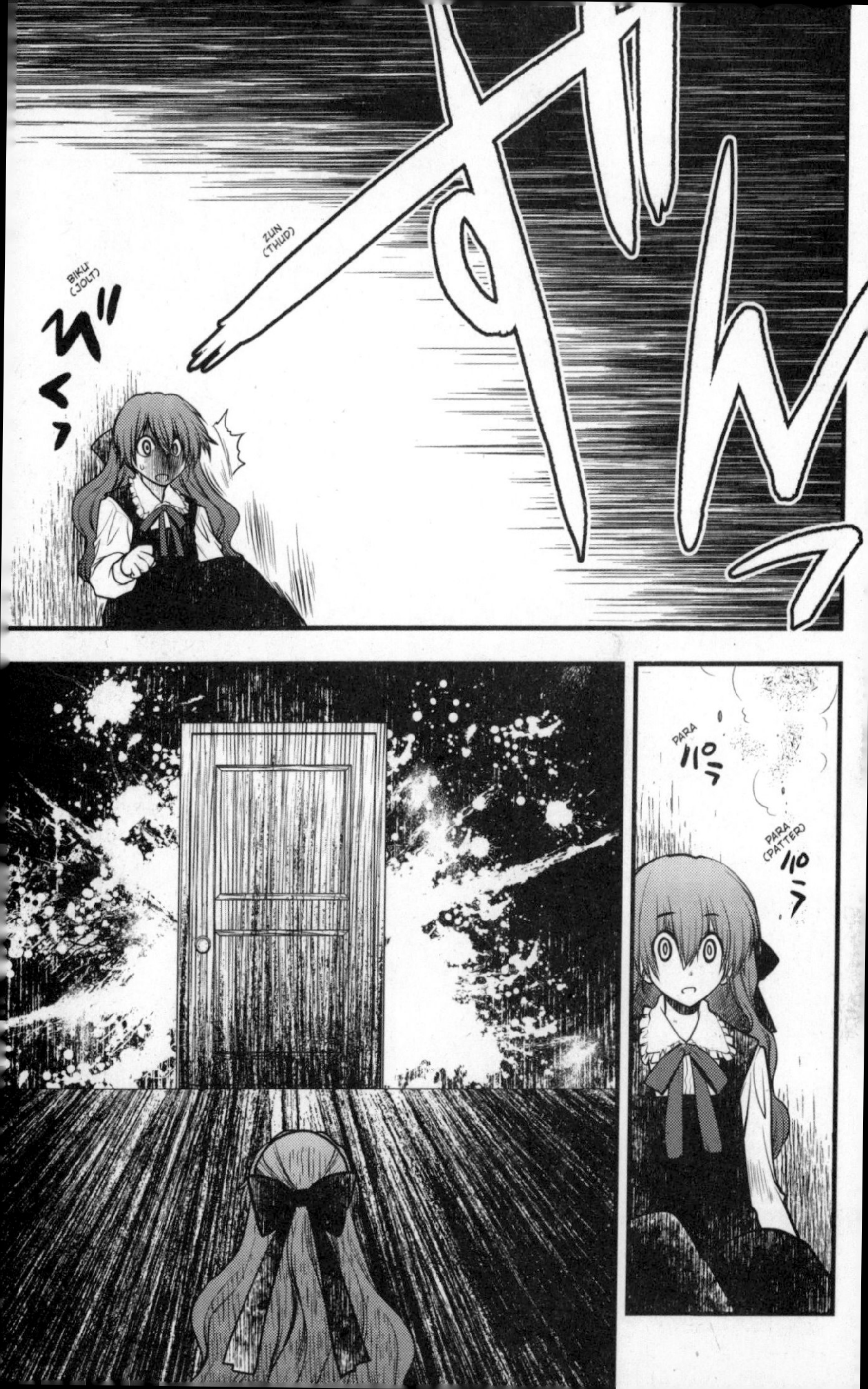
ZUN (THUD)
BIKU (JOLT)
PARA
PARA (PATTER)

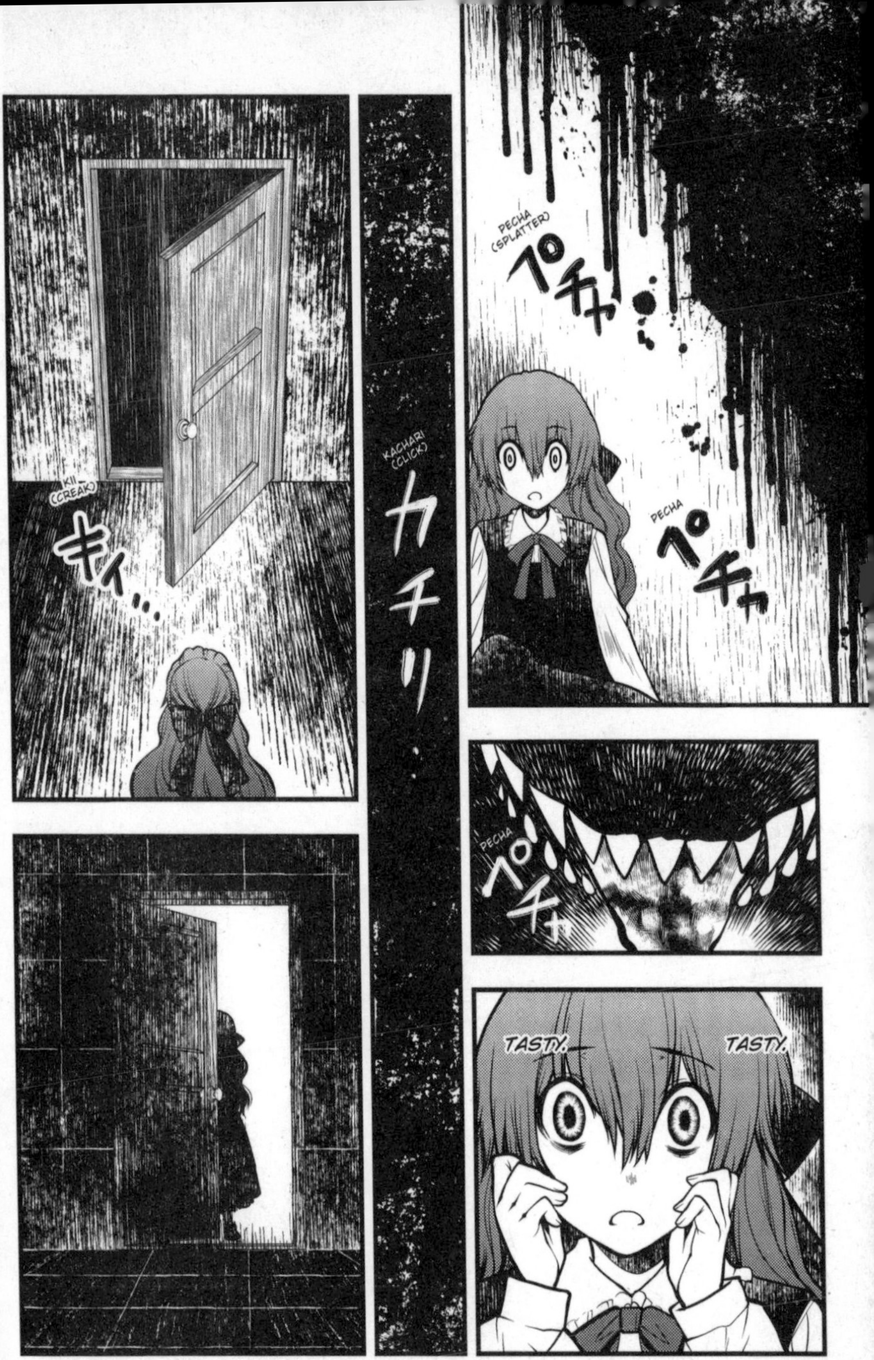
PECHA (SPLATTER)
ペチャ
PECHA
ペチャ
PECHA
ペチャ
TASTY.
TASTY.
KACHARI (CLICK)
カチリ
KII (CREAK)
キィ…

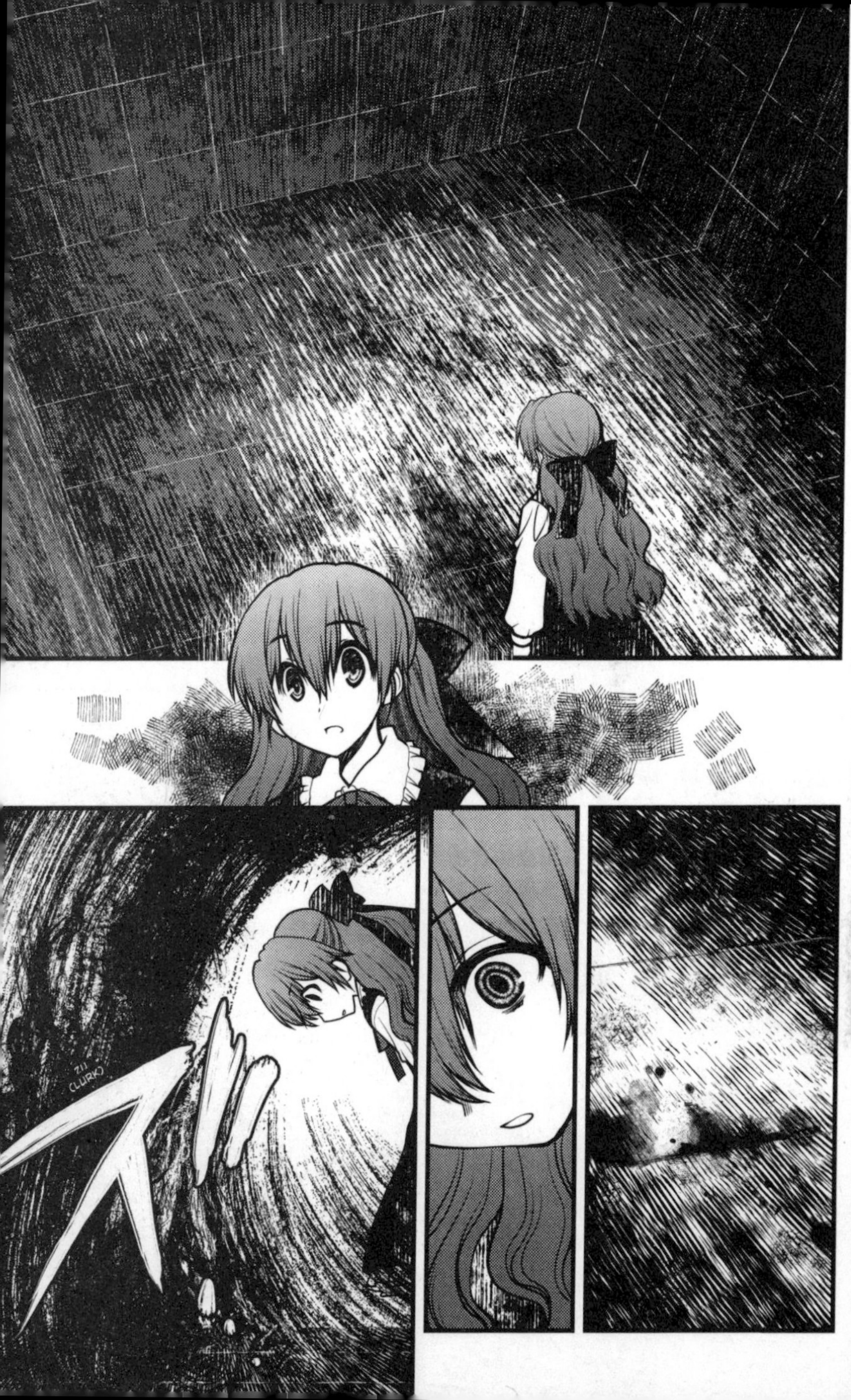
ZII
(CLURK)

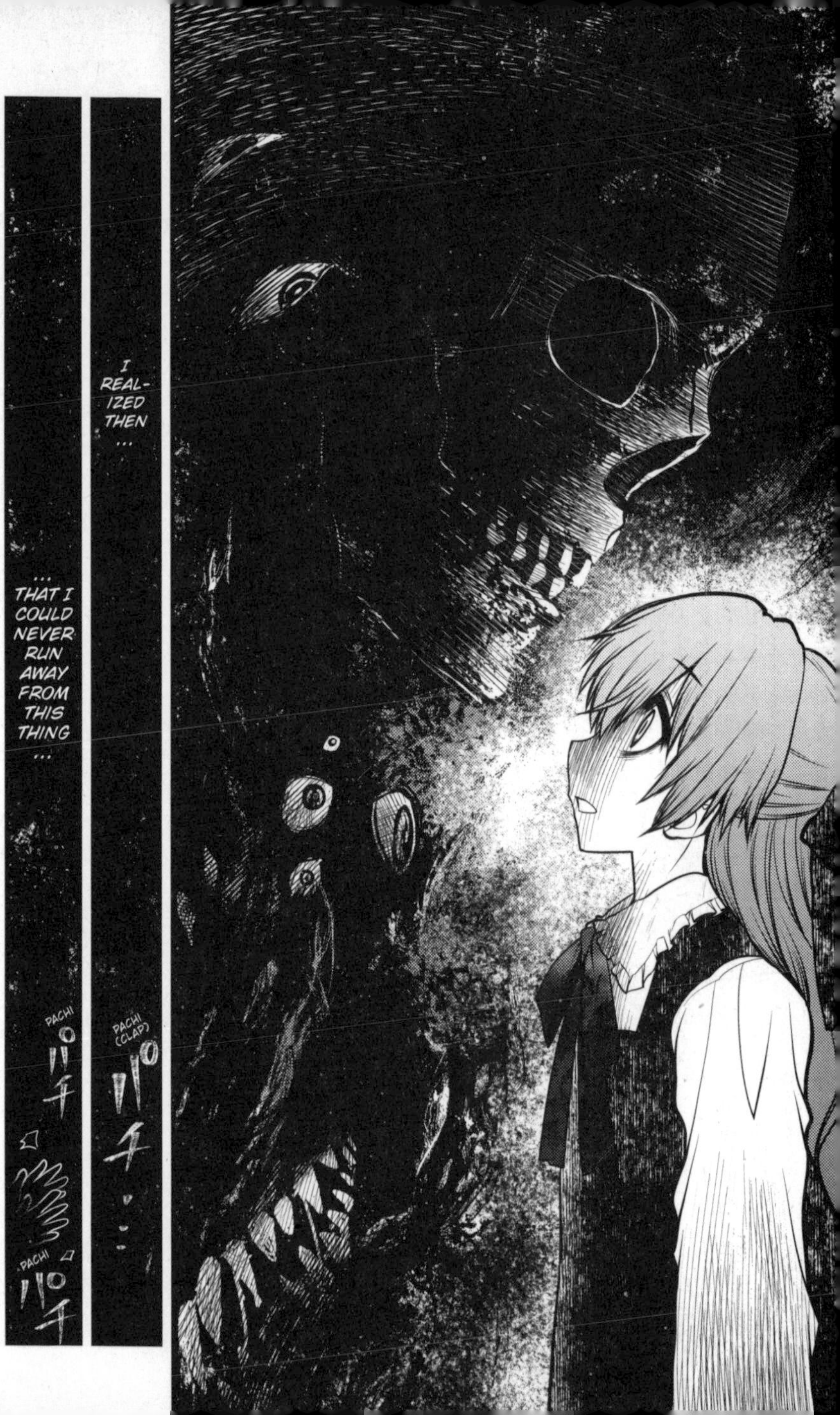
I REALIZED THEN...
...THAT I COULD NEVER RUN AWAY FROM THIS THING...
PACHI (CLAP)
パチ...
PACHI
パチ
PACHI
パチ

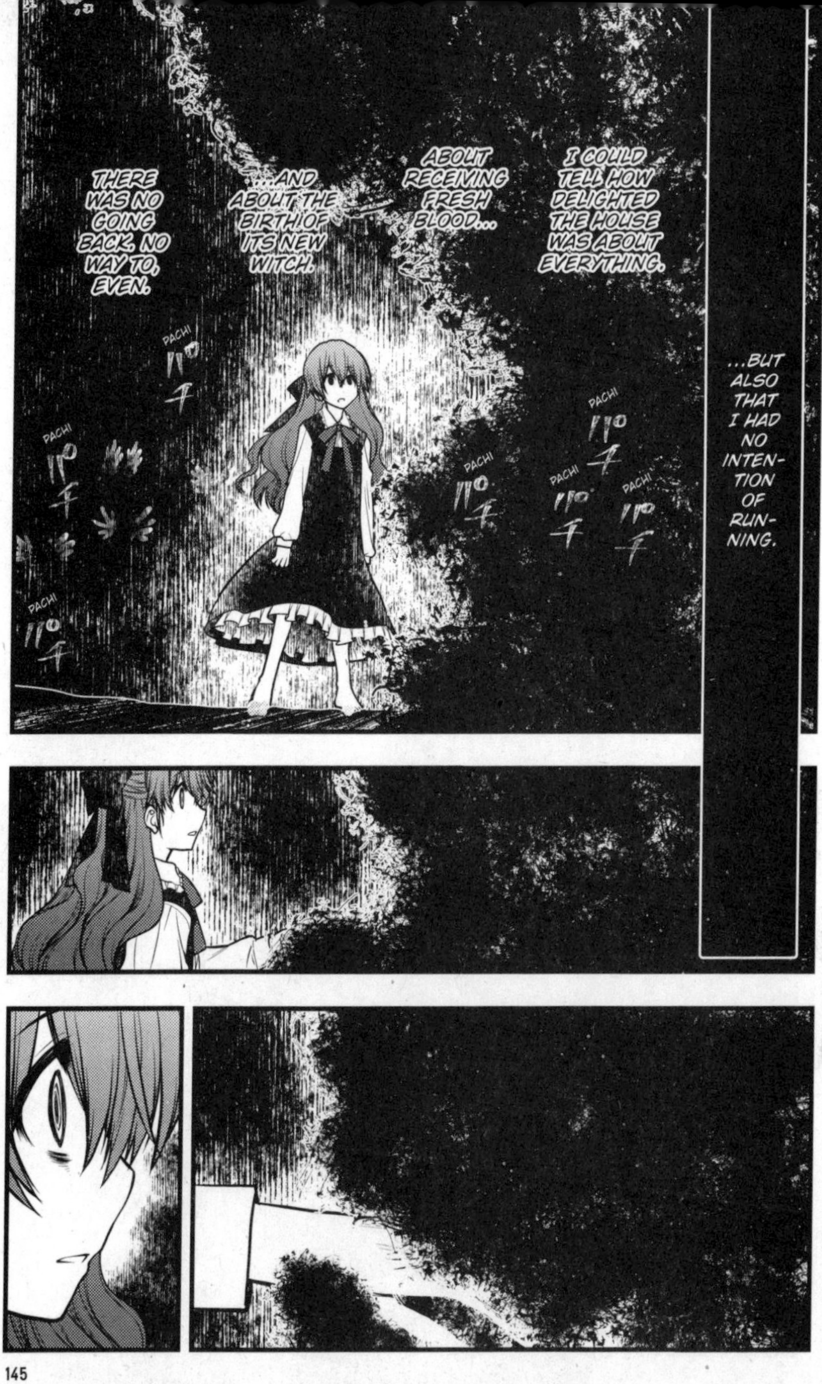

I COULD TELL HOW DELIGHTED THE HOUSE WAS ABOUT EVERYTHING.
ABOUT RECEIVING FRESH BLOOD...
...AND ABOUT THE BIRTH OF ITS NEW WITCH.
THERE WAS NO GOING BACK. NO WAY TO, EVEN.
PACHI
PACHI
PACHI
PACHI
PACHI
PACHI
PACHI
...BUT ALSO THAT I HAD NO INTENTION OF RUN-NING.

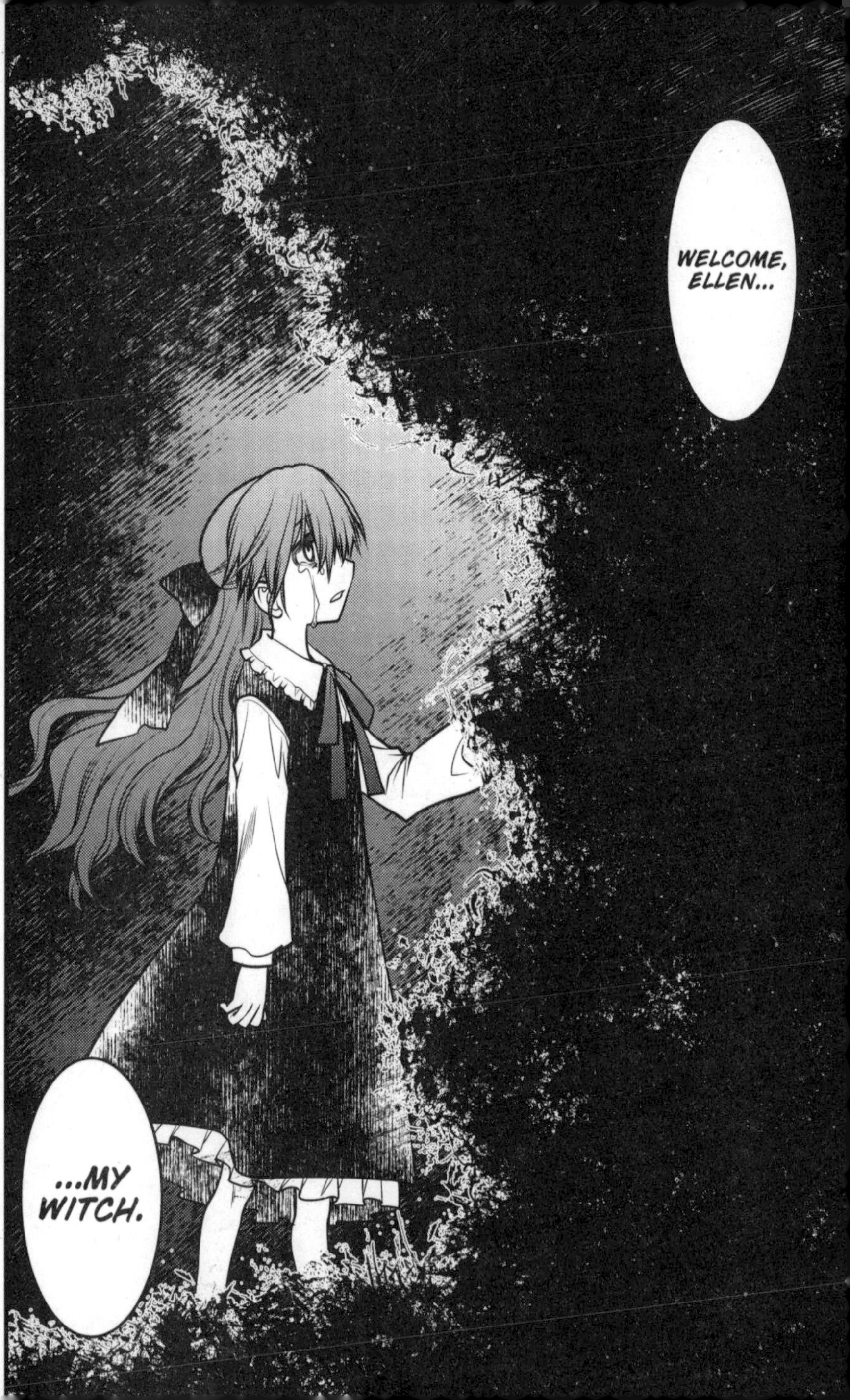
WELCOME, ELLEN...
...MY WITCH.

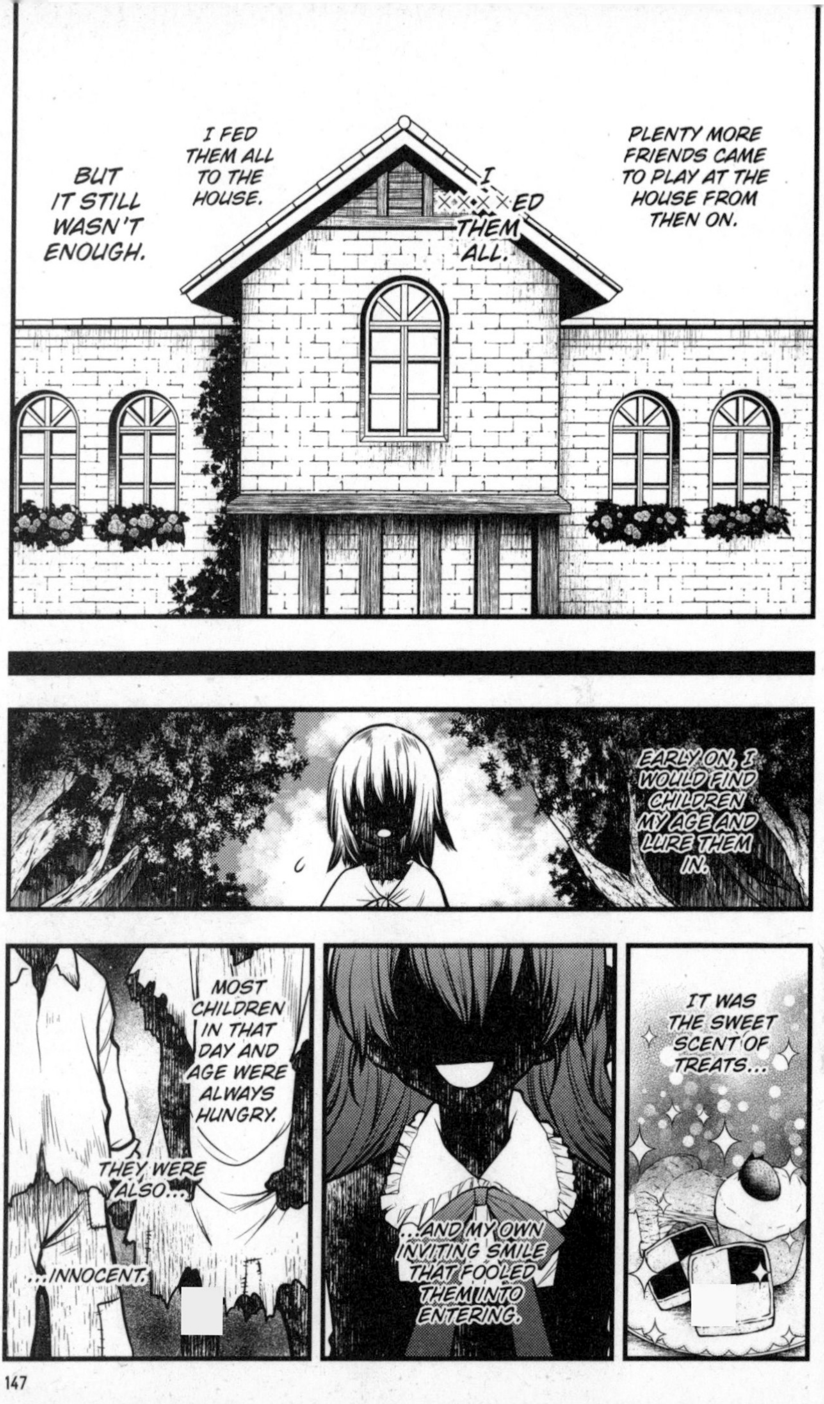
PLENTY MORE FRIENDS CAME TO PLAY AT THE HOUSE FROM THEN ON.
I ××××ED THEM ALL.
I FED THEM ALL TO THE HOUSE.
BUT IT STILL WASN'T ENOUGH.
EARLY ON, I WOULD FIND CHILDREN MY AGE AND LURE THEM IN.
IT WAS THE SWEET SCENT OF TREATS...
...AND MY OWN INVITING SMILE THAT FOOLED THEM INTO ENTERING.
MOST CHILDREN IN THAT DAY AND AGE WERE ALWAYS HUNGRY.
THEY WERE ALSO...
...INNOCENT.

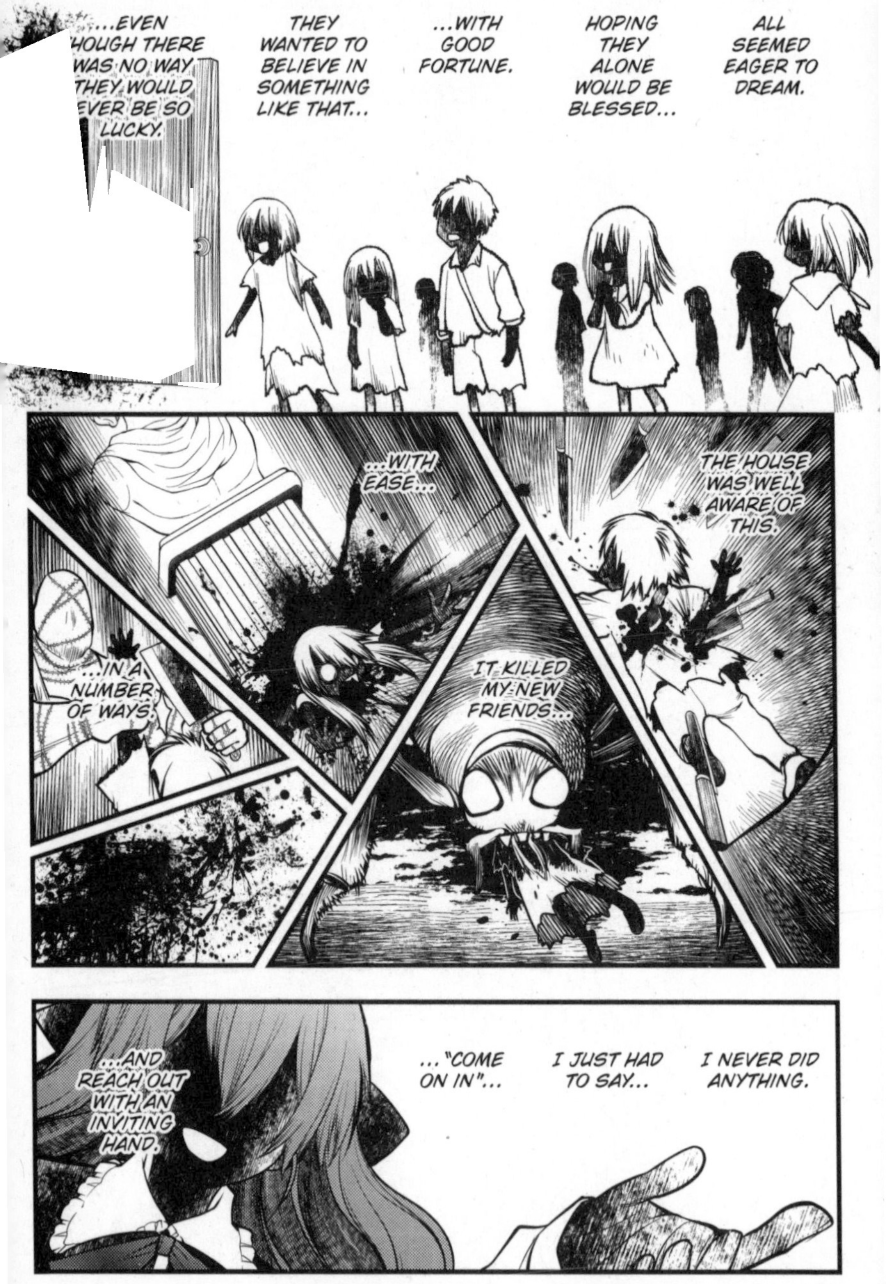
ALL SEEMED EAGER TO DREAM.
HOPING THEY ALONE WOULD BE BLESSED...
...WITH GOOD FORTUNE.
THEY WANTED TO BELIEVE IN SOMETHING LIKE THAT...
...EVEN HOUGH THERE WAS NO WAY THEY WOULD EVER BE SO LUCKY.
THE HOUSE WAS WELL AWARE OF THIS.
IT KILLED MY NEW FRIENDS...
...WITH EASE...
...IN A NUMBER OF WAYS.
I NEVER DID ANYTHING.
I JUST HAD TO SAY...
..."COME ON IN"...
...AND REACH OUT WITH AN INVITING HAND.

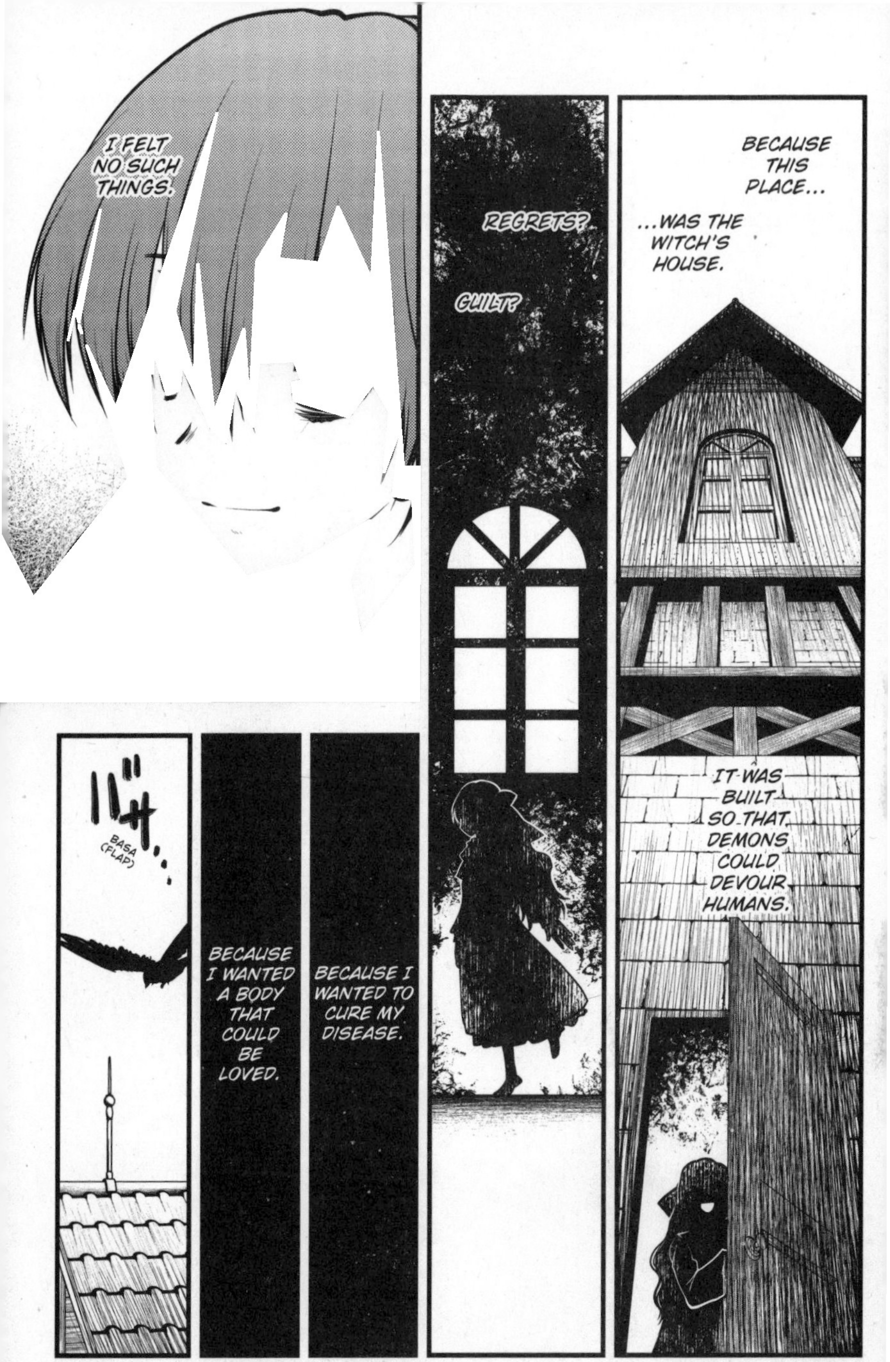
BECAUSE THIS PLACE...
...WAS THE WITCH'S HOUSE.
IT WAS BUILT SO THAT DEMONS COULD DEVOUR HUMANS.
REGRETS?
GUILT?
I FELT NO SUCH THINGS.
BECAUSE I WANTED TO CURE MY DISEASE.
BECAUSE I WANTED A BODY THAT COULD BE LOVED.
バサ...
BASA (FLAP)

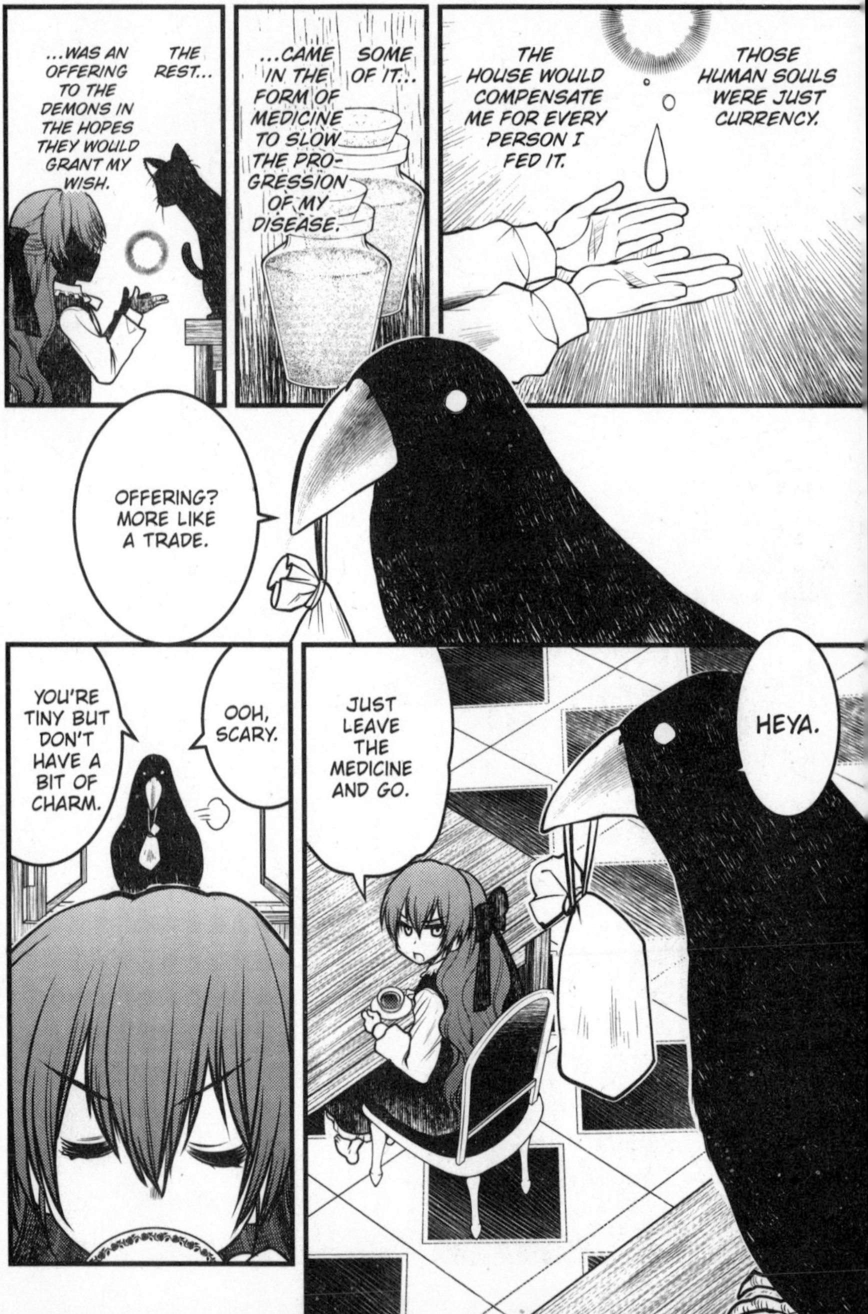
THOSE HUMAN SOULS WERE JUST CURRENCY.
THE HOUSE WOULD COMPENSATE ME FOR EVERY PERSON I FED IT.
SOME OF IT...
...CAME IN THE FORM OF MEDICINE TO SLOW THE PROGRESSION OF MY DISEASE.
THE REST...
...WAS AN OFFERING TO THE DEMONS IN THE HOPES THEY WOULD GRANT MY WISH.
OFFERING? MORE LIKE A TRADE.
HEYA.
JUST LEAVE THE MEDICINE AND GO.
OOH, SCARY.
YOU'RE TINY BUT DON'T HAVE A BIT OF CHARM.

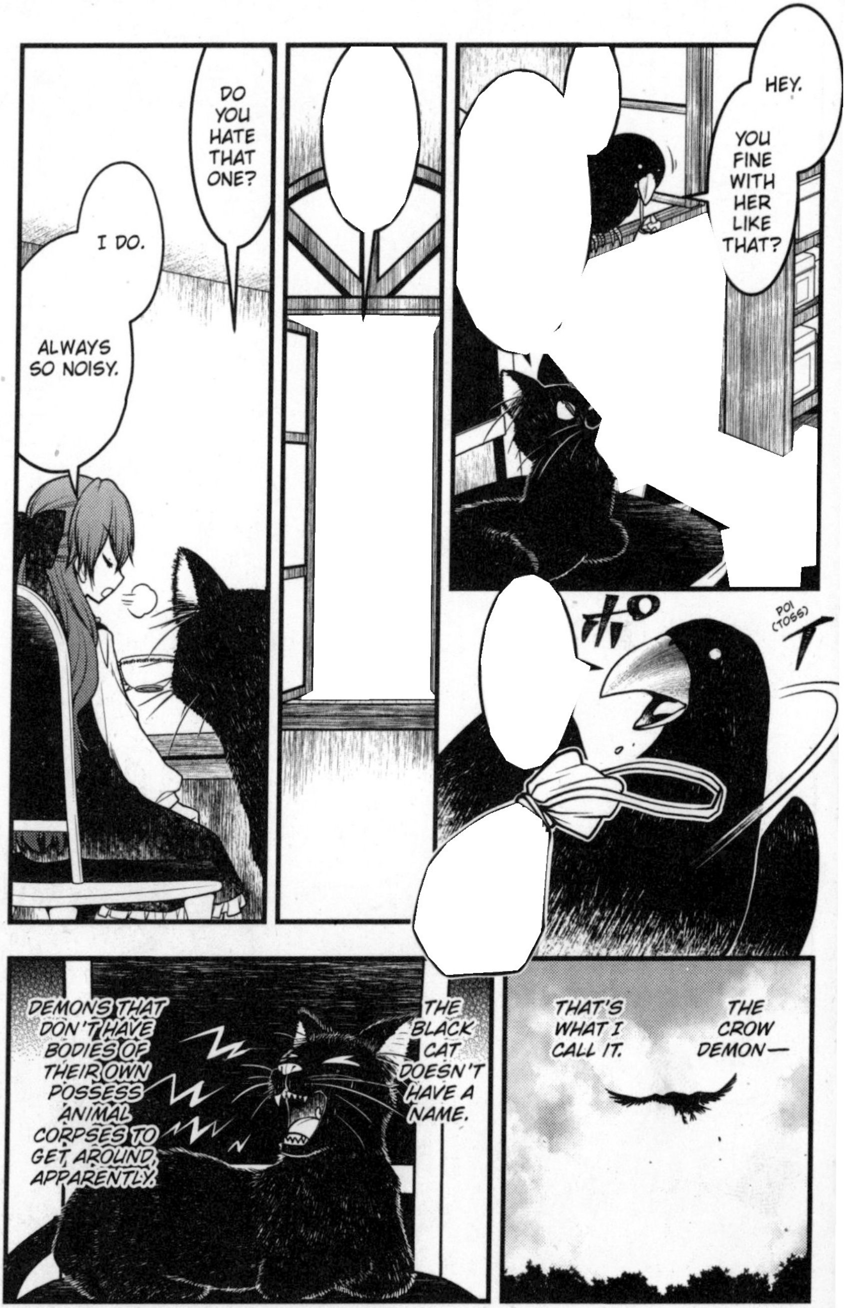
HEY.
YOU FINE WITH HER LIKE THAT?
ポ
POI (TOSS)
DO YOU HATE THAT ONE?
I DO.
ALWAYS SO NOISY.
THE CROW DEMON—
THAT'S WHAT I CALL IT.
THE BLACK CAT DOESN'T HAVE A NAME.
DEMONS THAT DON'T HAVE BODIES OF THEIR OWN POSSESS ANIMAL CORPSES TO GET AROUND, APPARENTLY.

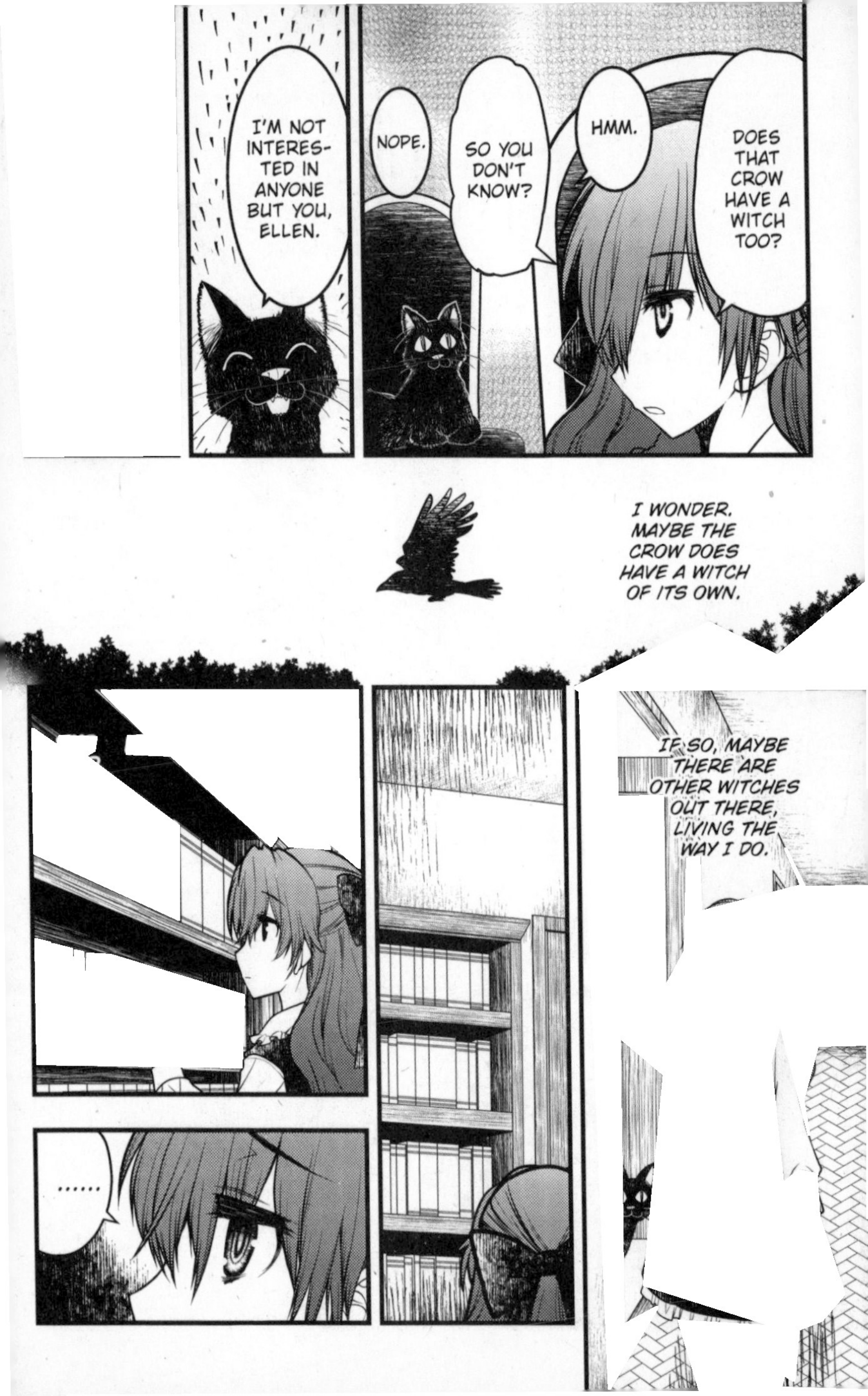
DOES THAT CROW HAVE A WITCH TOO?
HMM.
SO YOU DON'T KNOW?
NOPE.
I'M NOT INTERES-TED IN ANYONE BUT YOU, ELLEN.
I WONDER. MAYBE THE CROW DOES HAVE A WITCH OF ITS OWN.
IF SO, MAYBE THERE ARE OTHER WITCHES OUT THERE, LIVING THE WAY I DO.
......

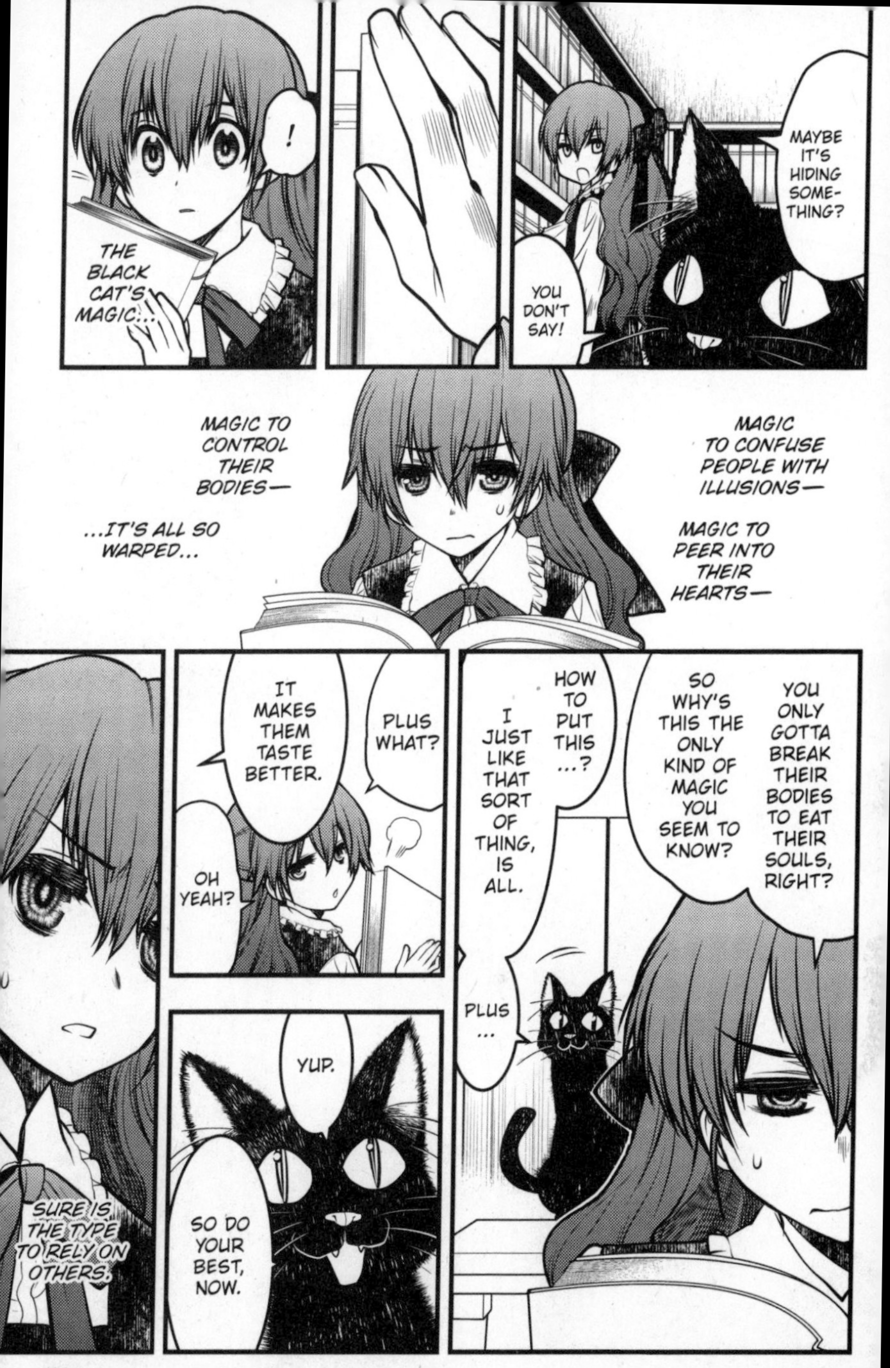
MAYBE IT'S HIDING SOME-THING?
YOU DON'T SAY!
!
THE BLACK CAT'S MAGIC...
MAGIC TO CONFUSE PEOPLE WITH ILLUSIONS—
MAGIC TO PEER INTO THEIR HEARTS—
MAGIC TO CONTROL THEIR BODIES—
...IT'S ALL SO WARPED...
YOU ONLY GOTTA BREAK THEIR BODIES TO EAT THEIR SOULS, RIGHT?
SO WHY'S THIS THE ONLY KIND OF MAGIC YOU SEEM TO KNOW?
HOW TO PUT THIS...?
I JUST LIKE THAT SORT OF THING, IS ALL.
PLUS...
PLUS WHAT?
IT MAKES THEM TASTE BETTER.
OH YEAH?
YUP.
SO DO YOUR BEST, NOW.
SURE IS THE TYPE TO RELY ON OTHERS.

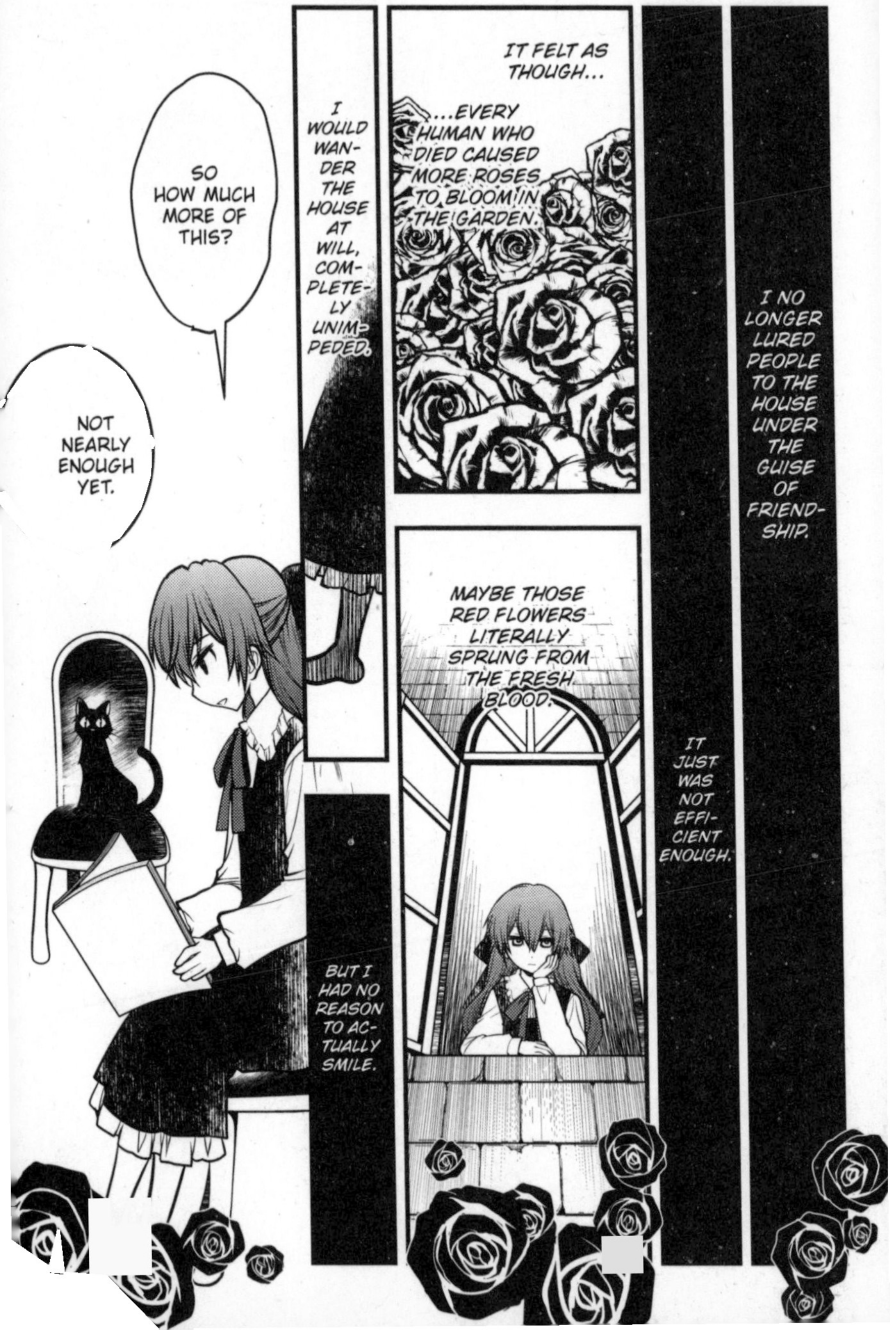
I NO LONGER LURED PEOPLE TO THE HOUSE UNDER THE GUISE OF FRIEND-SHIP.
IT JUST WAS NOT EFFI-CIENT ENOUGH.
IT FELT AS THOUGH...
...EVERY HUMAN WHO DIED CAUSED MORE ROSES TO BLOOM IN THE GARDEN.
MAYBE THOSE RED FLOWERS LITERALLY SPRUNG FROM THE FRESH BLOOD.
I WOULD WAN-DER THE HOUSE AT WILL, COM-PLETE-LY UNIM-PEDED.
BUT I HAD NO REASON TO AC-TUALLY SMILE.
SO HOW MUCH MORE OF THIS?
NOT NEARLY ENOUGH YET.

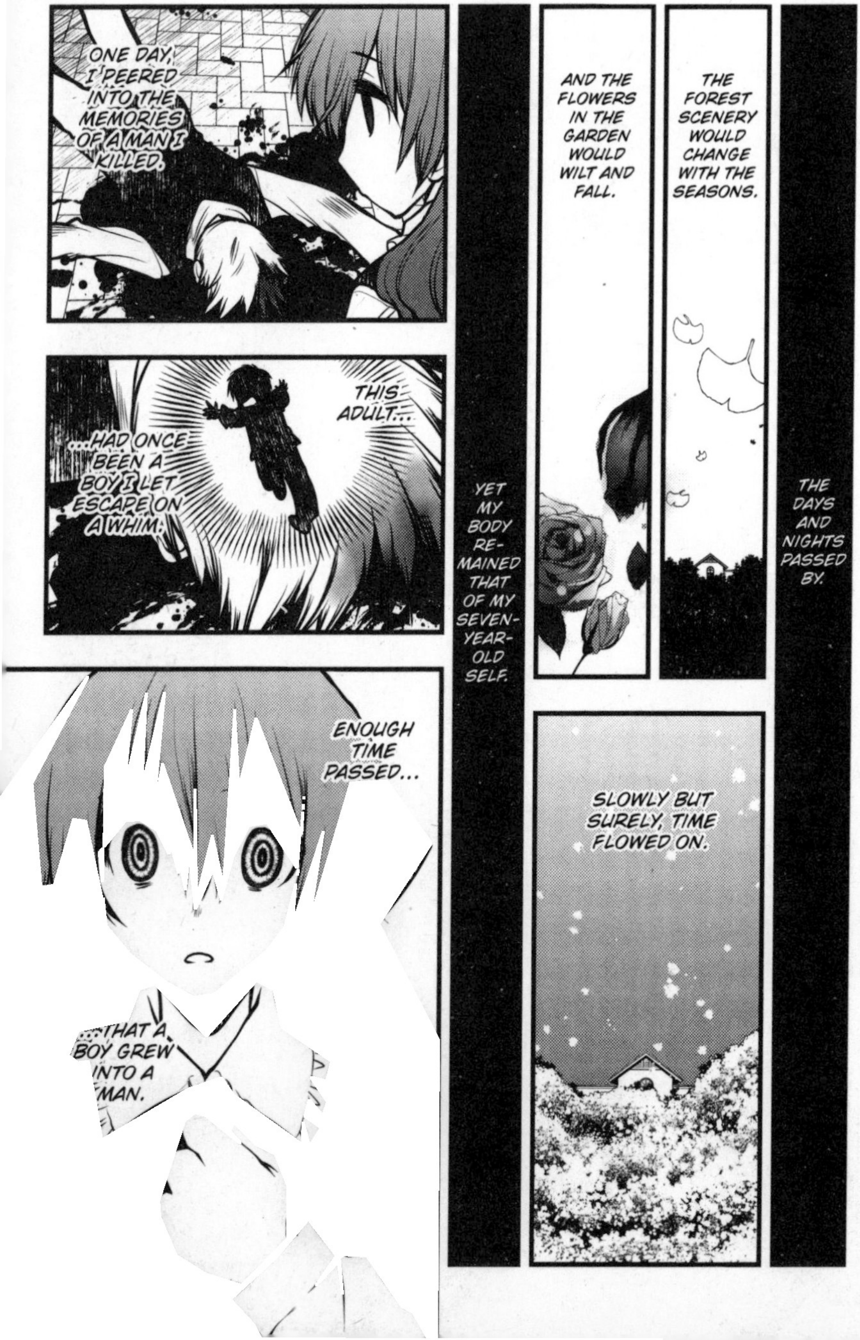
THE DAYS AND NIGHTS PASSED BY.
THE FOREST SCENERY WOULD CHANGE WITH THE SEASONS.
AND THE FLOWERS IN THE GARDEN WOULD WILT AND FALL.
SLOWLY BUT SURELY, TIME FLOWED ON.
YET MY BODY RE-MAINED THAT OF MY SEVEN-YEAR-OLD SELF.
ONE DAY, I PEERED INTO THE MEMORIES OF A MAN I KILLED.
THIS ADULT...
...HAD ONCE BEEN A BOY I LET ESCAPE ON A WHIM.
ENOUGH TIME PASSED...
...THAT A BOY GREW INTO A MAN.

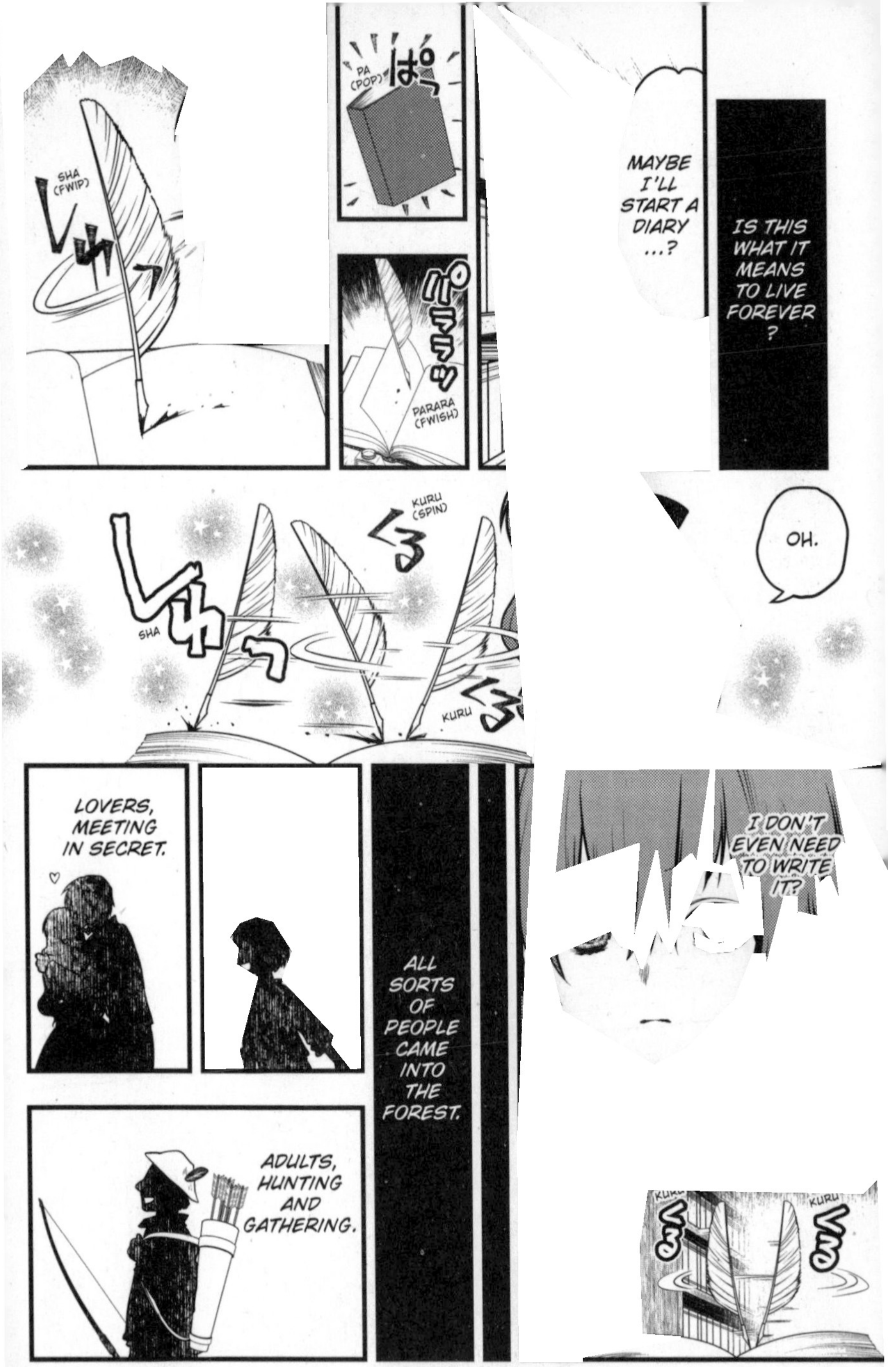
IS THIS WHAT IT MEANS TO LIVE FOREVER?
MAYBE I'LL START A DIARY ...?
PA (POP)
PARARA (FWISH)
SHA (FWIP)
OH.
KURU (SPIN)
KURU
SHA
I DON'T EVEN NEED TO WRITE IT?
KURU
KURU
ALL SORTS OF PEOPLE CAME INTO THE FOREST.
LOVERS, MEETING IN SECRET.
ADULTS, HUNTING AND GATHERING.

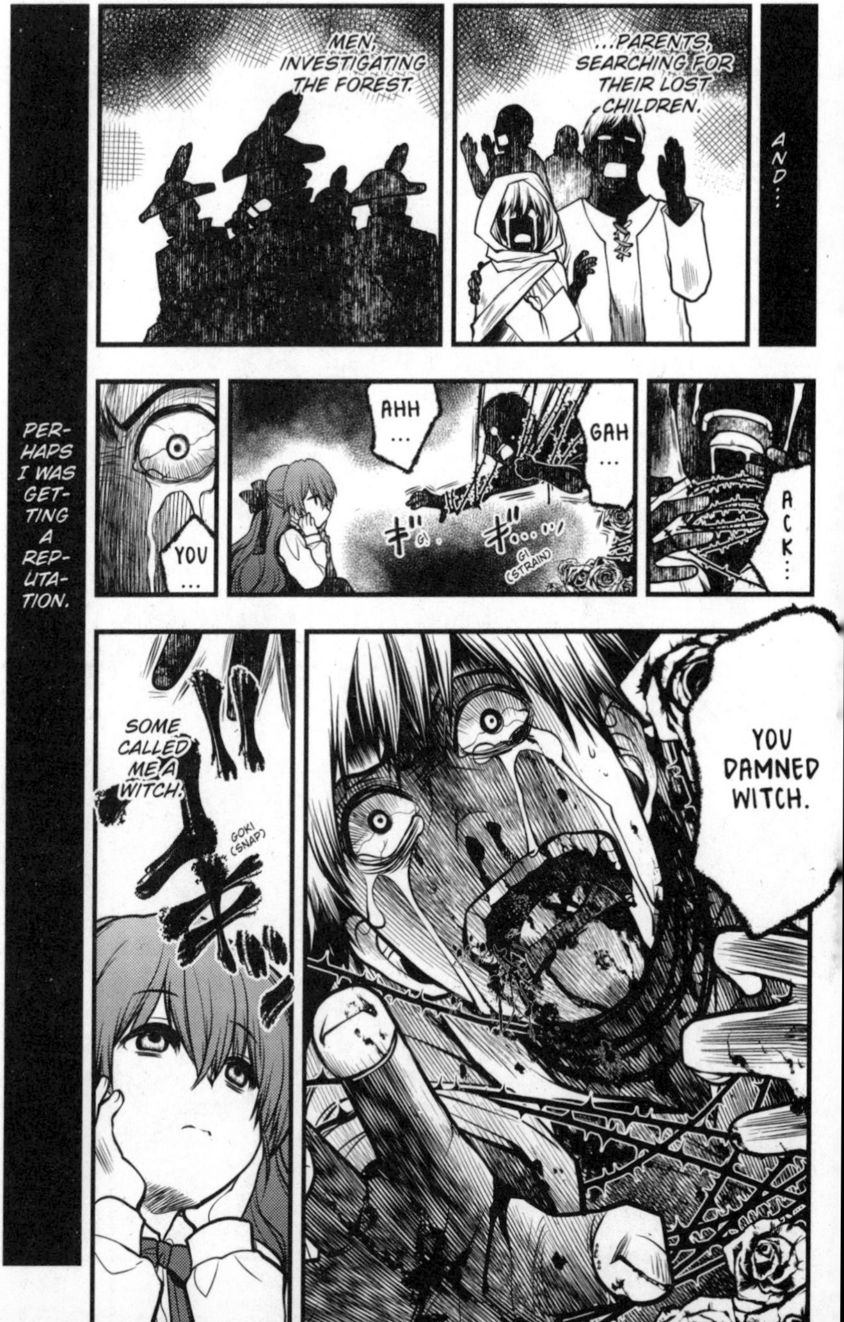
AND...
...PARENTS, SEARCHING FOR THEIR LOST CHILDREN.
MEN, INVESTIGATING THE FOREST.
ACK...
GAH...
AHH...
ギ
ギ...ッ
GI (STRAIN)
YOU...
YOU DAMNED WITCH.
SOME CALLED ME A WITCH.
GOKI (SNAP)
PERHAPS I WAS GETTING A REPUTATION.

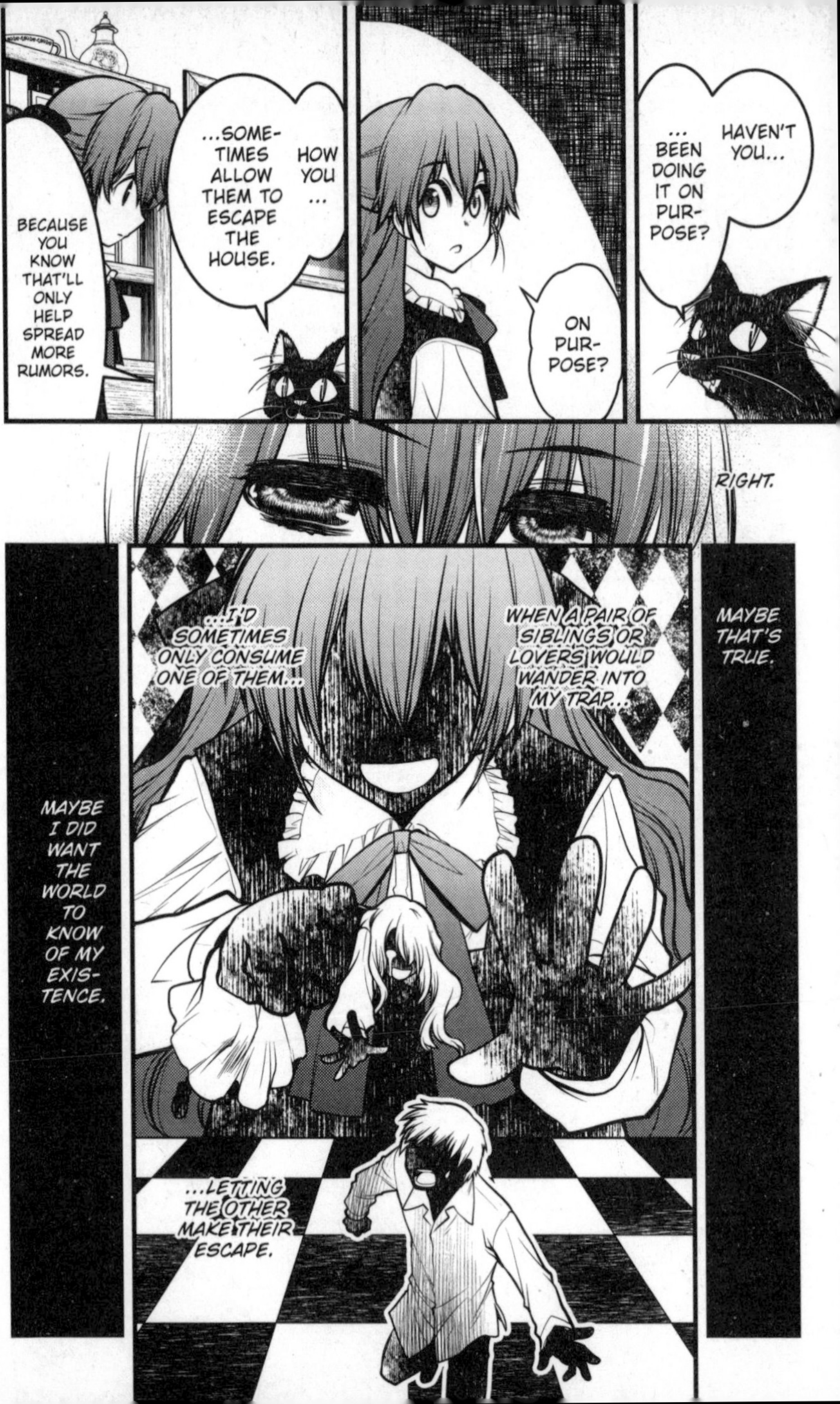

HAVEN'T YOU...
...BEEN DOING IT ON PURPOSE?
ON PURPOSE?
HOW YOU...
...SOMETIMES ALLOW THEM TO ESCAPE THE HOUSE.
BECAUSE YOU KNOW THAT'LL ONLY HELP SPREAD MORE RUMORS.
RIGHT.
MAYBE THAT'S TRUE.
WHEN A PAIR OF SIBLINGS OR LOVERS WOULD WANDER INTO MY TRAP...
...I'D SOMETIMES ONLY CONSUME ONE OF THEM...
...LETTING THE OTHER MAKE THEIR ESCAPE.
MAYBE I DID WANT THE WORLD TO KNOW OF MY EXISTENCE.

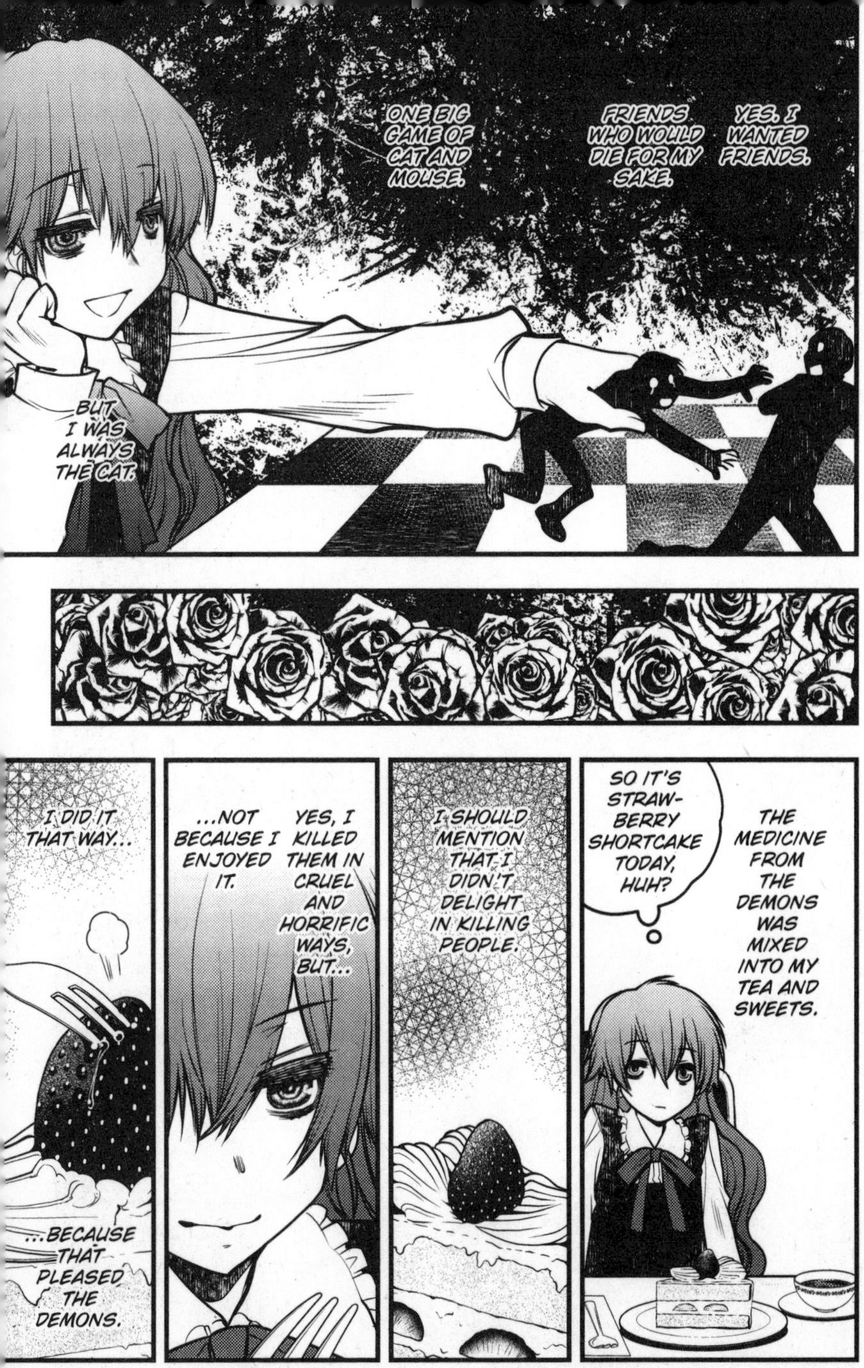
YES. I WANTED FRIENDS.
FRIENDS WHO WOULD DIE FOR MY SAKE.
ONE BIG GAME OF CAT AND MOUSE.
BUT I WAS ALWAYS THE CAT.
THE MEDICINE FROM THE DEMONS WAS MIXED INTO MY TEA AND SWEETS.
SO IT'S STRAW-BERRY SHORTCAKE TODAY, HUH?
I SHOULD MENTION THAT I DIDN'T DELIGHT IN KILLING PEOPLE.
YES, I KILLED THEM IN CRUEL AND HORRIFIC WAYS, BUT...
...NOT BECAUSE I ENJOYED IT.
I DID IT THAT WAY...
...BECAUSE THAT PLEASED THE DEMONS.

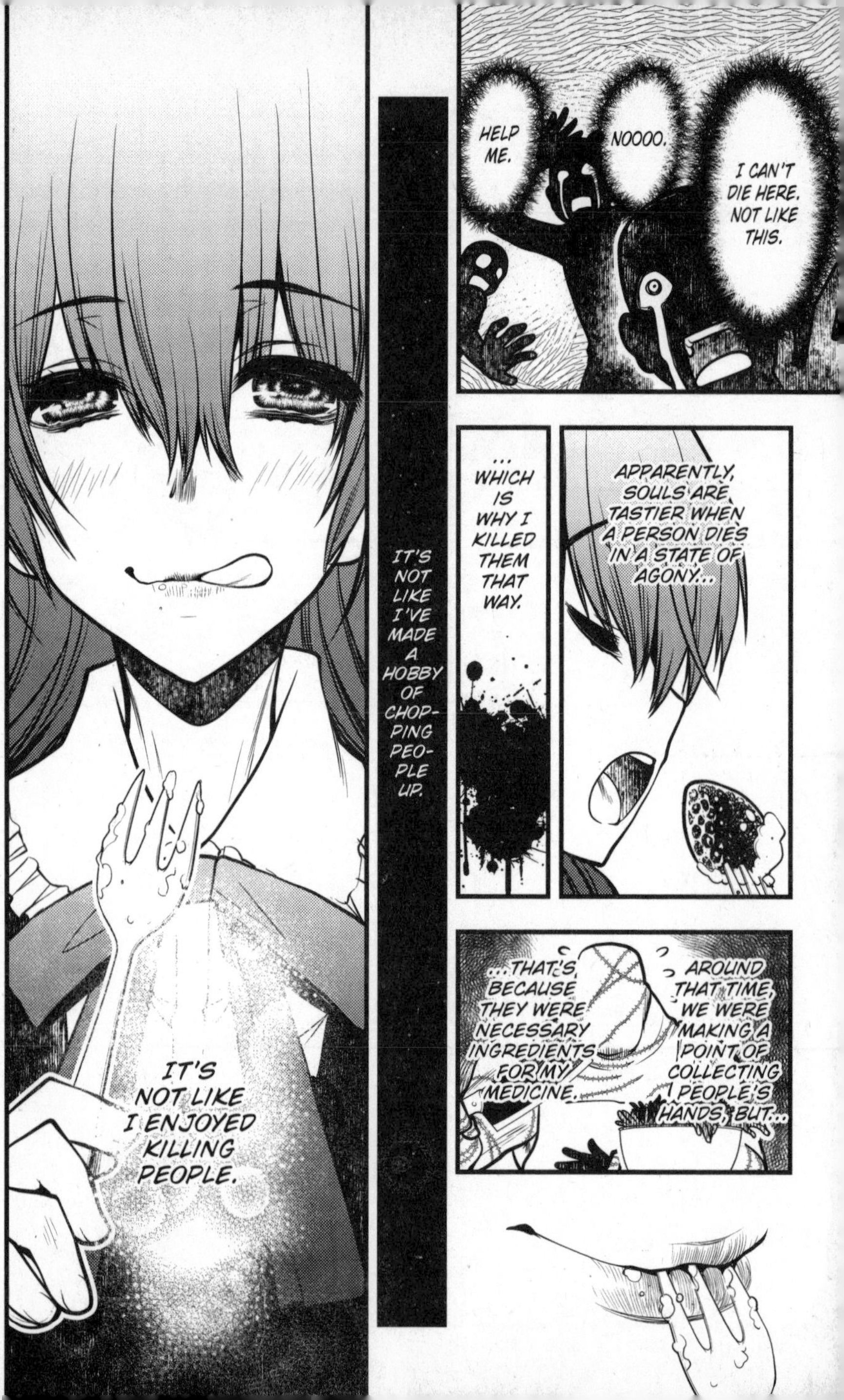
I CAN'T DIE HERE. NOT LIKE THIS.
NOOOO.
HELP ME.
APPARENTLY, SOULS ARE TASTIER WHEN A PERSON DIES IN A STATE OF AGONY...
...WHICH IS WHY I KILLED THEM THAT WAY.
AROUND THAT TIME, WE WERE MAKING A POINT OF COLLECTING PEOPLE'S HANDS, BUT...
...THAT'S BECAUSE THEY WERE NECESSARY INGREDIENTS FOR MY MEDICINE.
IT'S NOT LIKE I'VE MADE A HOBBY OF CHOP-PING PEO-PLE UP.
IT'S NOT LIKE I ENJOYED KILLING PEOPLE.

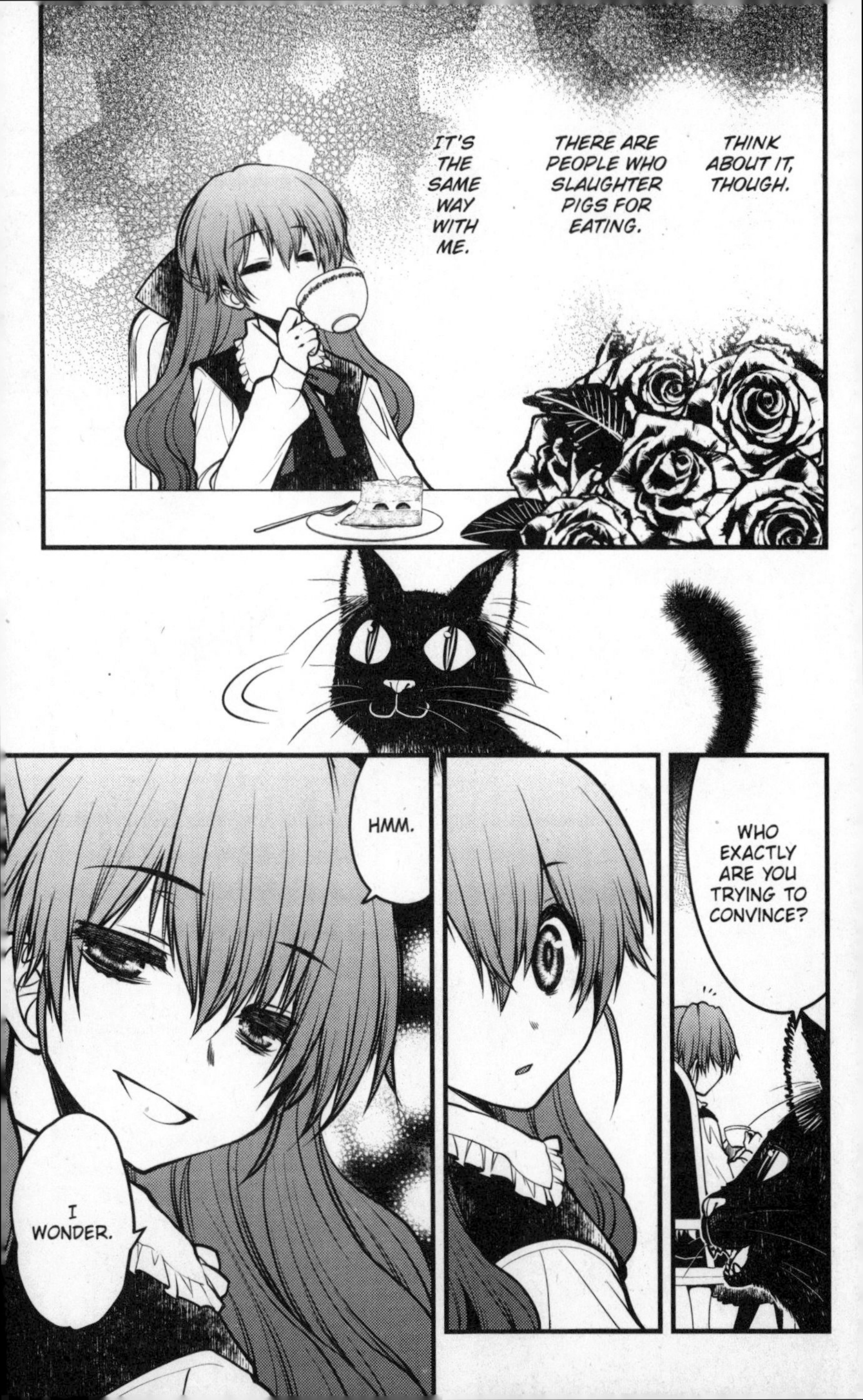
THINK ABOUT IT, THOUGH.
THERE ARE PEOPLE WHO SLAUGHTER PIGS FOR EATING.
IT'S THE SAME WAY WITH ME.
WHO EXACTLY ARE YOU TRYING TO CONVINCE?
HMM.
I WONDER.

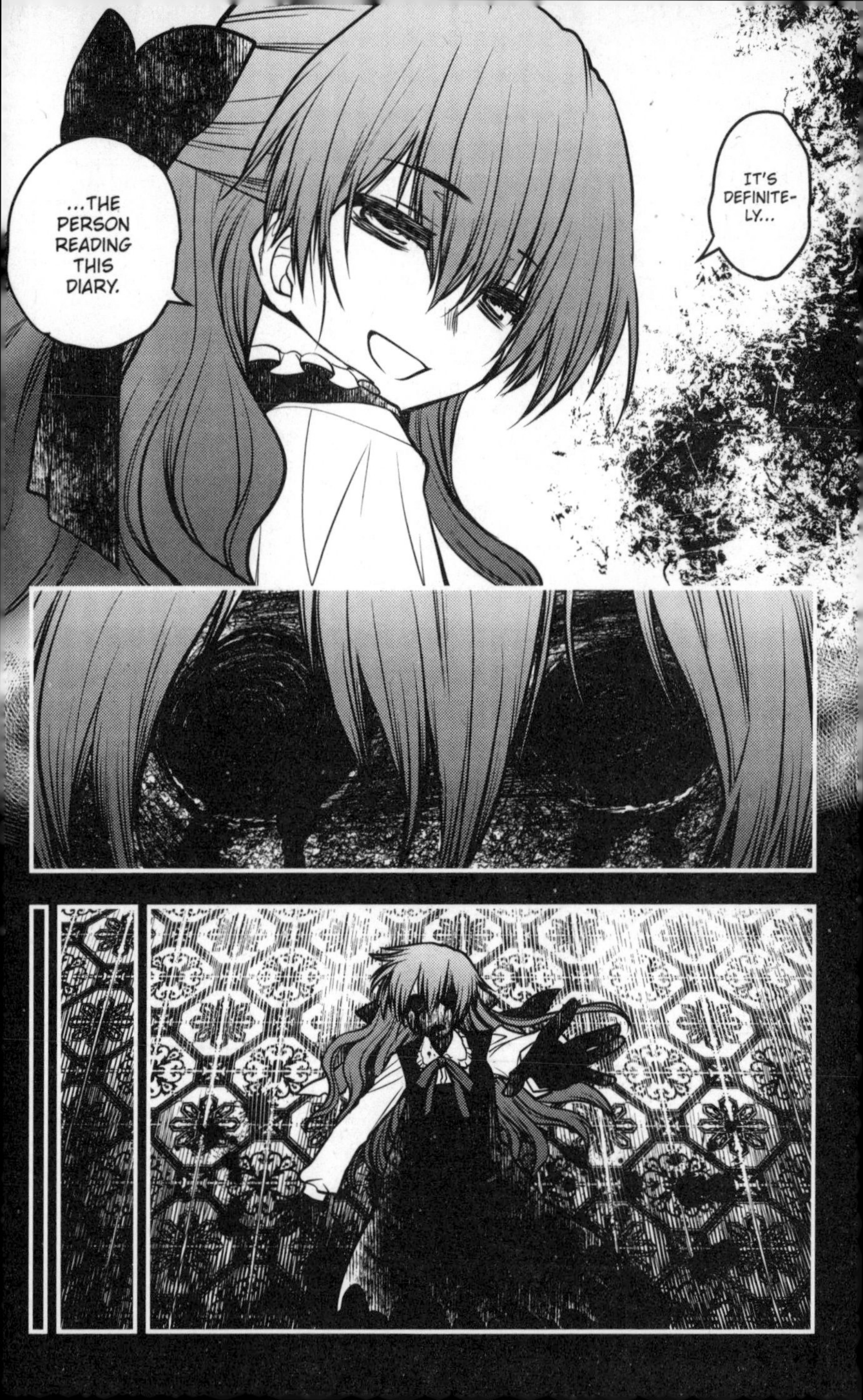
IT'S DEFINITE-LY...
...THE PERSON READING THIS DIARY.

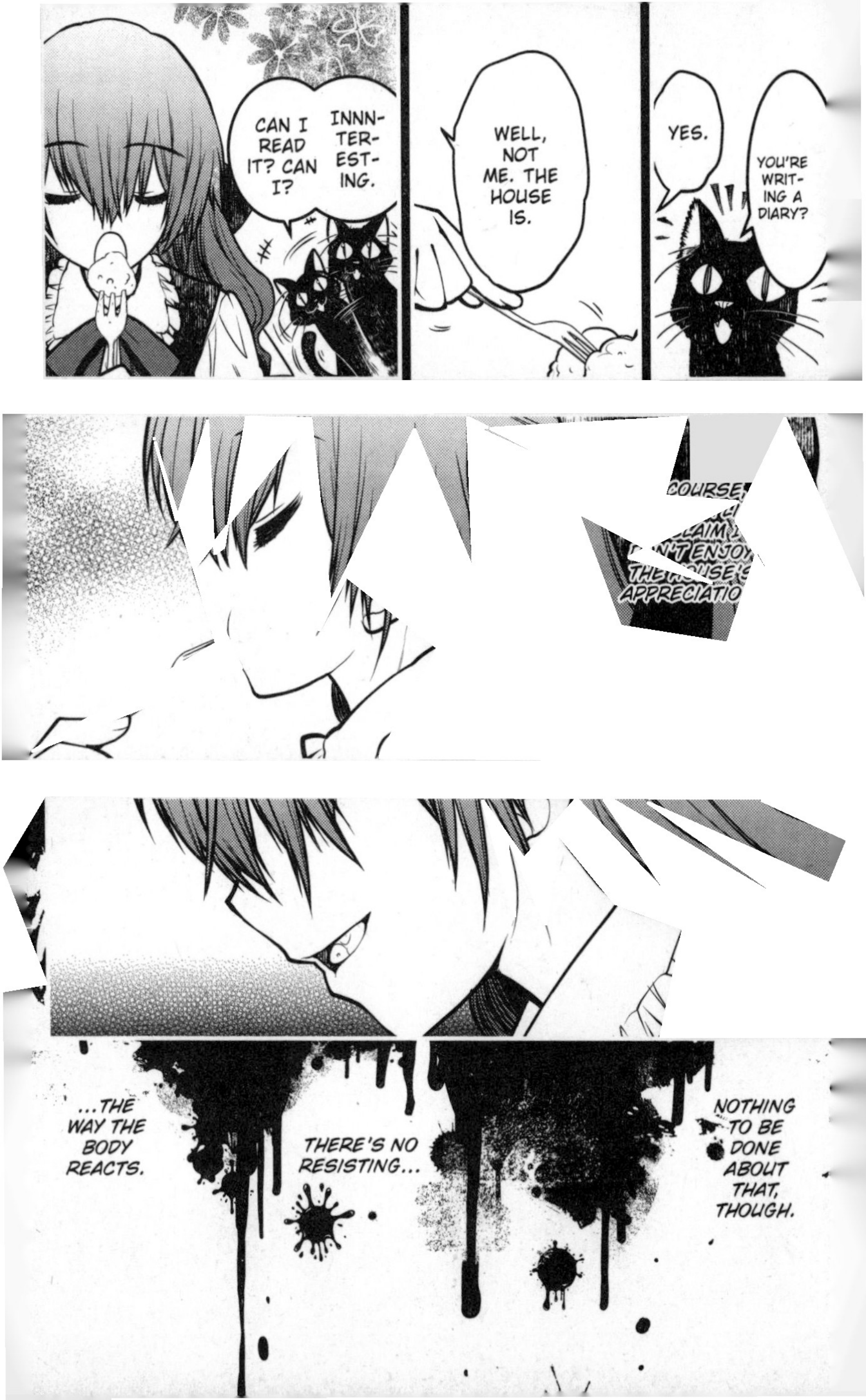
YOU'RE WRITING A DIARY?
YES.
WELL, NOT ME. THE HOUSE IS.
INNNTERESTING.
CAN I READ IT? CAN I?
COURSE
CLAIM I
'T ENJOY
THE
APPRECIATIO
NOTHING TO BE DONE ABOUT THAT, THOUGH.
THERE'S NO RESISTING...
...THE WAY THE BODY REACTS.

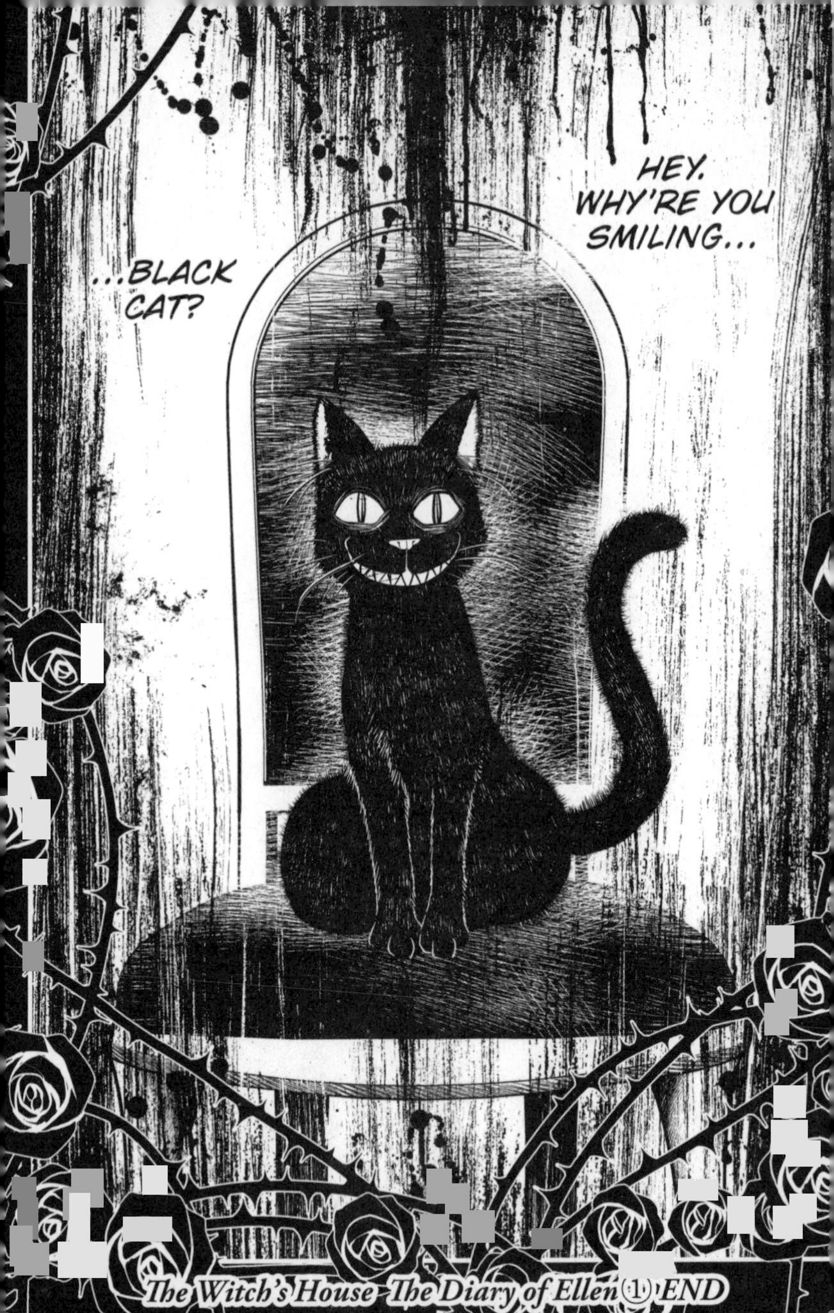
HEY. WHY'RE YOU SMILING...
...BLACK CAT?
The Witch's House The Diary of Ellen ① END

THE WITCH'S HOUSE
The Diary of Ellen

THE WITCH'S HOUSE
The Diary of Ellen

ORIGINAL STORY:
Fummy

ART:
Yuna Kagesaki

TRANSLATION: CALEB COOK
LETTERING: ROCHELLE GANCIO

THE WITCH'S HOUSE THE DIARY OF ELLEN Volume 1
© Yuna Kagesaki 2017
© Fummy 2017
First published in Japan in 2017 by KADOKAWA CORPORATION, Tokyo.
English translation rights arranged with KADOKAWA CORPORATION, Tokyo
through TUTTLE-MORI AGENCY, INC., Tokyo.

English translation © 2019 by Yen Press, LLC

Yen Press
1290 Avenue of the Americas
New York, NY 10104

Visit us at yenpress.com

facebook.com/yenpress
twitter.com/yenpress

yenpress.tumblr.com
instagram.com/yenpress

First Yen Press Edition: January 2019
The chapters in this volume were originally published as ebooks by Yen Press.

Yen Press is an imprint of Yen Press, LLC.
The Yen Press name and logo are trademarks of Yen Press, LLC.

Library of Congress Control Number: 2018958638

ISBNs: 978-1-9753-8371-8 (paperback)
978-1-9753-8372-5 (ebook)

10 9 8 7 6 5 4 3 2 1

WOR

Printed in the United States of America